Praise for
Freedom Journeys:
The Tale of Exodus and Wilderness across Millennia

"Arthur Waskow and Phyllis Berman are among the most creative interpreters of Torah in the past forty years, and *Freedom Journeys* is one of the most exciting interpretations of Exodus in contemporary Jewish literature. Combining very personal takes on the text with a profound rereading of traditional commentaries, Waskow and Berman have created a book that should be used at every Seder and in every synagogue in America."
—**Rabbi Michael Lerner**, editor, *Tikkun Magazine*, www.tikkun.org

"A powerful retracing of the Exodus story that reminds us all of our obligation to move against oppression and toward freedom in our own lives and in our own time. Waskow and Berman bring the iconic Jewish journey into our time, making the fights against evil and the searches for food, for health, for justice and for peace a part of what it means to be a Jew in the twenty-first century. Study is important, the sages say, because it leads to action; this book tells us why and how to put the teachings of our Torah to work building community and creating greater democracy. Waskow and Berman remind us that we are all on our own Freedom Journey. They look into our history and use it as a mirror to reflect on the issues of our day, noting the work of many in the twentieth century who led fights for freedom and suggesting how we should be picking up the challenge."
—**Ruth W. Messinger**, president, American Jewish World Service

"It was the Exodus story that undergirded the civil rights movement; but as Arthur Waskow and Phyllis Berman demonstrate in this fascinating book, even Martin Luther King didn't plumb the entire story, which we need now more than ever."
—**Bill McKibben**, author, *Eaarth*; founder, 350.org

"The story of Moses, Pharaoh, and the Exodus is familiar to Jews, Christians, and Muslims, but the familiarity is often superficial. *Freedom Journeys* encourages us to consider the deeper meanings of this story, and challenges us to apply the understanding we gain to transform and heal our broken relationships with each other and with the rest of creation."

—**Sheila Musaji**, editor, *The American Muslim*

"Many of the Hasidim saw the world as God, wrapped in robes of God so as to seem material. Yet they knew that God's Own Self was fractured in the world we live in, and so both world and God need our acts of healing. Today, a new paradigm of a Judaism is emerging that is in harmony with *tikkun olam* and will help heal that brokenness for all humanity and all our planet. *Freedom Journeys* helps us to bring to birth a new world as God and our forebears did in the Exodus so long ago."

—**Rabbi Zalman Schachter-Shalomi**, co-author, *Jewish with Feeling* and *A Heart Afire*

"This collection is a lush tapestry of visionary, incisive, and inspiring reflections on the Exodus and Wilderness stories. May Arthur's and Phyllis's inspired writing move many to work together for liberation from oppressive structures of our own day, both globally and locally."

—**Rabbi Amy Eilberg**, Jay Phillips Center for Interfaith Learning; first woman ordained by The Jewish Theological Seminary

"With fresh, bold, insightful interpretations on the well-known Exodus texts, *Freedom Journeys*, written by two of this generation's most compelling prophetic voices, eloquently invites us to remember and to rethink how our ancient mission addresses the most urgent crises humanity faces today."

—**Rabbi David Saperstein**, director, Religious Action Center of Reform Judaism

"The stories of the Israelites' journey to freedom have inspired Jews, Christians, and Muslims throughout the centuries. Waskow and Berman retell the tales yet again, weaving in the voices of fellow travellers, ancient and contemporary, from among the children of Abraham. The result testifies to the incredible enduring power of these narratives, their connection to the lives of men and women confronting the challenges of their own times. The authors answer the question 'Study or action?' with a resounding 'Yes!'"
—**Rabbi Nancy Fuchs Kreimer**, associate professor and director of Multi-faith Studies and Initiatives, Reconstructionist Rabbinical College

"Rabbi Arthur Waskow has spent a lifetime showing, through study and action, how the biblical tradition calls us to a way of living marked by care for the neighbor and care for the earth. In this wonderful little book, he—along with Rabbi Phyllis Berman and several Christian and Muslim colleagues—invites us 'to relearn and rethink' the Exodus story in order to grasp its essence as a journey of freedom. In this way, we see the text's immediate relevance to the pharaohs and plagues of our era."
—**Michael Kinnamon**, general secretary, National Council of the Churches of Christ in the USA

"A deep meditation on the timeless—and timely—relevance of the Exodus narrative. In the grand tradition of mystical exegesis, Waskow and Berman reflect upon Exodus not only as an event that happened 'then' and 'there,' but a paradigm of movement that is happening here and in the now, for all of us, Jew and Muslim, Black and White, male and female. A joyous, wondrous, and profound classic."
—**Omid Safi**, professor of Islamic studies, University of North Carolina; author, *Memories of Muhammad*

"Provides those who wish to embrace or encounter a liberal reading of the Exodus story the book they have been seeking. In their inimitable words as well as the essays they have collected from Christian, African American, and Muslim writers, Arthur and Phyllis have created a repository of exegesis and interpretation that will offer inventive, very liberal, and innovative pathways to understanding the narratives and *midrashim* that have been a part of this ongoing and changing story for the past two thousand years."
—**Rabbi Steve Gutow**, president and CEO, Jewish Council for Public Affairs

"The Exodus is one of the most powerful stories in the Bible, telling of a people's liberation from captivity to freedom. Waskow and Berman, gifted storytellers in their own right, also show how others see it as an archetype for similar stories in Christianity, Islam, and the southern freedom movement. *Freedom Journeys* is a book that will be informative and inspiring for those involved in current movements for justice."

—**Jim Wallis**, president, *Sojourners*; author, *Rediscovering Values*

"It is educational to learn of freedom journeys of the past, but awe-inspiring when these authors show how they can be experienced by people of all faiths today."

—**Laleh Bakhtiar, PhD**, first woman translator of the Qur'an

"Brings the Exodus story freshly and powerfully into our contemporary lives, offering a moving Torah of transformation that will undoubtedly impact many hearts and minds alike."

—**Rabbi Danya Ruttenberg**, author, *Surprised by God: How I Learned to Stop Worrying and Love Religion*; editor, *The Passionate Torah: Sex and Judaism*

"A prophetic book for the challenges we face in today's troubled world. Chapter after chapter contains the biblical foundation for addressing poverty, care of the earth and living in peace together on this fragile planet as brothers and sisters. I recommend this book of universal wisdom to people of *all* faith traditions."

—**Bob Edgar**, president, Common Cause; former general secretary, National Council of Churches; former president, Claremont School of Theology; former member, United States House of Representatives

"Opens the way to fresh, rich, and challenging readings of biblical tales of exodus and exile, return and reconsecration. Join these wise guides on this spiritual journey and experience the text renewed and illuminated by their brilliant interpretations and deep immersion in stories that cross boundaries and bring together all who value and seek freedom. You will be richly rewarded."

—**Rabbi Sue Levi Elwell, PhD**, union rabbi and worship specialist, Union for Reform Judaism

Freedom
Journeys

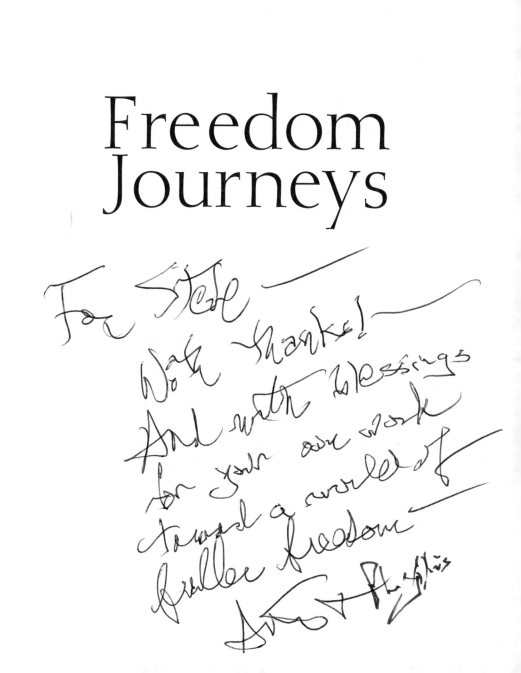

For Steve —
With thanks!
And with blessings
for your own work
toward a world of
fuller freedom —

Other Books by Arthur O. Waskow and Phyllis O. Berman

Tales of Tikkun: New Jewish Stories to Heal the Wounded World

A Time for Every Purpose Under Heaven:
  The Jewish Life-Spiral as a Spiritual Path

Other Books by Arthur O. Waskow

America in Hiding
  by Arthur O. Waskow and Stanley L. Newman

Becoming Brothers
  by Howard Waskow and Arthur O. Waskow

Before There Was a Before
  by Arthur O. Waskow, David Waskow, Shoshana Waskow, and Amnon
  Danziger

The Bush Is Burning:
  Radical Judaism Faces the Pharoahs of the Modern Super-state

The Debate over Thermonuclear Strategy

Down-to-Earth Judaism: Food, Money, Sex, and the Rest of Life

The Freedom Seder: A New Haggadah for Passover

From Race Riot to Sit-in, 1919 and the 1960s:
  A Study in the Connections between Conflict and Violence

Godwrestling

Godwrestling—Round 2: Ancient Wisdom, Future Paths (Jewish Lights)

The Limits of Defense

Seasons of Our Joy

The Shalom Seders

The Tent of Abraham:
  Stories of Hope and Peace for Jews, Christians, and Muslims
  by Joan Chittister, Neil Douglas-Klotz, and Arthur O. Waskow

Torah of the Earth: Exploring 4,000 Years of Ecology in Jewish Thought
  (Jewish Lights)

Trees, Earth, and Torah: A Tu b'Shvat Anthology
  by Ari Elon, Naomi M. Hyman, and Arthur O. Waskow

Other Books by Phyllis O. Berman

Getting Into It: An Unfinished Book
  by Phyllis O. Berman and Dave Blot

Freedom Journeys

The Tale of Exodus and Wilderness across Millennia

Rabbi Arthur Ocean Waskow
and Rabbi Phyllis Ocean Berman

For People of All Faiths, All Backgrounds
JEWISH LIGHTS Publishing
Woodstock, Vermont

Freedom Journeys:
The Tale of Exodus and Wilderness across Millennia

2011 Hardcover Edition, First Printing
© 2011 by Arthur O. Waskow and Phyllis O. Berman
"Exodus in African America: A Great Camp Meeting" © 2011 by Vincent Harding
"Exodus in the Life and Death of Jesus" © 2011 by Ched Myers and Russell Powell
"Exodus in the Qur'an: Mercy, Compassion, and Forgiveness" © 2011 by S. Ayse Kadayifci-Orellana

For information regarding permission to reprint material from this book, please mail or fax your request in writing to Jewish Lights Publishing, Permissions Department, at the address / fax number listed below, or e-mail your request to permissions@jewishlights.com.

Library of Congress Cataloging-in-Publication Data
Waskow, Arthur Ocean, 1933-
  Freedom journeys : the tale of Exodus and wilderness across millennia / Arthur Ocean Waskow and Phyllis Ocean Berman.
     p. cm.
  Includes bibliographical references.
  Summary: This book calls us to rethink the story of Pharaoh, the Exodus, and the wilderness to learn from it ways we can address our modern-day enslavements that echo the ancient ones—corporate greed; making "strangers" into pariahs; the climate crisis and other ecological disasters like the ancient "plagues." By examining the archetypal tale of the Hebrews' liberation from Egypt and the various ways the story has been retold throughout history, we gain new perspectives on the destructive effects of top-down, unaccountable power; the importance of replacing it with new forms of community; and the role of action in the quest for freedom.
  ISBN 978-1-58023-445-0 (hardcover)
  1. Bible. O.T. Exodus—Criticism, interpretation, etc. I. Berman, Phyllis Ocean, 1942- II. Title.
  BS1245.52.W37 2011
  222'.1206—dc22

                                                                  2010051361

10 9 8 7 6 5 4 3 2 1

Manufactured in the United States of America

Jacket Design: Tim Holtz
Interior Design: Kristi Menter
Jacket Art: "Burning Bush" (© 2003) was created by Michael Bogdanow, an artist, lawyer, author, and musician living in Massachusetts. "God's messenger was seen ... in the flame of a fire out of the midst of a bush ... the bush is burning with fire and ... is not consumed" (Exodus 3:2). The artist's contemporary, spiritual works of art inspired by Judaic texts can be seen on www.MichaelBogdanow.com.

Published by Jewish Lights Publishing
A Division of LongHill Partners, Inc.
Sunset Farm Offices, Route 4, P.O. Box 237
Woodstock, VT 05091
Tel: (802) 457-4000   Fax: (802) 457-4004
www.jewishlights.com

~

*"Tell it to your children on that day, saying,
'This is what the Breath of Life,
the Wind of Change,
did for us,
bringing us forth from slavery to freedom.'"*
THE PASSOVER HAGGADAH, FROM EXODUS 13:8

~

For our children:
David and Ketura; Shoshana and Michael;
Joshua; Morissa and Jason;
For the children of our children:
Yonit, Elior, Shifra, Kalman, and Yaela;
And for all children.

May they be blessed
with a world of freedom and community,
with their own Red Seas to cross, Sinais to climb,
and a Wilderness of open possibility.

Contents

Why Should We Relearn the Story?

*If a Pharaoh fell in the Red Sea but nobody
    told the story,*
Did it actually happen? —No.

*If no Pharaoh fell in the Red Sea, but we
    told the story for three thousand years,*
Did it actually happen? —Yes.
Is it still happening? —Yes.

To people brought up in the modern mode of focusing on cold, hard facts, these responses may seem ridiculous. What's this, the Jewish version of a koan? Either it happened or it didn't.

But let's leave aside for a moment the emotional and intellectual freight, positive or negative, of "the Bible." Imagine for a moment you are forced into making a choice. Here on one table are the factual, historical chronicles of the kings of Denmark. What really happened: alliances with Norway, wars with England. On another table are all the copies in the world of Shakespeare's play *The Tragedy of Hamlet, Prince of Denmark*. And you are forced to choose: burn to ashes what is on one table or the other. Would you choose to burn the fiction or the facts?

Suppose that we can find no evidence beyond the Bible and Qur'an that our ancient stories of Exodus and Wilderness "actually" happened the way we have learned them. Shall we throw them out? Or is there some profound value for our generation of retelling the story of Exodus, of Sinai, and of Wilderness?

This is no idle question. Modern historians and archaeologists report that so far they have found little or no evidence outside the biblical text (which is reinvoked and retold in the separate revelation of the Qur'an) that the Exodus ever happened in the usual sense of historical fact. No evidence of a series of ecological disasters in the narrow land astride the Nile, no evidence of sudden simultaneous deaths in every Egyptian family, no evidence of a shattered Egyptian army, no evidence that hundreds of thousands of people trekked forty years in the Sinai Wilderness.

Yet the story lives, more powerful than its factuality, because it speaks to deep strands of arrogance, fear, despair, and courage in the human process. It speaks:

- To the intertwining of the fates of earth and human earthlings.
- To broad histories of great political struggles, and to private personal struggles of the heart and soul.
- Far beyond the Jewish community, to influence deeply not only the "religious" traditions of Christianity and Islam, but also many modern "secular" liberation movements rooted in class, in nation, in culture, in gender—even some currents in the effort to free and heal the earth itself from destructive exploitation.
- To the interior spiritual and psychological struggles of individual human beings confronting their own "internal pharaohs"— some one aspect of their selves taking over the whole person, twisting and perverting full humanity by turning other facets into slaves, calling forth a yearning to free and integrate the self.

"April," we learn from T. S. Eliot, "is the cruelest month, mixing memory with desire, stirring dull roots with spring rain." April, when the flowers and the barley rise up against winter, when the people rise up against Pharaoh, when Christ rises up against death. "Mixing memory with desire"—weaving together our memory of the past with our hope for the future, a profound description of the intertwining of Exodus with Passover, Passover with the Mass, Moses with Martin Luther King.

"Mixing memory with desire" is what the biblical account of Exodus does by weaving together the description of the Exodus itself as a moment in the utter present—hope and desire turned into action— with detailed instructions of how to celebrate the transformative moment, remembering it through festivals far into the future.

This interweaving is done so subtly that on the first three or four readings of the story, one might almost miss the point. But if we keep our eyes alert to memory as well as desire, we see something remarkable in Exodus 11–13. Just as the story of the conflict/dance among Moses and Pharaoh and God reaches its climax in the moment of darkness, death, blood, and birth, the story turns itself into a story. It says that the cataclysmic moment must be relived year by year, the story must be retold, memory must be invoked. Verse by verse the story slips and slides between the present and a future where the past becomes the present. A Möbius strip in time.

Why do we think these stories are still happening? Why do we feel drawn to reread and reexamine them? Why do we need to hear them anew, to tell them differently?

Looking at the world today, we see and feel the whole human race, the whole planet in a crisis that dwarfs any crisis before. Several elements of that crisis remind us of the archetypal tale of Pharaoh, the Exodus, the transformative experience of Sinai, and the struggle to shape a new kind of community during a generation of experience and experiment in the Wilderness.

Some might say: Doesn't every generation see itself in a great crisis? What is so extraordinary about this generation as to call forth this kind of language?

Of course, as we look back, we realize that some generations are indeed more convulsed by crisis than others:

- The Exodus/Sinai/Wilderness. Even if much of this story is a heightened fiction, some experience of traumatic change inspired it.
- The exile of the Jewish people to captivity in Babylon.
- The Roman Empire's decimation of the Jewish community in the ancient Land of Israel after 135 CE.
- The expulsion of Jews and Muslims from Spain in 1492, and the beginning that same year of the European conquest of the Americas.
- The worldwide blood-drenched period from 1930 to 1975 of the Soviet destruction of the peasant kulaks, the Nazi Holocaust, World War II, and the Chinese "cultural revolution."

Each of these generations has been seen by historians and by the survivors as crucial times of crisis. But what is unique about the generation in which we live, and why does it remind us of the era of Pharaoh and the Exodus?

According to biologists, we ourselves are living through by far the greatest extinction of plant and animal species since the human race came into existence—indeed, since a great meteor hit planet earth sixty-five million years ago. And human behavior has precipitated this.

Moreover, according to an overwhelming majority of the world's climatologists, oceanographers, and epidemiologists, human behavior is heating up the earth's oceans and atmosphere in a way that is already disrupting climate patterns and is likely to bring about radical changes in polar and high-mountain ice, ocean levels, rainfall, crops, and the spread of disease. These predictions warn about huge movements of new kinds of refugees, deepening of the gulf between the extremely rich and the desperately poor, and widespread collapse of many governments and their ability to govern.

And here too, the great majority of scientists insist that these disruptions are being and will be caused by human behavior—by the addiction of a large part of the human race to the overuse of fossil fuels, and by the actions of some hugely profitable global corporations that have used their power to make it very hard for some societies to radically reduce the use of coal, oil, and natural gas.

Why does this pattern recall to us the ancient archetypal story of Pharaoh? According to the biblical tale, Pharaoh's army impoverished and enslaved peoples at home and beyond its borders; his cruel and stubborn arrogance brought on his own country the ecological disasters that we call the "plagues."

But the echo does not stop there, hearing disaster; the ancient story sows the seeds of hope as well. Today, in our own era, we are seeing seeds sown of new forms of grassroots community. To us they recall the ancient story of liberating efforts by the Breath of Life Itself, and the yearning for new wisdom, a compassionate community, and a new relationship with the earth (as exemplified in the Shabbat and Sabbatical year) that drew the runaway slaves to Sinai, to adventures in the Wilderness, and toward the Promised Land.

So we believe that whether the story of Pharaoh, the Exodus, and the Wilderness "actually happened" or not, our present situation calls us to relearn and rethink the story—to learn from it in ways that our forebears did not, to hear some aspects of the story that were always there but did not rise up into our consciousness until our own crises taught us to notice and draw upon them. To learn in order to act.

To that end, we have organized our retelling into eight parts. Each one begins with a brief summary, to help us understand where we are going. The first seven emerge from the text of the Hebrew Bible:

1. Leaving free nomadic life in the first place and being squeezed into the Narrow Land (which is what the Hebrew word for Egypt, *Mitzrayyim*, means).

2. The early efforts to resist the slave society and birth a new peoplehood through the Narrow birth canal, culminating in Moses's encounter with God at the Burning Bush.

3. The freedom movement's struggle against Pharaoh's arrogance and power, culminating in triumph at the Red Sea.

4. The efforts of a straggly band of runaway slaves to find their Center, and their success at Sinai.

5. Their struggle in the Wilderness to shape the supernal Sinai insight into boundaries of communal space, time, and personhood.

6. Facing death, rebellion, and war.

7. Preparing to cross the Jordan into a more ordinary life.

And then there is part 8, to look across millennia, beyond the stories in the Hebrew Bible, to examine how the freedom story has been transformed at several moments of history and is being transformed again today.

When Before Now Has the Story Been Renewed?

We are not the first generation that is living through Pharaoh once again and searching once again for our Sinai and our "promised land"—suffering through a transformation that gives birth to both tyranny and new forms of community. In this book, we have brought together some examinations of several crucial moments when the story of Exodus, Sinai, and Wilderness was central to new bursts of religious community.

One such moment occurred when the Roman Empire under Caesar seemed to the Jewish community of the ancient Land of Israel to be echoing the oppressive behavior of the Egyptian Empire under Pharaoh. There were two responses. One came from the Jewish sages and activists who reframed how to celebrate the Exodus in new ways and how to understand in new ways the Torah that came from Sinai. We ourselves have explored this rethinking of the story, in the first three chapters of part 8.

The other response to Rome was that of Jewish teachers and activists, deeply steeped in the stories of Exodus and Sinai, who shaped a powerful moment of insurgency against Rome, led by Rabbi Jesus—the moment that Christians now call Holy Week—into a new way of understanding both Exodus and Sinai. We asked Ched Myers and Russell Powell, two Christian theologian-activists, to show how the Torah story affected what became the Gospels and how the Gospel retelling changed the ancient story.

There are two other moments for which we asked others to examine ways of renewing the biblical tales. One was the appearance in the Qur'an of a somewhat changed version of the Exodus as it was revealed to Muhammad, who himself fled Mecca under pressure from its power elite as Moses fled Egypt, who returned with a liberating message as did Moses, and who had heard these stories from Christian and Jewish communities in Arabia. We asked S. Ayse Kadayifci-Orellana, a Muslim scholar who in our own generation is involved in interfaith work and in peace-committed and feminist evolutions of Islam, to write her assessment of the place of the Exodus in the Qur'an.

The other was the central place the Exodus story took in the freedom struggles of the southern Black community in the United States, during and after its own enslavement. We asked Vincent Harding, a Black Christian scholar-activist, friend, and co-worker of Dr. Martin Luther King Jr., to look at how the Exodus shaped the songs and actions of the Black community in the civil rights movement.

And in a final chapter, we ourselves look at the tentative beginnings toward a new way of applying the Exodus/Sinai/Wilderness stories in our own cultures, our own celebrations, our own forms of community, and our own politics today.

Study or Action?

The biblical account itself intertwines a call to action—a call to create the act of Exodus—with the command to tell the story of the action.

They are interwoven so closely that the "act" and the "telling" seem to become one fabric. It is as if the Torah has been asked, "Which is greater—the action or the learning?" and answers, "The action—only if it leads to learning."

A thousand years later, confronting a new incarnation of Pharaoh—the Roman Empire—one of the great rabbis, Akiba, turned the answer upside down. Rome had imposed the death sentence for either study of Torah or deeds of Torah. "Which is greater, study or action?" Akiba asked. For which shall we risk our lives? And he answered, "Study—if it leads to action."

In whichever direction we affirm the teaching, it is clear that both generations, both communities, saw that study and action, memory and desire, were deeply intertwined.

To act as well as study required the creation and commitment of bottom-up grassroots community. So the story does not end when (as the Black southern song tells it), "Well, Moses stood on the Red Sea shore / Smote the water with a two-by-four / Pharaoh's army got drownded / O Mary, don't you weep!" The story continues into the creation of a new community at Sinai and a new relationship between land and people, earth and earthlings, in the land across the Jordan River.

And today it is from the grassroots "bottom up" that efforts are being made to see not only human beings but trees, ozone, carbon dioxide, and wind as part of the planetary community; to see the Interbreathing of all life as the fullest metaphor for the Divine in our own generation; to see that when this Interbreathing, the exchanges of oxygen and carbon dioxide between animals and vegetation—is in most danger, that is when its sacred wholeness most needs to be celebrated and healed. This is when we need a new kind of "Sinai" to reaffirm our caring for this Interbreathing, a new kind of Wilderness in which to live out our uncertainties and experiments toward a new kind of "promised land" in which we can sustain our lives.

This crisis between human earthlings and the earth is not the only crisis we face that is reminiscent of the archetypal tale of Exodus:

- Today the nature and meaning of the family, sexuality, child rearing, and neighborliness are being transformed—at first by enormous economic and cultural pressures from the top, and more recently by creative responses from the grassroots "bottom" to shape new forms for the family and neighborhood.

- Today millions are born into an early death by starvation—not because the earth cannot produce enough food but because some institutions are gobbling up the abundance of the planet while leaving others to starve.
- Today millions are driven by war and drought and famine from their homes to other places—becoming "immigrants" and "refugees" without rights or sustenance.
- Today bombers and rockets fly high above the earth to destroy whole civilian neighborhoods whose faces they cannot even see—our analogue to the horse-drawn chariots that imperial Pharaoh mobilized to rise above the farmers and shepherds whom he conquered.

Is our global crisis tied to the overweening power of some modern Pharaohs? Is it true for us, as it was in the ancient story, that the remedy for Pharaohs is not merely overcoming them, but creating whole new forms of community?

These questions focus on specific aspects of tyranny and freedom. Beneath even these profound questions are several even deeper, about the process of learning that infused the ancient Freedom Journey and might instruct our own:

- What do we learn about the nature of journey itself? The story describes a newborn near-community tugged between the desire for freedom and the desire for safety, between demanding the next day's food and trusting in the bounty of the earth, between the hunger for decisive leadership and the desire to do what they wanted, between the stirring beauty that they could weave and color and build themselves and the searing beauty of the jagged mountains, between tangible gods and the evanescent Breath of Life Who would always be Becoming. Not only geographically but spiritually, the Wilderness was in-between. Was that journey itself—the in-between—the most important "destination"? Is it still?
- Can we usefully draw on this story of one ancient empire in one narrow land and its one ethnic band of runaway slaves and rag-

tag rebels, to face the present global crisis with planetary "pharaohs" and many "oppressed peoples"?

- Can the story speak anew, with truth and passion, to the communities that treat it as Holy Writ but often see that Writ with jaded eyes and act it out with rote and stale behavior? Can the story speak anew to the communities far beyond the ones that call it holy, stirring millions to new understanding of their own place in making history?

- How do we understand the God Whose universe can birth both a Pharaoh and a Moses, a Hitler and a Martin Luther King, arrogant empires and creative communities, I–It and I–Thou, the flowering of millions of varied abounding life-forms, and the power of one of those life-forms to extinguish thousands of species that have lived for many million years? How do we understand the God Whose universe gives birth, most of all, to the life-forms and the people who are themselves internally, eternally, fluidly shape-shifting mixtures of these starker models that we are wont to call reality?

- And the question that underlies and goes beyond this book: In that God-given universe of multiplicity and creativity, how do we answer the question Akiba faced before the Roman Empire tortured him to death—study or action? Can we draw not only wisdom but also wise action from the study of this ancient story? How do we move from study to action? What actions might arise for us from a fuller, deeper reading of the story of the Freedom Journey that we call the Exodus?

Perhaps the nature of the journey to freedom itself calls forth a new understanding of the story.

Time then to hear the story. Blessed is the Holy One, the Breath of Life, Who breathes into us the wisdom to know that we become holy by breathing together with each other and with all of life, by shaping our breath into words, and by shaping our words so that they aim toward wisdom, becoming words of Torah.

॥⁄

PART I

From Nomadic Freedom to Imperial Slavery

The Bible's great "Freedom Journey" began with a journey out of freedom into slavery. A small family of nomadic shepherds from the hinterland, literally the "children" of Israel (or Jacob, his childhood name), threw themselves into an encounter with great imperial Egypt.

Furious with their younger brother Joseph, who had with their father's connivance been lording it over them, the brothers sold him as a slave into Egypt. There Joseph repeated the same pattern that had defined his family life: arrogance bringing on his own humiliation. In Egypt, too, he rose in power and from a place of arrogance was brought down to prison; rose and fell again; rose once more—into becoming the right-hand man, prime minister, and viceroy to a benevolent despot, Pharaoh. From that place he did not fall—but in the long run, the rhythm culminated in the enslavement of his people.

Joseph's story takes up one-third of the book of Genesis. Then we leap across a chasm empty of words and history into not a family but a national saga in another book of Torah—Exodus. We find ourselves deep in the darkest, narrowest, most dangerous part of the journey—living under a different Pharaoh, tyrannical and murderous. So this rhythm in Joseph's life of arrogance, degradation, and triumph—followed again by arrogance, and on into the same spiral—becomes not only the biography of a single tormented family but a broader cautionary tale about the danger that arrogance will lead to disaster.

I

Entering the Tight and Narrow Place

Mitzrayyim is the Hebrew word for Egypt. But it is not merely a geographical expression; it means the "Tight and Narrow Place," that *-ayyim* ending making it a noun of twoness, as *oznayyim* means "two ears," *eynayyim* "two eyes." Narrowness doubled, as in English we might say, "Between a rock and a hard place," "Between the devil and the deep blue sea."

Perhaps it was originally a geographical description, pointing to the land that stretched for a thousand miles in a narrow band along both banks of the Nile, totally dependent on the river for its livelihood. To ancient Israelites it became as well a political and cultural critique: the narrow-minded land, a rigid place of slavery that cramped the body and the soul. Occasionally the Bible hints that any land could become *Mitzrayyim*; there was a danger that even an Israelite king could enslave his people, return them to *Mitzrayyim*.

Joseph's Life Pattern

In many great myths or legends, the beginning of the tale is a crystal of the whole. This great story begins with the tale of a younger son of the man known as Jacob, a "heel" in all its English senses, who transformed himself into Israel, the "Godwrestler." That son, Joseph, entered alone into slavery in *Mitzrayyim*.

Why and how? Because he drew on his father's favor to lift himself above his older brothers. In the traditional culture of the ancient Near East, not only in the era of the Abrahamic clan but much later as well, the older sons were expected to be favored. Yet Jacob himself had won favor above his older brother, Esau, and Jacob's father, Isaac, had won favor over his older brother, Ishmael. Indeed, the family memories were that God had affirmed these reversals—and that in the long run, the alienated brothers had been reconciled with each other.

Perhaps those memories were why Jacob felt justified in reversing expectations by favoring Joseph. Perhaps he felt from his own life history that God was trying to set a new standard of equality and justice, undermining the automatic power of the older, stronger sibling.

But Jacob's sons did not accept these reversals as a family value for their unique clan. They reacted with far more bitterness and rage than Ishmael had brought upon the head of Isaac or than Esau had brought upon the head of Jacob. They looked upon their father's special privileging of Joseph and Joseph's eagerness to play this role as a kind of family treason. They made sure this upstart would fall beneath them—first throwing him into a physical pit and then selling him into Egypt as a slave. Then they told their father that he had been killed by a wild animal. So they got rid of the one and broke the other's heart.

Once Joseph experienced this pattern, this rhythm of rise and fall, with such emotional power—love and power intertwined in his family like a choking noose—he repeated the rhythm so that it became the pattern of his life. He was joined in the pattern by three other men, surrogate fathers who in succession lifted him above his equals—and let him down.

Joseph became a slave in the household of Potiphar, a leading official. But he didn't remain an ordinary slave for long. He so impressed Potiphar with his administrative skills in running the household that Potiphar (like Jacob) lifted him above the rest of the household—to power limited only by his master's writ. But this disturbance of the usual household pattern robbed Potiphar's wife of her special role, flung her down the stairs of privilege.

What Happened with Potiphar's Wife?

Potiphar's wife used the one power she had left—the power to trick Joseph into a sexual seduction. He rejected her, but she accused him of attempted rape anyway.

Here we might open ourselves to "read" the blank spaces, the unwritten stories, that the Rabbis called the "white fire" of the Torah text. The Torah, they said, was not written in black ink on white parchment, but in black fire (the letters) on white fire (the spaces). They said we must learn to read the white fire as well as the black fire.

So let us turn our imagination to the blank spaces in the story of Potiphar's wife. Perhaps one way of bringing herself back into power in the household would have been to share Joseph's bed. It is also easy to imagine that if he had responded to her sexually, she would have exposed him just as she did when he rejected her. That would have gotten rid of him entirely and restored her to her wifely power in the household—as it did according to the story that can be read in the letters themselves, the black fire.

Whatever Joseph did, hidden beneath sexual attraction or seduction was power (in a way, as the contest for power had corrupted Joseph's loving childhood family). Potiphar's wife responded to her humiliation much as Joseph's brothers had, by having him thrown into a dungeon. His imprisonment thrust him even lower than the humiliated role into which his rise to household chief had thrust her.

From Down to Up, Again

In prison, Joseph replayed the pattern again. (It seems he could no longer choose whether to replay it or not; it had become the shape of his persona.) This time it was the prison warden who played the role of Joseph's father and of Potiphar. With the warden's help, Joseph lifted himself above his fellow prisoners. They fawned on him in the hope of winning advancement for themselves. But even the prisoner he did help did not reward this upstart. Instead, he evidently resented the pretensions of his equal to become his superior. Just as Potiphar's wife had tricked Joseph into prison, just as his brothers had thrown him into a pit, the other prisoner forgot Joseph's sage dream interpretation and left him in the dungeon.

Finally, Joseph got the chance to play out his life pattern with the highest authority in the world—the Pharaoh, ruler of the world's greatest empire—and at last his effort seemed to have succeeded.

Pharaoh lifted Joseph from prison to advise Pharaoh (by interpreting dreams) how to deal with an impending economic, political, and ecological disaster—a seven-year famine in the fruitful land of Egypt and far beyond as well.

What was the result of Joseph's advice? During seven years of plenty, surplus food was stored in Pharaoh's custody. When famine came, the food could be doled out to meet the people's needs. That could have been done at no cost to the yeomen farmers, with no disruption of their land holdings. But Joseph's advice, which the Pharaoh followed, was that the food the yeomen peasant farmers had grown not be freely returned to them when the need arose.

Instead, the people were required year by year to give Pharaoh their money, their cattle, and finally their land itself, in order to get bread to eat and seed to sow. Thus Joseph reduced them to sharecroppers. He could have honored and protected them, as he could have honored and protected his brothers, his fellow slaves in Potiphar's household, his fellow prisoners. Instead, he demeaned them as he had demeaned these earlier "equals" in his life. He converted all their land into Pharaoh's property (except for some reserved for ownership by the priesthood that served the gods and god-kings of Egypt).

The ex-slave, ex-prisoner not only rose to preeminence in Egypt, second only to the king himself, as he had been second only to his father, to Potiphar, and to the prison warden; this time was different: Joseph seconded his master so well that there was no one able to rebel and cast him into another slavery.

Or so it seemed, as long as Joseph lived and for more than a century beyond.

2

Controlling the Family

J ust as Joseph fulfilled what he had come to think of as his destiny on the huge political landscape of the world's greatest empire, he fulfilled it as well—at last!—in the intimate embraces of his family.

They, living still in the nomad's land of Canaan, were also caught in the widespread famine. They came to Egypt to seek food, and Joseph used his political preeminence to succor and protect them— but also to test whether harshness and jealousy still consumed them.

Joseph discovered they had changed by testing them. Under pressure, would they abandon their youngest brother, Benjamin, to an Egyptian prison to save their own skins, as they had long ago (for much less reason) abandoned Joseph to slavery in Egypt? Would they once again bring grief and despair on their father's head by abandoning his beloved son Benjamin, as they had done long ago by pretending Joseph had been killed by a wild animal? No. They insisted on protecting Benjamin; they passionately appealed to their unknown brother, the prime minister, not to break their aging father's heart.

Upon discovering that his brothers were open to turning themselves toward compassion instead, Joseph revealed to them who he was.

What Inspired the Brothers' Compassion?

What had changed in the dynamics of this dysfunctional family to make the brothers respond with honor and compassion?

We know of two major events in the family's history that may have caused the change. One is a horrifying episode involving their sister Dina. She was raped by a local prince in a town of Canaan near where the clan of Jacob had been living. The prince then fell in love with her and asked to marry her.

Her brothers, with their father Jacob's permission, agreed—on condition that all the men of the tribe agree to be circumcised as befitted those who might want to join the heirs of Abraham. The prince persuaded all the townsmen to agree, and on the third day after the circumcision, when they were most crippled by their pain, the two oldest brothers, Shimon and Levi, killed them all.

Jacob cried out that they had made his reputation stink in the noses of the whole countryside. But Shimon and Levi answered, "Shall our sister be treated like a whore?" (Gen. 34:31).

In the whole episode, the one person who never got to have a say was Dina herself. Her brothers, her father, the prince, the Torah itself never gave her a voice. No one asked her what she wanted. The story seems to be about the "honor" and reputations of the men in the family, not about compassion for Dina's plight or even the pursuit of justice.

Perhaps Jacob responded so obliquely in the moment—expressing concern over his own reputation, not about the immorality of the murders—because he feared that in their rage, his sons might kill him too. (After all, they had brought him Joseph's coat drenched in blood. Had he been killed by a wolf or by these wolfish brothers?) Years later, living in Egypt with Joseph to protect him, now in old age on the brink of his own death, Jacob accused Shimon and Levi outright of murder and once again denied them the honors due his firstborn sons.

During all those years between, what was life like in this blood-streaked family? If Jacob was silent out of fear, did his fear, his silence, his disgust weigh down the family? Had his sons begun to feel some guilt, perhaps even repentance? Or were they caught in sullen rage? When in Egypt they faced the mysterious power of the prime minister whose name they did not know, did they respond out of a bully's fear when confronted with a bully still more powerful, or out of late-grown caring for their father?

The Transformation of Judah

The second family episode involved another brother, Judah. He had married one of his sons to a woman not of the Abrahamic clan, Tamar. His son died. In accordance with the law about raising up a family to the dead man through a marriage to his brother, he married

Tamar to his second son. This one also died. Judah decided Tamar might be a jinx and kept her apart from the remaining son to whose marriage bed (and child) she was entitled.

But Tamar was not willing to bear the insult and the social dislocation of this unlawful widowhood and childlessness. During the great spring sheepshearing festival—one of the celebrations that is later woven into the Exodus festival of spring—Judah set out on the road to the shepherds' gathering place. Tamar disguised herself in a booth along the way as a priestess with whom the shepherds evidently celebrated the fecundity of springtime through a sexual encounter. Judah had sex with her. She became pregnant.

Back home, Judah was about to have his daughter-in-law executed for adultery (in the marriage to which he had denied her access). But she held out to him the staff and seal he had left with her along the way.

Judah cried out, "You are more righteous than I!" (Gen. 38:26), freed her, and took as his heirs the twin boys whom she bore.

This story shows that Joseph's brother Judah had matured beyond the harshness and contempt of his earlier life. Unlike the story of Dina, it shows both that a woman—Tamar—could act on her own and vigorously challenge the injustice put upon her and that Judah could respond directly to a woman's plight, even when it discredited his own reputation.

When Joseph forced Judah to choose between saving his own skin or abandoning Benjamin, we can almost hear the cry, "Benjamin is more righteous than I!" coming from Judah's lips. Judah's self-transformation made it possible for Joseph to reveal his true identity and resolve the estrangement from his family.

Resolving the Sibling Battles

Joseph brought his father to Egypt, introduced him to Pharaoh (who treated him like an equal), and deferred to his father as head of the family. During these last years of honor and comfort, Jacob did one thing that transformed the future of the family. He had Joseph bring his two sons, Ephraim and Menasheh, for a grandfather's blessing. Jacob gave the blessing with his left hand on the firstborn's head and his right hand on the younger's head. When Joseph protested that he had it backwards, Jacob—who knew from his own life about reversing the blessings due the first- and second-borns—insisted he knew what he was doing.

But what Jacob did to his grandchildren was quite different from what he had tricked his father into doing to him. Jacob had conspired to cheat, lie, and steal to win the blessing due his older brother, Esau. Not till the deed was done did Esau learn what had happened, and the blessing he then received was stingier than the one that Jacob got, ambiguous in meaning rather than wholehearted and full-throated. The result was decades of estrangement and hostility.

But Jacob's grandsons got his blessing at the same time, and they both knew what was happening. What's more, it was the same blessing for them both: "Forever and ever may the children of our people be blessed to be like Ephraim and Menasheh" (Gen 48:20). (And still, three thousand years later, that's how Jews bless their male children.)

What happened at that moment? Here was the culmination, the final case, of the brothers' struggles that had run all through Genesis, but this one was very different. In each of the others, the warring brothers were ultimately reconciled: Isaac and Ishmael, Jacob and Esau, Joseph and his brothers. But it took decades in every case. Decades of alienation, conflict, anger, fear, before they were reconciled.

Jacob, who had himself been through this process, dissolved it all between his two grandchildren in a single moment. If he had blessed them with the "correct" hands, he would have been perpetuating the official status quo of elder privilege. If he had acted like his father and grandfather, he would have created decades of distrust before they might have accomplished reconciliation. By bringing them together himself in a single moment, hands crisscrossed, he didn't leave it to the two of them to spend decades solving the problem. He himself intervened, bringing to bear his authority—moral and, you might say, political. He had more power than they, and he had the moral authority to do it.

And so we hear no more of bitter struggles between the siblings of a single family. When we meet Miriam, Aaron, and Moses, we hear of several conflicts among them—but mostly of cooperation and shared honor through most of their long lives. As we will see, the "firstborn" question did not disappear—but it took a whole new turn after Jacob's transformative act.

\\\//

3

Controlling the Realm

When Jacob died, Joseph, with the support of Pharaoh's officials, gave him a monthlong burial worthy of a king. The brothers were frightened—they assumed that only Jacob's supervision was still protecting them from Joseph's revenge. But now that Joseph was the indisputable head of the family, he responded with forgiveness and compassion. He did not bring upon his brothers the abasement he brought upon the farmers of Egypt.

The Hand of Fate

But there is something strange and unexpected about this compassion. For Joseph explained it not in terms of his own emotional and spiritual growth or, for that matter, the spiritual and emotional growth of his brothers. He explained it rather as a product of God's inscrutable will. Though his brothers meant him harm by selling him into Egyptian slavery, Joseph said, God had used precisely this evil to create good—for it had brought Joseph where he could save the family's lives and fortune. So, he explained, there was no reason for him to seek revenge upon his brothers and no reason for them to fear him.

Was this an obvious way for a member of the Abrahamic clan to think and feel? No. Joseph's forebears, women and men, all had a sense of choice, of freedom to choose. For them this freedom had come from their direct encounters with God: visions, voices, laughter, even wrestling.

But Joseph experienced God only through dreams, semi-visions in the dark of night. And Joseph's experience led him to a dark vision of

11

a God Who imposed a history devoid of freedom: not only did human beings become slaves to a tyrant, but also they were slaves to fate.

Was the Famine Fated?

Joseph first expressed his determinism when he interpreted the doubling of Pharaoh's dream—not only seven lean cows devouring seven fat cows, but also seven withered ears of grain devouring seven good ears—as proof that the future famine was inevitable. Only top-down control by Pharaoh and Joseph could match God's fateful top-down imposition of a famine.

Was this the only way to save the family and all Egypt from starvation? Wasn't Joseph free to choose another way?

For a moment, facing Pharaoh, Joseph said he could not interpret the dream; he had to ask God. But he did not wait to ask God. Do we have any hint of what God might have said?

Yes. A hint, that's all. (As the Rabbis taught, dreams are a hint of prophecy—one-sixtieth.) We have, much later in the Torah, God's command of how to prevent famine in the Land of Israel. Every seventh year, the land must lie fallow and all debts must be forgiven. If this seventh year of restfulness is not granted to the land as is its right, then scarcity—famine, drought, exile—will follow (Lev. 25:2–22, 26:34–35, 26:43–45; Deut. 15).

The seventh year? How evocative! Is this seven-year rhythm of abundance and scarcity only an accidental brush with the seven-year cycle that Joseph perceived in Pharaoh's dream? Or is there an integral connection?

Perhaps God—Reality—the inner processes of all abundance and all fallowness—intended Pharaoh's dream to teach: There will be seven years of plenty. If you reap all seven years, there will follow seven years of famine. If you rest and let the land rest in the seventh year, you will have enough to eat. Abundance will spring from self-discipline. *If*—the word of freedom, not of fate.

Could the Famine Have Been Addressed Another Way?

What Joseph taught Pharaoh in Egypt is like a photographic negative of what God teaches Israel at Sinai—dark where Sinai is light, light where it is dark.

Sinai taught that God owned all the land; Joseph taught it was Pharaoh—who claimed godship for himself—who owned all the land.

Sinai taught that the priestly tribe of Levi were to hold no land at all. Their religious power was to be checked by making them materially dependent on the tithing of the other tribes. But in Joseph's practice, the only Egyptians other than Pharaoh who still owned their land were the priests. Thus in Egypt they had both spiritual and material power.

Sinai radically decentralized power into families; Joseph's practice radically centralized power.

Sinai freed the earth to make its own Shabbat; Joseph's practice enslaved the land itself to constant work.

Sinai provided that once a generation, every family could return to its own original piece of land. Joseph tore the Egyptians from their native turf, sending them hurtling into unknown regions of the Egyptian Empire.

Walking in the Dark

Joseph walked in the dark because he had no light from God. Given no vision that would light a path of free choice, Joseph became convinced there was no free choice, and so he abolished freedom for the people of Egypt.

No spiritual freedom, no personal psychological freedom, no political freedom, no economic freedom, no freedom for the earth— all these slaveries meshed.

After a lifetime in which all Joseph's choices turned inside out upon themselves—so that when he chose domination, it led to slavery, and when he fell into slavery, it turned into domination—Joseph was drawn to determinism as a theory of life. That was how and why he could absolve his brothers of their guilt for selling him into slavery. It was all God's decree.

Joseph had walked in the dark because he saw no light from God, no conversation with the universe but only a diktat. Was it his fate to be denied the light that had shone so brightly to his forebears? Or—by joining with his father in turning so early in his youth to rise above his brothers—had they together darkened Joseph's path? Had the two of them called forth a version of the universe and God that was filled with fate, not freedom? Driven by dreams that seemed to predict the future, did he become convinced there was no free choice to be had? Bereft of a clear vision that might have taught compassion, did he think the only path was seeking power, the only choice the one between more power and the pit?

And at last the pattern worked. It took decades of his life, but finally it worked. At last he stood on the pinnacle of the world, and no one could throw him in the pit again.

Or so it seemed, until long after his death.

The Future: Another Degradation?

When we roll the parchment forward to the early passages of Exodus, we discover that Joseph's people, whom he had made so prosperous when Egypt was suffering from famine, had been flung into slavery by a Pharaoh who did not cherish Joseph. We may wonder whether the spiral had spun once again.

Every time before, Joseph's effort to rise above his fellows had ended up by casting him beneath them. Did his ultimate triumph in becoming Pharaoh's viceroy simply postpone and worsen the fall— into a pit of slavery for all his people? Did the whole people suffer in slavery for the sake of Joseph's triumph, for his turning Egyptian peasants into serfs, for his believing that neither he nor others had real freedom to make choices, for his conviction that only a dark vision of a darkly absent but insistent God was the world's reality?

PART II

Midwives and Moses

Just as the Bible's story of losing freedom is told as a "biographical novel" centered on Joseph, the Bible crystallizes the ascent from slavery to freedom with the biographical novel of the life of Moses.

The Exodus story is said to be a heroic epic unusual in world literature in that the hero is not a single individual but an entire community that suffered many vicissitudes before achieving—or not quite achieving—the heroic goal. Yet within that story, Moses can certainly be seen as himself a hero, journeying to the edge of—but not quite into—the treasure of his vision.

Like Joseph going into slavery in Egypt, Moses foreshadowed his people's future—in his case, coming out of slavery in Egypt, going forward into a journey of freedom. Joseph's family and his whole life history had engrained in him a sense of fatalism, unfreedom in the hands of a benevolent but despotic God. Moses, on the other hand, learned that at the roots of life and history was freedom. He learned to be guided by a God whose very Name beckoned him and everyone into a future of open possibility—even the possibility of arguing with God, confronting God, disobeying God.

The Family of Moses: Solidarity, Not Struggle

Moses's story began even before his birth. The small family of the "Children of Israel" had become a teeming, swarming multitude. The Pharaoh, frightened, ordered a pair of midwives to murder the Israelite boy-children as soon as they were born. They refused, and the Pharaoh

15

ordered the newborns to be murdered by anyone and everyone in sight.

Now one Israelite family took center stage in the national drama, a family united by love and solidarity, markedly different from Joseph's family history of anger and dissension. Their youngest child, not yet named Moses, was saved by sister Miriam's stratagem from the murderous death decreed by Pharaoh. Miriam enlisted the motherly feelings of the Pharaoh's own daughter to rescue the infant from exposure on the Nile.

From that point on, our journey is strongly connected with Moses as hero. The pathmarks are almost all connected with his experiences, triumphs, and failures. They come in three great sections of his life—each, according to tradition, approximately forty years long. We will briefly see his life as a whole in the light of these three stages of growth and then focus on the first two, which moved the people of Israel from abject slavery to the Sea of Transformation, when they became a band of runaway slaves and the imperial power that had enslaved them collapsed.

Three Lives in One

The first phase of the three forty-year periods of Moses's life began with a babyhood of deadly danger and of doubled birth (from the womb and from the Nile) and duplicated mothers (his own, his sister, and Pharaoh's daughter). From this danger and deliverance in the midst of birthing waters, he grew into adulthood in Egypt. His tumultuous babyhood was followed by a silent time of many years, capped and ended by the first traumatic stirrings of Moses's resistance to tyranny, his failure, and his sudden flight from Egypt to escape once more the danger of an early death (Exod.1:15–2:15).

The second phase began again with danger and deliverance at water's edge, in a struggle against injustice at a wellspring in the hill country of Midian. That struggle drew him into marriage with another daughter of a leading local family—this time the daughter of a priest of God, not an imperial ruler. Then Moses lived through a silent time of many years of calm and inner reflection as a husband, father, and shepherd. These quiet years were followed by, capped by, and ended by a startling, enlightening encounter with God as the Voice of the Burning Bush and with another startling danger to his life (Exod. 2:16–4:26).

The third phase of Moses's life—a forty-year struggle for liberation and community—began with about two years full of incident and excitement. His return to Egypt to face Pharaoh and demand freedom for the people was punctuated by a series of ecological and social disasters—the "plagues"—that grew out of Pharaoh's arrogance, stubbornness, and cruelty. The first of these was Moses's challenge to the Nile that had been his birthing-waters of danger and deliverance. With God's help, he transformed the Nile from water to blood, an echo of his birthing. The plague year ended with the shattering of Pharaoh's power and the liberation of the Israelites as they crossed the Reed (or Red) Sea. Again a body of water became both a danger and a deliverance (Exod. 5:1–14:31).

There followed at once a year filled by an encounter between God and the entire people at the Mountain of God; by the building of a colorful and portable Shrine for God's Presence; by the sufferings of the people, their repeated rebellions against Moses's and God's authority, and their battles against other peoples; and by God's decision that they must stay in the Wilderness until the generation that left slavery had died out and a new generation was ready to create a new society.

These two intense years were followed by almost thirty-nine years of silence, capped and ended by Moses's retelling of the story of the journey to the new generation, along with his visions of victory to come and faithlessness to follow—and finally, the death he had escaped at the ends of his two earlier phases of life. This time the waters of another river became the marker of his dying. For Moses died just as the people prepared to cross the Jordan River into the Land that God had offered them. He pleaded with God to let these dangerous waters become once more for him (as well as for the people) the waters of deliverance and rebirth, but it was not to be.

A Rhythm: Tumult, Calm, Tumult

We should notice that within all three of these phases of Moses's life, we see tumult at the beginning of the phase, almost nothing about many years along the way, and an explosive event at the end.

This pattern—action, long period of calm, action—especially repeated three times in this way, is unique among the Bible's tellings of various heroes' stories. The Torah's silence about these three sets of middle years may invite midrashic tales to fill the open space or may be understood to point toward the need for long periods of calm and reflection if the hero and his people were to achieve a new stage of their liberation.

The same pattern is unveiled at another level as well: Moses's family time in Midian lay between the two more turbulent and politically active times in Egypt. Again, the teaching seems to be that the ineffective activist of early adulthood needed a period of reflection and calm to become the far more effective leader of the Exodus.

4

From Benevolent Despot to Vindictive Tyrant

As the book of Genesis ends, we see two things: a benevolent Pharaoh ruling over Egypt, owning all the land except for the holdings of the priests who celebrated him as a god; and a flourishing family of the children of Jacob, also called Israel, living as shepherds in a region separate from most Egyptians.

There is a large blank space in the Torah scroll as we move from Genesis to Exodus. As we have already seen, any blank space, even between two letters, is really "white fire," which calls out to be read—interpreted—just as the writing, "black fire," does. But this is not merely the space between two letters or two words. This expanse of white fire is enormous, leaving us to read the silent stories of several hundred years.

To glimpse what may have happened in that long blank space, we must first look at the black fire of the text of Exodus.

A New Kind of Pharaoh: Unkind

As the book of Exodus begins, the Children of Israel had been multiplying, swarming, and their very numbers and success had frightened the king.

Pharaoh had lost all emotional connection with these folks. Though he had certainly heard plenty about his ancestor's prime minister Joseph, he did not "know" him (Exod. 1:8). And here, in the use of the word *yodea*, we get an insight into a kind of outlook that is foreign to most modern ears.

In biblical Hebrew, *yodea* meant physically making love (as in "Adam *yodea* Eve, and she conceived" [Gen. 4:1]), as well as emotional connection ("Pharaoh did not *yodea* Joseph"), intellectual exploration ("I [Job] *yodea* that You can do everything" [Job 42:2]; "Do you *yodea* the dimensions of the earth?" [Job 38:5]), and spiritual experience ("The *yodea* of God will fill the earth as the waters fill the sea" [Habakkuk 2:14]). All these, when they were working right, the intellectual and spiritual as well as the others, were as interrelational as sex. And *yodea* sex was filled with spiritual, emotional, and intellectual interrelationship—it was not only a physical coupling.

This approach, in which *yodea* in all its uses could be translated "know," evidently still made sense when the King James Version of the Bible was translated from Hebrew to English, about five hundred years ago. But now modernity has split the meanings along with splitting the realities. On the one hand, lovemaking is supposed to be romantically "blind" (closing your eyes when you kiss someone is just a physical aspect of the romantic ideal). And intellectual "knowledge" is now intended to be coldly "objective" (and objectifying), the "cold facts." The sense of interrelational exploring in body-mind can't be accessed anymore. Imagine a modern university in which learning was as interrelational as making love!

The only adequate translation in current English for *yodea* is "grok," which is unfortunately but unsurprisingly only an English loanword—a word from Martian. At least it is according to Robert Heinlein. It's worth reading his book *Stranger in a Strange Land* just to get what the word "grok" means—that is, to grok the word "grok" fully.

So this Pharaoh didn't grok Joseph. (The negative gives us an interesting backward-looking glance at the deep connection between Joseph and the Pharaoh whom he served—who became a substitute father for him, in all the complexity of that role in Joseph's life.)

Turning Immigrants into Pariahs

Even more important than this new Pharaoh's failure of historical memory, even more important than his own inner thoughts and feelings, were the words he spoke aloud to the nation. He warned that the Israelites were too numerous and too dangerous; they might side with Egypt's enemies and "rise from the ground" (Exod. 1:10).

Now let us try to read the white fire of the blank parchment by drawing on the modern life experience of our own day.

Egyptian yeomen farmers had been turned into serfs and their lives had been saved through the clever advice of a renowned, now almost legendary, foreigner named Joseph—an Israelite, would you believe, one of those shepherds (pfui!) who lived off by themselves in the land of Goshen!

The Great Egyptian Famine and its transformation of society were being recalled with awe in storybooks and fireside tales. But now that the frightening famine of a seven-year drought had become a distant shuddery memory, the serfs were not so happy with their lot. Yes, they had enough to eat, but only by the king's grace.

The muttering was turning into grumbling. "My granddad says his granddad said they owned a sweet forty acres where the Nile bends—so."

"How could we take back our land again?"

Pharaoh was of course not terribly pleased to hear this grumbling. He was also not pleased with a cohesive bunch of folks who claimed some special privileges because some legendary leader they had long ago had saved his forebear's life and career. They talked a different language, they were mostly shepherds (pfui!), and they lived in a cluster with little supervision by his army and police.

And they had become extraordinarily numerous. "They reproduce like rabbits, like insects," he snarled. "If the Babylonian army invaded, who knows what they might do?"

So Pharaoh tried something new—or maybe old, even then: he turned the grumbling of his people against the strangers.

※

5

Giving Birth to Freedom

The frightened Pharaoh invented a new political tactic—genocide—and there arose in response another new political invention: non-violent civil disobedience.

Pharaoh called into his presence two midwives and ordered them to kill every boy newborn to Israelite women.

Midwives—Not Murderers

The Hebrew description of these two women is best translated as "midwives / Hebrews" (Exod. 1:15). Does this mean midwives who themselves were Hebrew or women who were midwives to the Hebrews? The grammar and the meaning are not clear. It would seem Pharaoh might have more likely expected Egyptian women to kill the Israelite babies than Hebrew women, but it is still not clear whether they—Shifra and Puah are their names—were themselves both Hebrew women, or both Egyptian women, or perhaps one each.

Perhaps the reason that the text is so ambiguous is that its writer does not care and is trying to teach us not to care. The important thing is that two women, of whatever ethnic background, banded together to disobey the king—perhaps an international feminist conspiracy.

The passage says that they revered God and would not kill the babies. It does not mention a Voice or a Vision of divine revelation. Perhaps they heard God in every baby's birth-wail, saw God in every baby's face—or every mother's.

22

When Pharaoh called them back to him again, angry that no babies were being killed, they sidestepped his anger. They did not say, "God forbids us to kill these innocents." Instead they played with Hebrew words—a pun to placate the king while explaining their actions. They told him that the Hebrew women were so "life animated" (Exod. 1:19) that they gave birth, unlike Egyptian women, before the midwives could arrive to kill the boys.

What was the pun? In English, there is an overlap in meaning between "animal" and "animated" and an overlap in meaning between "wildlife" and "lively." Saying to Pharaoh that the women were like animals or wildlife (*chayot*, from the root for "life") in their swiftness to give birth would play to his racist contempt for the Israelites. Yet the Hebrew word could also simply mean that the women were "animated," "lively."

The midwives told a truth that was also a lie. This first step into civil disobedience was a sidestep, rather than direct and challenging resistance. It set the stage for more direct resistance later.

Far from suffering from their disobedience, the midwives prospered. The Bible says that God gave them "households" (Exod. 1:21). What does this mean? Wherever a male hero of the Bible is given a "household," the Rabbis interpreted this to mean a wife and children. For these women, does "household" mean that they were given husbands and children? Or—now here's a stretch, no doubt influenced by the history of our own generation—could the story be hinting that the midwives were given "wives" because they were what we would today call lesbians? (The Bible does not denigrate lesbianism in the way it does some aspects of male homosexual relationships; so this notion is not as outlandish as it may at first blush seem.)

An International Feminist Conspiracy

Instead of trying to enforce his original edict by punishing the midwives, Pharaoh now called on the whole Egyptian community to start killing the Israelite boys. That edict is what led to Moses's family's efforts to hide him in plain sight, cast adrift on the bosom of the Nile, to be reborn—they hoped—from the fruitful waters of the River. That is where Pharaoh's own daughter and a lowly slave girl—two women of different nations, religions, and class origins—did for certain create an international feminist conspiracy to save the life of Moses.

Notice that images of birth are rising to the surface of our story. Midwives—birth givers—were the first people to resist Pharaoh's tyranny. Moses was reborn and named by his foster mother, Pharaoh's daughter, with the help of his sister and his biological mother. But even these are not the first birth references in the story, or the last.

God's own Self, early in the story, called Israel "My firstborn" (Exod. 4:22). In the natural and historical senses, this was surely not true. Egypt was an older, bigger, stronger, more learned, more sophisticated civilization. God turned all this on its head.

This somersault at the level of nations echoes analogous somersaults at the level of families that appear again and again in the book of Genesis. In Genesis, Abraham and Sarah intervened to expel the elder son Ishmael from the family and make their Isaac the "firstborn" instead; Rebekah intervened to help her younger son Jacob steal from Esau the blessing of the firstborn; Jacob intervened to favor his son Joseph over all Joseph's older brothers; Judah's son Peretz took on the honors due the firstborn instead of his older twin brother Zerach; Joseph's son Ephraim was elevated by his grandfather Jacob in Menasheh's stead. In each generation, successive parents tried, with God's help and approval, to reverse the blessings due the firstborn. The special privileges due the firstborn were, in all these stories, handed over to a younger sibling.

Now the birth-order switching that had for so many generations in the book of Genesis focused on individual siblings leaps in the book of Exodus into a larger, longer category: whole peoplehoods. Now the special privileges that might have belonged to Egypt would be given instead to the people Israel—and the topsy-turvy somersault would be enforced by a threat to endanger all the firstborns of Egypt if the Egyptian Pharaoh did not let these "firstborn" slaves go free.

Topsy-Turvy Firstborns

In the book of Exodus, the earthly parents fade from sight. It is God who becomes the Father/Mother, God who acts on His/Her own to turn the history of great families—peoplehoods—topsy-turvy.

Among the sibling pairs in the book of Genesis, these somersaults had resulted in years of conflict and estrangement, ultimately followed by reconciliations. In the story of Egypt's displacement by its younger sibling Israel, there was certainly conflict—disastrous plagues and ultimately the death of all Egyptian firstborns. Where and when did the ultimate reconciliation between the displaced sibling Egypt with the favored "firstborn" Israel come? For this we have to turn to prophetic visions of the end of days (Isa. 19:24).

Once we begin to think "birth" and "newborn," moment after moment of the story takes on new meaning. Begin again at the beginning. What entered Egypt at the beginning of the book of Exodus was a tiny band of households, a nucleus, a cluster of cells. At that point, they sojourned in a broad and open space, a womb that was nourishing and spacious.

And then they grew with astonishing speed, like any fetus: they were fruitful, they swarmed, they multiplied, they grew strong beyond and beyond, the land was filled up with them (Exod. 1:7). This string of verbs echoes precisely the Torah's language of Creation; as the world itself was conceived with these verbs of overflowing growth, so was the people Israel. They grew not only in numbers but in self-awareness. They grew enough that they felt the nurturing space around them beginning to close in. They could feel their lives, pregnant with possibility, begin to point toward a destination. A birth.

As the birthing approached, the doorways of the Israelites, through which they would leave their houses to begin the Exodus, were sprinkled with the blood of lambs. These doorways echo the bloody doorway of the womb through which all human beings must pass to begin their independent lives. Those who walked through this bloody passage on the night of the Exodus became newborns, God's "firstborn."

The "breaking of the Sea" (Exod. 14:21), as the Bible calls the moment when the Israelites crossed the Sea of Reeds that had divided for them, echoes the breaking of the waters that precedes the birthing of a newborn. Whence comes the mistranslation that calls the water the "Red Sea"? Modern scholars think it comes from a linguistic habit of some Mediterranean cultures to name seas by their color to specify their geographic place. In that habit, the "southern sea" was the "Red Sea." But perhaps, more powerfully and poignantly, the image of the "Red Sea" is rooted in an image of the bloody drowning of all Pharaoh's army.

All the firstborn of Egypt's every family had to die for "firstborn" Israel to win its freedom. Out of this danger, woven into the ritual memorializing of the Exodus, is a ritual redemption of the firstborn of every Israelite family—a redemption from the danger of their own deaths.

Indeed, so strong is this message about the newly "firstborn" people that in the midst of the Torah passage about the Exodus and the Pesach celebration that will recall it, the Torah twice interrupts itself (Exod. 13:1–2 and 13:11–13) to command that the people make holy and redeem their own firstborn, throughout all generations. Just as the circumcision of all sons is to recall the covenant of fruitfulness with Abraham, Sarah, and Hagar, so the redemption of all firstborns is to recall the covenant of freedom.

It becomes clear that these firstborns of each family had been "priests" for the family, its channel to God. To redeem them from this role, this sacred burden had to be transferred to a tribe of priestly obligation. Perhaps this switch hints that the firstborns of Egypt were already "family priests" whose lives were owed and consecrated to the gods of Egypt—until they were forfeited by the God known to the Israelites.

The Narrow Birth Canal

As we learn our way into seeing *Mitzrayyim* as a narrow birth canal, and Mother Egypt travailing in a birth obstructed by Pharaoh's will to Mastery, we might wonder why this metaphor of birth was not one we all were taught, you might say, with our mother's milk.

And why has it arisen in the second half of the twentieth century?

Here is a case where we need to leap across the barriers of time, leaping three thousand years and more to understand the way the telling of the Exodus has taken on new truth.

When was this midrashic metaphor conceived? During the mid-1970s, a dozen men and a single woman sat together to test out an idea full of holy chutzpah. I, Arthur, was one of them. Could we, in our own generation, create a commentary to the Torah that could stand alongside the great collections of midrash from the past?

How come there was just one woman? At that moment in history, not many women could pass the official tests of "knowledgeable Jew"—set by male scholars who had just barely begun to relinquish their monopoly of the rabbinate. The one woman present was Lynn Gottlieb. She had wanted to enter the Conservative rabbinical seminary, but at that time they had refused to admit any women. She had kept on studying and was prepared—if they kept refusing—not to wait forever but to seek ordination by an independent committee of rabbis (and that is ultimately what happened).

As we settled into place, our chairman—a well-known and weighty scholar—proposed that we test ourselves in the classic way: we would pick a passage of Torah, go through it verse by verse, and say our say upon each verse. We had two days. Then we could decide whether the results seemed rich enough for us to do a whole new "Rashi" (the name of the twelfth-century rabbi who was the most respected commentator/collector of verse-by-verse midrash).

The passage we chose was the first portion of Exodus. We began moving one verse at a time around the table, the excitement building as we played with the richness of the Torah text. Each phrase, each word, was lovingly caressed. Lynn was silent; the men fell easily into filling all the space. An hour, two hours, went by; we had just barely reached verse 10.

Suddenly Lynn said, "Look! I've just noticed, down below, about the midwives ..." The chairman quirked an eyebrow at her: "Sure, Lynn, we'll get there. Let's keep going as we agreed, in order." The conversation resumed, got even more excited; the wind of words hovered even longer on each phrase of text. Half an hour later, Lynn broke in again: "Yes, look, see what the story says about the midwives ..." And again the chairman, slightly exasperated this time: "Lynn, look, we'll be there soon."

Women Birthing Torah Today

Suddenly Lynn grinned, shook her long hair, and said, "The Hebrew women are full of life to give birth *quickly*, before the midwife comes to them" (Exod. 1:19).

The rest of us laughed. We kept on with the text. But Torah—Torah straight from God, Torah *mamash* for real, had just happened. The medium and the message, the form and the content, had just merged. The newborn fact of women learning and teaching Torah had just found its voice, and the voice was an ancient voice, a Voice straight from the Torah text. The Voice was brash, persistent, disobedient, jokey—just as the midwives had been. They had made a pun, a wordplay, to ensnare the king and free the people. Lynn had made a play upon the ancient words, quoting them as a comment on our most immediate present—a kind of pun on the ironies of life. Gently, gently, she had raised the question: Who is Pharaoh? And who seeks to give new birth?

When at last we reached the midwife passage, Lynn pointed precisely to the theme of birth. Here, she said, is where the liberation started. Before Moses, before Miriam, here—these two women, maybe Israelites and maybe not, had asserted freedom by defending newborns. And later God says all Israel is God's firstborn. Somewhere here, she said, is a new way of looking at the story: a story of the birthing of a people.

From this spark, this past generation, has grown a glowing metaphor, a midrash that now seems obvious and utterly apparent from the Torah text, but once was utterly unheard of. Listen to the text with "birthing" on your mind, and suddenly the pieces of the story come together in a new configuration. Many ears have joined to hear it, many voices have joined to speak it: a piece of insight here, a new connection there.

And the story takes on a whole new shape. It does not lose the old shape, the shape of political freedom, of rising up against tyranny, of the triumph of the God Who sides with the despised against a resplendent emperor who claims to be a god. The new shape, the new metaphor, enriches the old one. And it also enriches and expands and transforms the community for which Torah is a collective family story.

This is indeed a confirmation, an enrichment, not simply an additional aspect of the story. For each birth brings into the world a being who is new, unpredictable, made partly from parental givenness and partly from unprecedented possibility. Each birth is an act of freedom. And the birth of a whole people—not only as an ethnic family but as a particular kind of community, one made up of the despised, the enslaved, who come forward to change history—makes for the birth of a new approach to life.

Indeed, the Torah teaches that not a "pure" ethnic stock of Abraham's descendants went forth from the narrow birth canal to freedom, but a "mixed multitude," an *erev rav* (Exod. 12:38), what ethnic purists might have called "riffraff." And the tradition adds that Pharaoh's daughter (in Hebrew, "Bat-Pharaoh" [Exod. 2:5]) was among them. She who was named only Bat-Pharaoh when she rebirthed Moses from the river, when at last she reached Sinai was herself reborn and took on the name "Bat-Yah": the daughter of God, daughter of the Breath of Life (*Vayikra Rabbah* 1:3).

This was not only a new people but a new kind of people that had just been born. And when did this birthing happen? In the springtime, when lambs were being born and barley was sprouting. The earth itself was giving birth, and human history joined in.

Indeed, when the Rabbis later wrestled with the shape of the Jewish calendar, they amended what could have been a purely lunar calendar to make sure that the month of Passover would always obey what the Torah says about the month of the Exodus: that it was "the month of *Aviv*," meaning "spring/sprouting/new-grain" (Exod. 13:4, 34:18). Thus the birth of the people and of freedom would always be recalled and celebrated in the time of year when earthy rebirth is occurring.

Torah Rebirthing Women

What do we learn from this "rebirthing" metaphor of the Exodus, and to what changes—what new birth of ourselves—does this midrash call us?

For me, Arthur, the most powerful answer to this question came in a moment's revelation on a Shabbat morning in New Orleans. I had been invited to teach Torah at a synagogue there, one whose custom it was to follow the sermon with an open discussion—usually rich and thoughtful, I was told, full not just of questions but of independent comments. I came during the time of year when we were reading the story of liberation from *Mitzrayyim*. So I focused my talk on the Exodus as a birth.

As advertised, the discussion afterward was full of life and creativity. After the service, a member of the congregation came up to me to say how extraordinary the discussion had been. "But—why?" I said, puzzled and embarrassed. "I was told the discussions are always full of life. What was so special?"

"Oh," he said, "the women. They never join in. Today they did."

Oh.... Oh! So not only did the seed of this fruitful midrash come from a woman, but the midrash itself invited women into Torah in a new way, even when it happened to be a man who midwifed it in their particular community.

I do not think it is an accident that this new metaphoric midrash arises in our midst for the first time in the first generation when women are studying Torah and men can be present in the birthing room. Always before in Jewish life, the two worlds were totally separate. Now the barriers have broken down.

It matters that the barriers have broken down—matters to what we see in Torah, and matters to what Torah will make of us. The metaphors that women learn about themselves from other women matter to their perceptions of the Torah—including the metaphor of birth and mothering, even among women who are not themselves mothers. (Lynn Gottlieb was not yet a mother when we met around that table.) The life paths that men walk matter to their perceptions of the Torah. The fact that I had been present and taken a hand, even a secondhand hand, at the moment of my daughter's birth—that mattered when I heard Lynn speak of Torah.

But the effect on me is far less important than the effect on women. For this process strengthens itself, brings on a "virtuous circle." The more women help to shape new midrash, new ways of understanding Torah, the more women will bring themselves into the process not only of Torah study but of shaping all the elements of Jewish life.

There is a second powerful effect of seeing the Exodus as birthing. It brings to consciousness again the earthy element of the festival of spring. It reminds us that history and biology, human earthlings and the earth, are intertwined. It reminds us that in a generation when the very cycles of the web of life on earth are stuttering and stammering, damaged by the changes we humans have worked upon our planet, we may need to reshape history in order to keep the cycles of future generations flowing. It gives a poignant depth to living in a generation when for some species birth itself has become problematic—when on the one hand human populations are exploding and on the other hand pollution of the earth and air and water has reduced male sperm counts and made many marriages infertile. It reconnects freedom and birth in a new dimension.

These two new learnings from the metaphor of Exodus as birth are connected. As women bring themselves into the process of Torah, the earth will bring itself into Torah as well. The male Rabbinic and kabbalistic traditions, as well as Christian tradition, mostly saw women as "earthy"—creatures of body and emotion, not of intellect and spirit as were men. The earth itself was "earthy," "feminine," not suffused with higher intellectual and spiritual meaning. Both women and earth lived on the edges, the fringes, of religious life. In our own day, it may be that earthy women and feminine earth will be intertwined in their return to the center of religious life.

What are the implications of seeing the Exodus in these new ways?

What does it mean for us to say those astounding words "Mother Egypt"? How might it change our outlook on our lives to see *Mitzrayyim* as not only the Tight Place squeezing the old life out of us, but the Narrow Canal through which we emerge to new life? Can we integrate into our spiritual and political lives this learning of how to move from the spacious womb that nourishes, to the womb that constricts, to the womb that insists on pushing us forward, to the open space beyond the womb—the open space that is again a new womb that at some point, as we grow, will become a constriction that pushes us forward yet again?

What does it mean for our yearly Passover celebrations of the Exodus? To this question we will return when we make a different leap through time—into the nature of the Passover Seder as the Seder itself is reborn in our own generation.

6

Drawn Forth, Drawing Forth

The midwives have set the scene for leadership by women, for the importance of birth, and for the first stages of nonviolent civil disobedience. Now we move into Moses's own life. It begins, of course, with his birth—not a simple story but a double story, of two births. And it begins with women's leadership, exercised through acts of activist, assertive nonviolent civil disobedience—not only by passive refusal to obey.

We begin with a mysterious, heroic birth. The child, younger than his sister Miriam and his brother Aaron, was born into a world where the Pharaoh had ordered him to be killed on sight. To save his life—or at least to prevent an obvious and easy murder—his sister illegally set him adrift in a protective "ark" on the Great River, the birthing waters not of one lone mother's womb but of all the Narrow Nation.

Challenging Pharaoh's Law

There the tyrant's daughter found him and, joining with his incognito sister, decided to break the law and return him to his mother to be nursed under the protection of the palace. Notice that this act, in some ways like that of the midwives Shifra and Puah, was both more challenging and less public than theirs had been. They had refused to do the evil Pharaoh had commanded; Miriam and Pharaoh's daughter acted affirmatively to do the good that Pharaoh had forbidden—one more step toward assertive nonviolent resistance.

And crucially, Pharaoh's daughter gave Moses his name. Just as his life wavered between Egyptian and Hebrew culture, so did his name waver between its meanings in Hebrew and Egyptian. It speaks in Egyptian and in Hebrew, and even suggests an ungrammatical but prophetic Hebrew spoken by the Egyptian princess.

In Egyptian, "Moses" means "son of," as in the pharaohs Rameses, "son of the god Ra," and Thutmose, "son of the god Thoth." Thus Moses was simply "son of—" and a blank. "Son of—*who knows?*"

The Egyptian princess who named him in Hebrew got the Hebrew grammar wrong, as someone might who is clumsily trying to learn a different language. She who had drawn him forth from the water said that "Moshe" meant "the one who is drawn forth," but it actually meant "the one who will draw forth"—as he does ultimately draw forth the people from slavery. She was grammatically wrong but prophetically right.

All this effort to protect and nurture Moses gave him a family deeply different from the one that shaped the life and character of Joseph. Joseph's mother had died when he was young; his father had thrust him into danger; his brothers had almost killed him and did sell him into slavery. Moses's parents nurtured him; his sister saved his life; his elder brother, we will learn, assisted him at almost every turn in their lives; he ended up with a second or third mother—Pharaoh's daughter—and perhaps with an extra father, Pharaoh himself. When Pharaoh forced him to flee into exile, he found a place where he could be affirmed and sheltered by still another surrogate father. In none of these situations did he force himself into a haughty role; in none did he find himself the victim of jealousy and rancor.

The One-Time Terrorist

Moses's life was an experiment in the forms of resistance to tyrannical injustice. As a young man, he became a one-time terrorist: when he saw an Egyptian overseer beating an Israelite slave, he killed the overseer. How do we assess this act of violence today?

And how do we assess his motivation? Was this an act of ethnic or ethical solidarity? Was Moses responding with rage because he felt his own identity as a downtrodden Hebrew outraged, or his own identity as a human being, even though a prince? We do not know.

Just as the text may deliberately be never clear whether Shifra and Puah are Hebrews or Egyptians, so the text may be telling us precisely that here as well it doesn't matter—that this young man who was both Egyptian and Israelite had found a way to fuse his ethnic passion and his ethical compassion.

Or rather, the text may be saying that it matters enormously that we can't tell the difference. This is the first moment when Moses himself took on the heroic stance. Is this some teaching to each of us today, that the first step into our own best self is to integrate our commitments to our own community with our commitments to universal justice? Would we want others to say of us that the two were so intertwined that there was no way to tell them apart?

But then Moses overreached the bounds of good sense or concluded that he had already transgressed them. He intervened in a fight between two Hebrews—and one of them revealed that his killing of the Egyptian overseer was already known. So Moses fled his ambiguous home. Was he overcome by fear of punishment or by guilt over his own violence? When he said, "So the matter is known!" (Exod. 2:14), did he mean by the police or by divine authorities?

Again, we do not know.

It may be this very moment of self-questioning that sparked in Moses the quest for a different kind of resistance. If violence was self-destructive and the bravery of the midwives was not sufficient, what kind of resistance could end a life of tyranny and transform the future?

The ancient Rabbis, trying to understand this still more ancient story, thought it was a sin to kill the overseer without a trial in court. They questioned the Torah text that says God told Moses he could not enter the Land of God's Promise because much later in the Wilderness he struck a rock till water flowed from it when he was supposed to speak to it. The Rabbis suggested that God's prohibition was rooted in a sin much earlier and much worse: that Moses struck the overseer till blood flowed from his body.

In our own generation, it took a ten-year-old boy in a Sunday-school class to say that the two reasons were the same: that Moses had smashed the rock as if he were still full of rage against that overseer, rather than speaking to the rock as God had told him—treating it with caring and compassion. Said the ten-year-old, "God did not want him to rule over the people in their new land if his instinct was still to hit and smash."

A Wellspring of Well-Being

So Moses fled the turmoil of his birthplace. He may have had no idea where he was fleeing to. But what he found was a place of peace and quiet—the rocky hillside pastures of nomadic Midian. Even there his first encounter was with burly shepherds who were harassing seven young women at a well where they were trying to water their sheep. Moses drove the troublemakers off.

The young women turned out to be daughters of a Midianite priest and shepherd named Reuel—a pun on two Hebrew words that could mean "God's shepherd" and "God's seeing." Moses married one of the seven daughters he had rescued: Tzipporah.

This episode stands in a long series of ancient storytelling about wells:

- God's shepherd Abraham's sealing his ownership of a well with an oath over seven ewe lambs. (Were God's shepherd's—Reuel's—seven daughters an echo of these seven ewe lambs?)
- Hagar's discovery of a well she named the "Well of the Living One Who Sees Me," which saved her and the son Ishmael she bore to Abraham from dying of thirst.
- The well at which Abraham's servant found a wife for Abraham's son Isaac.
- The well at which Abraham's grandson Jacob met his wife-to-be, Rachel.

So the story linked Moses to four different moments in the saga of the wandering shepherds of the Abrahamic clan, and not to random moments but to moments of healing, nurturing: one well of peace-making, one well of life saving, two wells of loving marriage.

From these four moments we realize that the hero did not spring on his own from slavery or luxury. He had forebears in the ancient heroes of his people. It had taken the silences of wandering with the flocks to let those ancient heroes hear the Voice; it had taken caring for the lambs to breed in them compassion for community. Now Moses, the child of hubbub, had himself become a wanderer. Not till he had lived the nomadic life that they had lived could his ears hear the Voice that they had heard.

Now he was ready.

7

The Fiery Voice at the Burning Bush

Earth's crammed with heaven
And every common bush afire with God:
But only he who sees, takes off his shoes ...
ELIZABETH BARRETT BROWNING

Moses saw. And heard. From amid the bush that burned and burned, yet was not consumed, the Voice of God commissioned Moses to return to Egypt and call for the liberation of his people.

Hearing, Moses demurred, "I am not a good public speaker, I gave up the turmoil of politics for this simple shepherd's life, I like spending time with my beloved wife and children ..."

Sez Who?

The Voice insisted.

So finally Moses said, "Who should I tell them sent me?"—figuring perhaps that God would not unveil the Inner Being of Divinity and he'd be off the hook.

"Stop wasting My time, Moses," said the rattle of the leaves that burned and would not burn. "You know—I am I, the I of all the universe. Listen to your own heart, you will hear it beating, I, I, I, I—

"All right, that's not enough? I am the God of your fathers, of Amram your father, Jacob your grandfather, Isaac and Abraham their fathers."

Moses talked back:

"You think that will convince them? Off here with the sheep and the wellsprings and the mountains, You must have forgotten what it's like to live in slavery. I've already tried to invoke That Name to my people, men and women! Yes, before I ran away, I said exactly this to them. When they asked who had sent me to keep them from killing each other, who had put me in authority over them, I told them the God of our fathers had sent me.

"The men laughed. They slapped their knees and laughed at me. 'The God of our fathers!' they said. 'Where was He when our fathers knelt to Pharaoh? This God we know, this God we knew, this God we have always known. No hero. At best He hates us, at worst He forgets us.'

"And the women—much worse. They clicked their teeth at me: 'You men! This God of your fathers is useless to us. Will your freedom come from Him? If it comes from anywhere, it comes from us! Your mothers and midwives gave you birth when Pharaoh said to kill you. Your sister drew you from the river, to make it birthing instead of drowning waters. This God of your *fathers*—what has He ever said to us? At worst He excludes us, at best He ignores us. We must have a new birth of freedom, and no father-god knows how to give birth.'"

Moses watched the bush of flame blow sideways, like a shrug. He heard the leaves muttering, "All right. Tell them it is the God of their fathers *and* mothers—Sarah, Rebekah, Rachel, and Leah as well. Then the men will know something new is happening, and so will the women."

Moses turned pale. "Can't do it. *Won't* do it. Won't even mention it. Once I do that, they will argue day and night. Some of the men will be angry. Some of the women won't think it's enough. I'll never hear the end of it. As for freedom—forget it."

For an instant the flames roared up like a furnace, and the tongues of flame roared words: "Someday, I will teach such a lesson!... *Some* day. All right. I'll wait. Someday there will be women who are willing to insist. And meanwhile ..."

The flames grew quiet. For many, many minutes, Moses stood in silence, trembling.

The Spiral of Becoming

Then the flames began to rattle. No, not quite a rattle. A cough? A chuckle? Could it be, a chuckle? Yes, a chuckle, and then: "Tell them, I was what I was, I am what I am, but I will be who I will be. Yes, I will be who I will be. And so will they. *Ehyeh asher ehyeh* [Exod. 3:14]."

> asher ehyeh asher
> ehyeh asher ehyeh
> asher ehyeh asher ...

The flaming bush became a spiral of fire.

"I who was once the God of your fathers, I learn from mothers how to give birth. I learn and you learn, you learn and I learn; I bear and you are born, you bear and I am born. We will become who we will become.

> *"Ehyeh asher ehyeh*
> *asher ehyeh asher ..."*

Moses found his arms inscribing in the air before his chest a spiral, in rhythm with the flames and the words the flames were chanting.

"They were slaves, but they can become free people. They were a tiny clump of cells, nestled in a nurturing womb—but they can grow to birth size, and the birth pangs will seize Mother Egypt if Pharaoh tries to block their birthing. They can become who they will become.

"I speak to the women as well. When the midwives heard Me, I spoke not from a bush but through a baby. I appeared in every mother's face, I was heard in every baby's cry. How else did they know they must disobey Pharaoh?

"And the women know My Name, as well. My secret Names.

"To Abraham I thundered that *El Shaddai* meant God-of-the-Mountains, All-Powerful; but to Sarah I whispered that it meant God-of-the-Breast, All-Nourishing."

Beyond Words

"Now I must speak to both Hebrews and Egyptians, so My name can be neither Hebrew nor Egyptian. What can be My Name for them both to understand? Only the word that is beneath all words, the word that is beyond all words, the word that is within all words, the word that holds all words within it. The word that is not shaped by human hands, or tongue, or lips—but comes from outward in, from inward out. A breath. *Only a breath. Entirely a breath. Nothing but a breath. Every in- and out-breath.*

"My name is *YHWH*. Do not put in a vowel, Moses! Do not try to call me Yahweh; not Jehovah; not *Adonai*, or Lord, or even Eternal. Just Yyyhhhwwwhhh, a Breathing.

"I am the breath of life, and the breath of life is what will set you free. Teach them that if they learn My Name is just a Breathing, they will be able to reach across all tongues and boundaries, to pass over them all for birth, and life, and freedom."

Some of that dialogue comes straight from the black fire of the Torah, and some is from the white fire—midrash. Somehow it seemed necessary not to talk *about* the Bush but to overhear the dialogue between the Bush and Moses. But "about" may also be a necessary way of understanding this crucial moment on the path of liberation.

For one thing, it happens at a thornbush—in Hebrew, a *sneh*. When Moses returns to the Wilderness at the head of a multitude of runaway slaves, it is at a burning, smoking, shaking mountain called *Sinai* that God speaks. The similarity in names is not an accident. Once again the individual hero is foreshadowing the journey of the collective hero.

Changing the Name of the Universe

When Moses challenged God, the Voice announced that an old Name of God was no longer operative. At the Bush, the Name of God changed. The shape of the universe, the way to understand and grok the universe, changed. How?

First of all, what was that previous Name, and what did it signify? It was, God says, *Shaddai*—the Name by which God was known to the early forebears of the nation, from Abraham to Joseph. Its last use as an invocation of the Holy One came in the very last passage of the book of Genesis, the last voice of an old era before we roll the scroll of history. It came at a climactic moment in the life of Jacob. He was blessing his son Joseph after all the turmoil of their lives had been resolved:

> May your father's God on high become your help,
> And may *Shaddai* become your blessing—
> Blessings of the heavens, from above;
> Blessings of the deep, crouching below—
> Blessings of the breasts [Hebrew: *shadai'im*]
> And of the womb.
>
> GENESIS 49:25

There are more clues: God used this name in Genesis 17:1, speaking to Abram when he was on the verge of becoming Abraham, "the father of a throng of nations," the initiator of the covenant of circumcision. It was *Shaddai* who foretold the birth of Isaac.

Isaac invoked the same name to bless Jacob: "May God *Shaddai* bless you, make you bear fruit, and make you many, so that you become a host of peoples" (Gen. 28:3).

And God bore this name when Jacob, returning from a foreign land, rediscovered his own transformation from "Heel" (Jacob) to "Godwrestler" (Israel). God said to him, "I am God *Shaddai*. Bear fruit and be many! A nation—a host of nations!—shall come forth from your loins" (Gen. 35:11).

Most English translations of Torah have used "Almighty" for *Shaddai*. This goes back to the Greek and Latin translations of the Bible, the Septuagint and Vulgate, which used the Greek and Latin words for "All-Powerful." Perhaps they drew on an ancient Rabbinic midrash that the name means "*Sheh-dai* [Who/Enough!]," the One who had enough power to say to the ocean, "Enough!" when it was about to swallow up the world.

But if we look back at the blessing Jacob gave to Joseph (Gen. 49:25), it is inescapable that the poet who wrote those lines meant: "*Shaddai* is the Breasted One." Why else would the quatrain of this blessing so connect *Shaddai* with *shadai'im*?

And if we look back at all the blessings in which *Shaddai* is over and over invoked, they were about fruitfulness and fertility. God was seen as Infinite Mother, pouring forth blessings from the Breasts Above and the Womb Below, from the heavens that pour forth nourishing rain, from the ocean deeps that birth new life.

Shaddai came first to command circumcision, to open up the thickened cover of the foreskin. For us today, uncovering this ancient metaphor may open up some blocked off, thickened coverings on our minds and hearts that have hidden from us an earthy, womanly God. Uncovering the Breasted God might "circumcise the foreskins of our hearts," as Torah has it (Deut. 10:16 and 30:6).

Jews have prided themselves on avoiding the "pagan" celebrations of the earthiness of earth, but the metaphor of *Shaddai* could recall for us what we have repressed.

But if this Name is so filled with profound value, why did God need a new Name? What was insufficient about *Shaddai*?

At the Bush, two new Names came forth. The first was *Ehyeh Asher Ehyeh*, which means "I Will Be Who I Will Be."

This Name that encodes possibility, transformation, was too much for the translators of the Bible into the King James Version. They mistranslated this clearly future-tense Hebrew into "I Am What I Am," unchanging. Perhaps this committee appointed by a king could not bear to say the Name of freedom, change, the overthrow of a Pharaoh.

In the context of the crisis at the Burning Bush, this Name meant that neither Egypt nor its subject people Israel was locked into the patterns of the past. The nature of the universe could change. Indeed, the nature of the universe *was* change. For Moses to conjure transformation by this Name would not be perjury.

Breathing Life

And then the Voice spoke a second Name. This one was *YHWH* (Exod. 3:15). At one level of reality—language, grammar, intellect—this Name was, like the other, rooted in the verb "to be." It could be understood as a shortened version of the formal "*Ehyeh* ..." for it encoded the past, present, and future of the verb "to be" into a brevity. It was as if God were taking on a nickname, a contraction of God's formal Name. Easier to use in an intimate relationship. And in its brevity a Möbius strip in time itself, through which a three-dimensional shape took on a single surface and a single edge. Uncanny.

Yet there is another aspect of Reality in this Name: its sound. "Pronounced" without a vowel, it becomes a breath.

For millennia, the Jewish custom has been not to try to pronounce this physically unpronounceable name, but to substitute the word *Adonai*, which means "Lord." From this habit grew the use in the Greek "New Testament" of the word *Kyrie* and in the Latin translation, the Vulgate, *Dominus*—and so in English "Lord" and in all the other languages into which Christianity has carried the Bible, their words for "Lord."

This substitution carried its own theology into the world: the sense of the Divine as King, Lord, Judge. The world as hierarchy, each being above another. It became easy to talk of the divine right of kings, though occasionally the definition of God as King was used to denounce the pretensions of earthly kings to divinity, or at least infallibility.

Now let us explore the implications of letting *YHWH* stand naked, unmasked, on our tongues. Divinity as Breath.

First of all, this Name transcends all languages. It is not Hebrew, though originally expressed in Hebrew letters. It is not Egyptian, or Sanskrit, or Latin, or Greek, or Arabic, or Chinese, or English, or Spanish, or Russian, or Swahili. Or rather, it is in all of them. It is the only sound that is.

And "breathing" is not what only humans do. All life-forms on this planet breathe.

And they do not each breathe in a separate lonely bubble. What we breathe in is what the trees breathe out. What the trees breathe in is what we breathe out. We breathe each other into life.

YHWH is the Interbreathing of all life.

A fitting Name for God?

A Name that is most fitting in the crisis of our generation? When the Interbreathing Itself—the interchange of oxygen and carbon dioxide—is in danger, as the proportion of carbon dioxide in our atmosphere rises and threatens to scorch our globe and condemn to death large numbers of the life-forms that make up our planet?

Naming God Today

Is the lesson of the Burning Bush that in a time of supernal crisis, we may need to conceive of the universe itself in different terms?

It is true that the crisis the Voice called on Moses to see, to hear, and to speak was a crisis of the oppression of some human beings by others. It did not seem to involve the broader earth—though soon we will see, as oppression brings on the plagues of earth-circling disaster, that the separation between human and humus, earth and earthling, is not entirely possible. But the deeper principle, that a transformation of action requires a transformation of perception and belief, is at the heart of the story of the Burning Bush.

When we need to rename God, we can realize that we are in a crisis of history and civilization.

Indeed, there are at such moments likely to be fierce battles between those who want to address God and understand the world in new categories and those who are satisfied: "Give me the old-time religion; it was good enough for Grandpa, it's good enough for me."

Today, many people find some of the old ways of naming God—King of the universe, Lord, Judge, for example—no longer adequate or honest.

Through this metaphor, we are defining ourselves as subjects, slaves, to a Ruler whose powers we have no way to exercise or challenge.

But in a generation when human beings can destroy life on this planet, can splice DNA to create species as radically new as the spider-goat, can overthrow pharaohs—all the powers we once located in a Ruler far beyond us—it no longer seems truthful to invoke such metaphors.

And many women, with some men, have pointed out that the old metaphors for God are overwhelmingly and pointedly masculine, bespeaking men's spiritual experience but rarely women's.

What then? Some people have poured scorn on the whole enterprise, avoiding the God word, perhaps identifying "biological evolution" or "the historical process" as the only sources of creativity and justice. We might say that those become new names of God. Few call them that because they seem—or their proponents claim—they are discoverable, reducible, weighable. They do not trail clouds of Mystery.

Others have renamed God as the "Eternal Thou" (Martin Buber), "the Power that draws us toward salvation" (Mordecai Kaplan), "the Wellspring of Life" (Marcia Falk), perhaps "the Web of Relationship" (some feminists). We usually speak in and through and to "Yahh," the "Breath of life, the Breathing-spirit of the world" (*ruach ha'olam*).

So here we are again today, facing pharaohs that bestride the narrowed earth like a colossus, stony, stamping underfoot the growth from grass roots of change and possibility and freedom. Who are our midwives, what Name can beckon us to grow?

The fiery Voice of the Burning Bush taught that an old name of God—*Shaddai*, the Divine Breasts of earthy fruitfulness—needed to be set aside in order to face the political and social crisis brought on by Pharaoh's unchecked tyranny. Today it is pharaonic global corporations that are pouring poison into the heavens and the earth. The two kinds of crisis have joined into a single danger. It is the aspect of

God's Self as the Breasted One that we are poisoning, and so condemning ourselves to drink a milk that is laced with poison.

In the *Aleinu* prayer close to the end of Jewish services, we envi-
sion a glorious future by chanting the phrase *Letakken olam
bemalkhut Shaddai*. In the past we have understood this as "To heal
the world in the Kingship of the Almighty." But now we can draw on
Shaddai as the Breasted One and hear ourselves call out, "To heal the
world through the Majesty of Nurture."

8

Toward Freedom—or Toward Death?

Now we are leaning forward as the story gathers energy. God just finished commanding Moses to return and liberate the Israelites from Egypt. God's final words instructed Moses to tell Pharaoh that the people of Israel are God's firstborn and that God has demanded, "Let My son go, that he may serve Me. If you refuse to let him go, here!—I will kill your son, your firstborn" (Exod. 4:22–23).

With no transition, the story then says that at a lodging place on the road Moses, his wife Tzipporah, and their two sons were journeying toward Egypt, following God's command, "*YHWH* sought to kill him" (Exod. 4:24). Him? Moses? The Moses who had only a sentence before been sent as the liberator to Egypt? Had God become a dark and terrifying joker, a jester in God's own royal court?

Or perhaps there is a strange carryover from God's threat to Pharaoh, as if the one sentence, "I will kill your son, your firstborn," belongs in both stories. Read that way, the story is saying that God threatened to kill Moses's firstborn.

Maybe so! For his wife Tzipporah responded to this threat by taking a flint to circumcise her son and throws his foreskin at "his legs" (Exod. 4:25). The legs of ... Moses? God? Her son? The pronouns are unclear.

"For a bridegroom of blood are you to me," she said (Exod. 4:25), and God let alone whoever had been about to die. Then she repeated, "A bridegroom of blood for the circumcision" (Exod. 4:26).

What a moment! Hearing the soul-lifting story of Moses's encounter with God at the Burning Bush, most of us are, with heart and spirit, ready to hear the story of how Moses did with the mission

God sketched out: Confront Pharaoh! Free the People! End their slavery! We can almost feel our legs ready for the journey, a song of freedom on our lips.

Our legs are ready—but the bloody foreskin was flung at someone's legs, and the liberator nearly died. How do we face this unexpected, this unimaginable story?

Do we feel gripped by terror as we hear this passage?

Was It All for Nought?

Does all our reasoning fly away? Are our mouths too frozen to shriek a warning, a challenge, a denial?

How can we understand that God could seek to kill Moses, whose life was saved by a "conspiracy" between his sister Miriam, his mother, and Pharaoh's own daughter who became Bat-Yah, "God's Daughter," by rescuing and rearing him, saving him from death, giving him life?

How can we understand that God could seek to kill the Moses who had saved the life of a Hebrew slave from an arrogant taskmaster, had saved his own life by running away from his home in Pharaoh's palace to take refuge in Midian?

How can we understand that God could seek to kill the Moses who gave new life to the seven daughters of the priest of Midian when shepherds barred them from watering their flocks at a well?

The Moses who was then embraced by Reuel/Yitro, the shepherdesses' father; the Moses who then was married to the Midian priest's daughter Tzipporah and stirred new life—his son Gershom—into being?

How can we understand that the God Who greeted Moses with a name to give new life—"*Ehyeh Asher Ehyeh,* I am forever becoming whom I am becoming"—could seek to kill Moses?

How can we understand that the God Who gave Moses a life-supporting brother and a staff filled with the magic life of serpentry could seek to kill that same Moses?

How can we understand that God could seek to kill Moses, whom God had picked out as the one to save from death and slavery, God's own "firstborn," the children of Jacob/Israel?

The God Who had warned that if Pharaoh refused, death would stalk his land, snatch away each firstborn?

How can we understand that this God Who promised life, and life, and life, and life, now sought to kill his messenger of life?

Moving from Fear to Awe

We cannot understand. Instead, we are filled with terror. And suddenly we realize: Moses was filled with terror. Not terror on the road, not even terror at facing the God Who sought to kill him, but terror ever since the Burning Bush, terror at facing the God Who sought to free him. Terror at the notion of facing Pharaoh's power.

Seeing Moses's pale, gaunt face imbued with terror, trudging hopeless on the path to death, God knew that he had to slay this terror-stricken Moses, had to kill the terror that was already emptying out Moses's life, making him impotent to face Pharaoh and free the slaves.

Facing a God on the brink of killing him was Moses's cure. Facing immediate death, he knew a Power more powerful than Pharaoh. His terror burned away, and he became the Moses about whom it is written, "Never again did there arise among the Israelites a prophet like Moses who knew *YHWH* intimately, face-to-face" (Deut. 34:10).

This terror is not encoded only in an ancient story. Let us all look at the terror in our lives. The fear of death, or disgrace, or some superior power that threatens our well-being. Or threatens our families, children like Moses's son "Gershom" (meaning "a stranger there"), every child born always—like his children—as "strangers in a strange land" that they must devote their lives to understanding (Exod. 2:22).

Face your own terror. Feel it. And hear Tzipporah save her husband's life, release him from his terror, make him her "bloody bridegroom."

Watch his face take on new life; hear him take up his mission with a hopeful heart.

And take from her swift healing act the blessing that the One Who blessed our forebears in their terrors will bless us to live beyond the terror that we feel, live beyond it to step fully into the tasks and missions that the One Who Will Be is calling us to live.

That is one way of understanding: learning from our own feelings as we read the story, feeling how it must have felt to Moses to live the story, how it feels to anyone who sets out on a path of transformation. Terror.

And then let us turn to the intellect God gave us to seek out a different kind of understanding.

Most traditional commentators think that God threatened to kill Moses for having failed to circumcise his son, that Tzipporah did it for him, and that Moses was the "bridegroom of blood."

Maybe. Or maybe God was demanding the boy be killed as a sacrifice, as once God demanded Isaac; maybe Tzipporah used the foreskin as Abraham used the ram, as a ransom and a substitute.

Was Circumcision Still Obligatory?

Or maybe Moses was threatened with death because he himself was uncircumcised, and when the text says Tzipporah circumcised "her son," it means she made Moses "her son" by saving his life, giving him life—and then greeted him, standing bloody before her, as her "bridegroom of blood."

Maybe all three—that is, maybe the story is deliberately leaving the pronouns unclear.

Either way, all three ways, the issues remain: Why this sudden attack on Moses's just-created mission? Why was it Tzipporah who acted, not Moses—the mother who did this circumcision that all tradition says is the obligation of the father? Notice that the Torah says "her son"—at this moment hers, for at this moment Moses was not acting like a father. Even if it was Moses who lacked the circumcision, when Abraham— Abraham our Father!—was in that situation, he did it himself.

One possible interpretation of the story arises from the experiences of a generation that has been hard and joyfully at work in making fresh, renewing, the meanings of Judaism. Some Jews accuse us of breaking with tradition even while they claim we pretend to care for it. They accuse us of playing with a new religion. Sometimes we ourselves are not sure what the boundary is. It is easy to imagine Moses exploring: where *is* the boundary?

In the white fire, let us read a few additional lines of conversation.

Tzipporah, speaking to Moses after he returned from the Burning Bush, ready to set out for Egypt: "We are returning to your people? Then we should circumcise Gershom, don't you think? Isn't that the tradition of your people? They won't be happy if we show up without ..."

Moses, the Bush still burning in his eyes, a little grandiloquent: "You don't understand! That's the old covenant, the one with Abraham. I was told God's Name anew. It all starts over now. We will have the Pesach lamb to sacrifice instead; our firstborns are redeemed from circumcision as from death."

Tzipporah: troubled, frowning, silent ... until the explosive God-fury suddenly threatened her son. Then she herself exploded into action, slashed with the flint ... turned to Moses, shaking in the aftermath of fear and fury: "Don't you see? You said the covenant of Abraham was over ... so God started back at the beginning, back where he was with Abraham. He wanted your son for an offering. But this time—thank God!—I was ready. You would have been my bridegroom drenched in blood!"

Then she turned back to God, truly exhausted, emptied out, calling Him as well a bloody Bridegroom.

"Motherizing" Fathers?

Such a scenario stirs ideas about old and new in religious growth, about the difference between tradition and renewal. But it also stirs up deeper feelings about fatherhood and motherhood. The social psychologist David Bakan, applying Freudian method to the Bible, has pointed to the inverse of Freud's Oedipus complex, where the son wishes to kill the father. Bakan suggested that both circumcision and the Passover lamb (and also the ram that Abraham found on Mount Moriah) were ransoms against the father's ancient tendency to kill his offspring—especially a son, who seems most like him; especially the firstborn, who comes as the shock to, the test of, his previously worked-out equilibrium.

So these rituals, Bakan said, are part of the Torah's overall effort to "motherize" men—to induce among men a sense of communion with their sons strong enough to prevent them from murdering their sons.[1]

Many of us have felt that tide of fury. The more my children grew into new people—not just an extension of me—the more I, Arthur, have felt the tug of fatherhood fulfilled against fatherhood frustrated. On the one hand, I have felt joy at truly fathering—that is, creating new and independent life; but on the other, I have felt the pride that what I have fathered is growing in the directions I have pointed. It is a more complicated tug than that, because the more different my children are from me, the less they feel like "mine"; and the more like me they are, the less it feels as if I have created someone new. So the two feelings work both with and against each other. When they are both most powerful, both working deep within me, I feel the most fury.

Jewish tradition says that all children have three parents: father, mother, and God. That is a way to celebrate the newness, the unpredictability of the child; in each child there is something that did not come from either parent but from the world's inexhaustible storehouse of freedom—that is, from God. But there is also what both parents give.

So if Bakan is right and the *bris* (*brit*, "covenant") of circumcision and the Passover lamb are both efforts of the father to say, "It's all right, despite the tension of these tugs inside me, I will not kill you!" they are also efforts to say that the reason for such gentleness is God—God's stern command against murder, God's sweet gift of newness and freedom. That is what Tzipporah understood; that is what the mothers had to teach—had to teach even Moshe Rabbenu, Moses our Teacher.

Covenants Old and New

So what Tzipporah taught was not to cast aside the old *bris*, the circumcision, for the new covenant of the passing-over of the Israelite firstborn. It would not be enough to make this ransom with a lamb each spring; the ransom would also have to be paid when a boy was born. The cycle of the seasons and the cycle of the generations must be connected. The old ritual, from Abraham our Father, must join with the new, she taught Moses: you cannot be a good teacher to the people of everything new you learned from God unless you have remembered what it means to be a good father, bearing something old.

The Torah reinforces the notion that what was at stake was the conjoining of circumcision with Passover. For when it commands the order of the Passover celebration, it insists with utter vigor that every man at the Passover gathering be circumcised. It does not think to specify this for Shabbat or the other holy days, nor even for the priestly celebrants of Temple sacrifice. It is as if Passover, with its echoes of the firstborn of Egypt dead, the firstborn of Israel redeemed, the lamb sacrificed as a ransom, is the one moment when people might think that circumcision is irrelevant. God's warning is like Tzipporah's action.

We know a history in which a "new covenant" decided that the covenant of circumcision was no longer crucial. That was the decision of what became the Christian church as it struggled to define its differences from Rabbinic Judaism. And Rabbinic Judaism, so different in profound ways from the practice and theology of the Bible and the Temple offerings, decided—like Tzipporah!—that the old covenant was still necessary.

There is a strange irony in the questions that have arisen as Judaism renews itself in our era as it did two thousand years ago. Today Jews ask again, does circumcision remain crucial to affirmation of the covenant? In our generation, girls and women are no longer mere baggage for the actual covenanting parties—men—but themselves are covenanting parties, yet are not circumcised. So the question has arisen, what role does this ritual still have for boys and men? In the transformational time we live in, women have done the opposite of what Tzipporah did: they have doubted, questioned, where she insisted. How Jews will answer the question is not yet certain.

The issues go beyond this one ironic resurfacing of that particular ancient ritual dilemma; they go beyond the one small people whose self-transformations we have been witnessing. Many similar uncertainties rise up again as all our old traditions and communities bend and crack and break and flow. What must remain? And what must change?

We too may be filled with terror as we start down the path into a new version of our traditions, our world, our selves. The pharaohs we must face are not only those who sit upon a public throne of military might or money, but our own old selves ruling over our habits and assumptions. Shaking ourselves loose to face these pyramids of power can be a terrifying process. How do we face the terror and live our way beyond it?

PART III

From the Palace to the Sea

Now we enter the third phase of Moses's life, when he became the hinge of history, the leader/liberator. Only now did his life become the reason to remember him.

Armed not with weaponry but with the knowledge that *YHWH* breathes the intertwining of all life and that *Ehyeh Asher Ehyeh* defines a universe that is always able to become, to change, Moses could invoke that unity and that freedom against the locked-down notion of a country fated to slavery and Pharaoh. With his brother and his sister beside him, he could unlock the energies of an enslaved people and a tormented earth.

He drew on the prestige of his early life in the palace to challenge not only the naked power in the palace—whips and swords, chariots and wealth—but also the mystique that clothed its power, preventing any challenge. Pharaoh was no god, he knew, despite all worshipful obedience. Only God, the Breath of Life, could bring the Winds of Change to reshape history.

Even Pharaoh, he knew, could change. But Pharaoh instead refused to change. And every refusal made the next refusal easier, the next offer of transformation harder to accept. Even when Moses's own people quailed at the harshness of the king's response, Moses did not waver. And the people learned.

It became clear that the acceptance of fate and inevitability was itself not fated or inevitable but itself a choice, a choice that could be transcended.

The waters that, when Moses was born, were intended by Pharaoh's orders to become the place of drowning and had instead become the waters of rebirth, after a titanic struggle became waters of both drowning and rebirth. Drowning for Pharaoh and his army, rebirth for the "Children of Israel" who had grown into a multitude and an identity. No longer could they be forced to die in the narrow birth canal.

So the power that Moses challenged in the palace fell to a watery grave at the Sea.

9

Facing Pharaoh

Having transcended his terror at the task he faced, Moses left the broad open spaces of the nomad's shepherding to reenter the Tight Place, the Narrow Land. In this land, he—and everyone—were "supposed" to choose between two narrow choices: oppress or be oppressed.

To make possible a wider choice for himself and for the people, Moses realized that he had two tasks: organizing the workers, especially his kinfolk and perhaps some others too; and challenging the tyrant who had turned them into slaves.

The Face within Pharaoh

When God sent Moses to face Pharaoh, the Torah text says that God said, *Bo el Pharaoh*. Most English translations say, "Go to Pharaoh" (Exod. 10:1). But *bo* means "come," not "go."

"Come to Pharaoh!"

How could God be saying "Come!" unless God was already there?—already within Pharaoh!

"Come toward Me."

And God's call to Moses continued, *Hikhbad'ti et libo* (Exod. 10:1), which is usually translated, "I have made his [Pharaoh's] heart heavy, hard."

But the Hebrew root *KVD* can mean "heavy," or "glorious," or "honorable," or "radiant." Perhaps the English sense of "gravity"—a force that reaches far beyond its source, radiating through the world—catches some elements of *KVD*. When a leader is said to possess "gravitas," it means he is a "heavy dude," worthy of honor, radiating forth his own glory to faraway places.

So the phrase can be read as "I, God, have put My radiance in his, Pharaoh's, heart."

In other words: "Come to Me—the Me who lives hidden inside Pharaoh. Don't be afraid of Pharaoh. What looks like *his* radiance, *his* glory, is really *My* radiance, *My* glory."

Courage and Compassion

From seeing God hidden within Pharaoh, Moses could learn both courage and compassion.

Courage as he realized that Pharaoh's seeming power was not his, but just a part of the enormous power of the flow of life, the Unity of the universe. If Pharaoh tried to grasp that power as his own, the river and the locusts, the frogs and the firstborns, would overflow his rigid boundaries and sweep away his power. No one need fear it.

Compassion as Moses recalled that even within Pharaoh was the *tzelem Elohim*, the spark of God. So he could resist the Pharaoh's tyranny while yet remembering the *KaVoD*—honor—due his spark of divinity.

Multiply courage by compassion, and what emerges is nonviolent resistance. "I will not obey my enemy, and I will not kill him either. I will pursue my own life journey."

Twice, Moses and Aaron faced Pharaoh saying, "Thus says YHWH ..." (Exod. 5:1 and 10:3). In their first encounter, Pharaoh answered, "Who sent you?"

Who indeed?

This is the God who spoke that Unpronounceable Name to Moses at the Burning Bush. Unpronounceable because there is no way to "pronounce" it but by simply breathing, "Yyyyhhhhwwwwhhhh." The Name that reaches across all barriers of language, present beneath all of them. The Breath of Life.

Moses tried to explain to Pharaoh who had sent this message, "Free the slaves," by simply breathing: "*YHWH* sent me."

But Pharaoh answered, "What do you mean, just breathing in my face? This is a god? This god I have never heard of."

A ruler who did not recognize the Interbreathing of all life? The disastrous end of Pharaoh's story was already present in that moment.

So Moses and Aaron added an explanation: "*YHWH*, the God of the *Ivrim* [Hebrews]" (Exod. 10:3).

So sad as almost to be funny: entangling the most universal affirmation of a Name beyond all languages with an ethnic claim!

The Boundary Crossers

Or perhaps they were entering a word play with Pharaoh. Perhaps "God of the *Ivrim*, the Hebrews," meant more than an ethnocentric boast. For *Ivrim* means "those who cross over," nomads, wanderers, the kind of people that in the twentieth century Stalin called rootless cosmopolites. It seems to have been used by the settled, "responsible" peoples of the Middle East as a contemptuous label for people who wouldn't stay put where they belonged. "Wetbacks."

Perhaps Moses and Aaron were warning Pharaoh that the Breath of Life—which blows where it wishes, cannot be captured and pinned down—was the God of those who cannot be pinned down to one place, one life path, one Narrow Space.

Moses insisted that the Boundary Crossers had to leave in order to celebrate a festival for the Breath of Life.

Often this is read today as an attempt to mislead Pharaoh. But if we imagine Moses groping his way toward a broader, stronger form of resistance, and if we ask ourselves what it would mean today to take on the task of nonviolent resistance against our generation's pharaohs, perhaps our varied religious festivals can embody that resistance.

Perhaps some festivals that we call "secular," as well: Martin Luther King Jr. Day, celebrating not a triumphant warrior but a nonviolent opponent of war, not a wealthy overlord but the suffering servant of the poor and disempowered. The Veterans Day that began as Armistice Day, the day to end the war to end all wars. The Fourth of July, a day of resisting a tyrant not by choosing a new one but by creating an alternative form of self-government.

When Soviet Jews began dancing for the Simchat Torah festival in the public streets of Moscow, facing what seemed to be a totalitarian regime, that was utterly different from the old Jewish custom of dancing with the Torah scroll in the hidden streets of the ghetto. Their new kind of dancing began to crack the rigidity of their pharaoh. And they called forth allies.

When American Jews celebrated Freedom Seders that demanded an end to the Vietnam War, and feminist Seders that affirmed new freedom for women within and beyond the boundaries of Jewish life, they cracked ancient rigidities that required both Jews and women to stay "in their place." They became *Ivrim*, "Hebrews"—boundary crossers.

And when they celebrated Tu B'Shvat, the midwinter festival of the Rebirthday of the Trees, by facing the corporations that were draining the Everglades and destroying ancient redwood forests, they invoked those kabbalists who knew that *shefa*, the divine abundance that fills and fulfills the world, needs to be renewed on earth as well as heaven. And they had allies.

When Israeli Jews celebrated the festival of "huts," Sukkot, they built "Sukkot Shalom"—huts of openness—to move toward peace with Palestinians. They too were facing the pharaonic rigidity of governments that were stuck in a narrow place. They too had allies.

When Christians reenact the Stations of the Cross by walking through a city's meanest streets—drug houses, gun stores, spots where the homeless try to sleep—they are learning that when we face "the least of these," it is God's Face we see. These values, expressed in Christian symbolism, invite new alliances beyond the Christian community.

When Muslims walk the Hajj in Mecca, as Ali Shariati taught, touching the skirt of Hajar brings them close to the downtrodden, the outcast; offering up their own "Ismail" means giving up the idols of ego and distraction; sharing the meat of a lamb with the poor reminds them that God wanted not that Abraham kill his son but that the poor be fed. These values, expressed in Muslim symbolism, invite new alliances beyond the Muslim community.

In all these ways, we see new explorations in what it might mean for every people to cross old boundaries by moving to a new place in its history, turning old festivals to new purposes.

Anciently, those Hebrews who fled Pharaoh hoped to settle down and make a decent society on their own, through military conquest of a small land for themselves. But over the centuries, that vision became indefensible in the face of the Roman legions.

So their descendants scattered around the world; ruefully accepted that the great powers of the world could not be drowned as Pharaoh had been; turned their attention to making holy their own communities; became *ivrim*, wanderers, once more; and gave up the hope of repairing the world at large. In that mode of scattering it seemed workable, though painful, to suffer pogroms and expulsions. But that vision too was shattered by the Holocaust: in the modern world, no place to hide or flee.

What then? Imagine reclaiming festivals as Moses did, facing pharaohs with that nonviolent challenge. And imagine making allies of other spiritual communities that might be ready to become *Ivrim*— the Boundary Crossers—in order to face the pharaohs of today, on behalf of the Breath of Life.

10

Who Hardened Pharaoh's Heart?

When Moses called upon Pharaoh to obey God's will and let the Hebrews go free from their forced labor, Pharaoh refused. When Moses began to invoke God's pressure to make Pharaoh change his mind, the Torah says that Pharaoh—time after time—hardened his own heart against compassion for the Hebrews and against obedience to God's warnings.

But later in the story, as the plagues mounted up that brought more disaster upon Egypt, the Torah says that God hardened Pharaoh's heart.

This aspect of the Exodus story has puzzled or angered many readers. What, they ask, happened to free will? What happened to repentance? Why did God prevent Pharaoh from changing his mind and heart?

Pharaoh did have free choice—until he gave it away. At the beginning, he freely chose to close his heart, chose to be stubborn, cruel, and arrogant. Then something happened to end the freedom of his choices.

What was this like? Use heroin once, twice, thrice—and you are making a free choice. But at some point the very makeup of your brain and body changes. Now you are no longer taking heroin; the heroin has taken you. Addiction has taken over, Reality has taken over, God has taken over.

Addicted to Power

If you choose hard-heartedness so long that you get addicted to it, at some point you are no longer choosing; God, Reality, starts hardening your heart.

And arrogance is not only a moral and spiritual malady. It breeds stupidity. For those who are utterly convinced of their own absolute rightness cannot hear the warnings of others, cannot pay attention to the signals from the world around them, cannot learn from their own mistakes.

Even when Pharaoh's own advisers shrieked at him, "You are destroying Egypt!" he could no longer turn back.

In the twentieth century, we witnessed and suffered from governments like this. Hitler, Stalin, Mao—they acted so brutally that their actions undermined their own societies. The minorities they targeted suffered, but so did the people they claimed they were protecting. And these ultimate cases, where millions died in a few short decades, were not the only ones. Even some governments elected by the people after public debate took on the hardened hearts that led to disaster.

How did this work in ancient Egypt?

First came the "plagues"—environmental disasters. The rivers became poisonous, undrinkable. Frogs swarmed everywhere and then died in stinking heaps. Vermin swarmed. Venomous bloodsucking flies followed. Mad cow disease descended. Airborne infections raised boils on everyone. Unprecedented hailstorms signaled radical climate change, shattering grass, grain harvests, trees, animals.

To the bafflement of Pharaoh and his advisers, Moses and Aaron had evidently become experts in the ecological balance. Again and again, their warnings had been borne out. Now they warned that the ecosystem was so ruined that a monstrous plague of locusts was about to strike.

And in this critical moment, Pharaoh's own advisers shrieked at him, "Do you not know that Egypt is destroyed?" (Exod. 10:7).

But Pharaoh hardened his heart once more, and the locusts came. And after that, so darkened were the eyes of all the people that the land itself was darkened as a thick dust swallowed up all vision. And then came an illness that left no house untouched by death. Yes, death.

How were Moses and Aaron able to foretell disaster? Why did Pharaoh fail? What glimmer of reality spoke through the king's advisers?

"Stuff Happens"

For Pharaoh, the "plagues" were a startling series of singular accidents. That was all. Each one was scary, but it did not portend another—or a broken system.

Moses and Aaron saw a deeper truth. They saw and felt the inter-connections that weave the world together. They understood that *YHWH* was the Interbreathing of all life. They may not have under-stood the details of how smashing a butterfly far up the Nile could bring down hailstorms on the country's farmland—but they knew that it could happen. They understood that oppressing and enslaving workers, forcing them to work the land beyond its limits, would leave the land defenseless against a horde of locusts.

That was their advantage over Pharaoh and over his advisers, who could through sleight of hand make a serpent appear where a staff had been—but could not cure tormented cattle from mad cow disease.

Finally, the advisers admitted their incapacities, spoke aloud Real-ity—and were ignored. The morning after they told Pharaoh he was ruining Egypt, his hardness-addicted heart drove him to march for-ward on the road to ruin.

Surely, in the thirty-five hundred years we have been hearing this archetypal story and taking its harsh lessons to open our own hearts, surely after millennia of political effort to create the checks and bal-ances in which what were the Pharaoh's "advisers" have become the sovereign democratic people, no government would be able to repeat such a crime, such a blunder.

Surely.

But in a front-page article on June 3, 2002, the *New York Times* reported that the United States had submitted to the United Nations, as required by treaty, a report on the expected impact of global scorching on the United States.[1]

The report was not written by radical outsiders, but by the presi-dent's own advisers. Indeed, said the *Times*, "phrases were adopted wholesale from a National Academy of Sciences climate study, which was requested last spring by the White House and concluded that the warming was a serious problem."

The report said the United States would be substantially changed in the next few decades, "very likely" seeing the disruption of snow-fed water supplies, more stifling heat waves, and the permanent disap-pearance of Rocky Mountain meadows and coastal marshes, for example.

The report emphasized that global warming would also carry potential benefits for the nation, including increased agricultural and forest growth from longer growing seasons and from more rainfall and carbon dioxide for photosynthesis.

But it said environmental havoc was coming as well. "Some of the goods and services lost through the disappearance or fragmentation of natural ecosystems are likely to be costly or impossible to replace," the report said.

"Other ecosystems, such as Southeastern forests, are likely to experience major species shifts or break up into a mosaic of grass-lands, woodlands and forests."

"Bureaucratic Hot Air"

This report came from the president's own advisers. And how did the president respond? The usually staid British press agency Reuters put this headline on its report on June 5, 2002: "Bush: Global Climate Report Is Bureaucratic Hot Air."

Reuters explained:

> President Bush on Tuesday called a recent report that blames humans for global warming nothing more than a product of government "bureaucracy" and said he would not accept an international accord to reduce heat-trapping emissions.
>
> The report by the Environmental Protection Agency, whose top officials are appointed by the president, appeared to back the view of many scientists who believe that global warming is primarily caused by emissions from automobiles, power plants, and oil refineries.[2]

This kind of response has not been limited to one country, nor has it been ended by one election. The dangers of top-down, unaccountable, irresponsible power transcend the borders and the centuries.

Wherever you live, measure whether that place is *Mitzrayyim*, imposing on you narrow choices. Hearken to any warnings called out by those who listen carefully to the Breath of Life that intertwines us all. And if at first you think they are doom-besotted radicals, listen to the pharaoh's own advisers.

Let us think of ourselves as Moses, Miriam, and Aaron did. If indeed we celebrate the interweaving of all life, the *YHWH*, what should we be doing?

Can we learn from this old story to look beyond specific issues—this war or that highway, this tax cut or that coal plant—to the issue of unaccountable power? Of power as pyramidal in its top-down shape as ancient pyramids?

II

Brickmakers' Union Number One

And the proof that God had entered into Moses, and that Moses had really been "converted," was that he had to go back and identify himself with his enslaved people, "organize them into Brickmakers' Union Number One" and lead them out of hunger and slavery into freedom.

A. J. MUSTE, 1943

B ut organizing the Israelites into Brickmakers' Union Number One was difficult.

At the Burning Bush, God had cited outcries of pain from "My people" as the reason for the Transcendent One to descend into the maelstrom of sorrow to rescue them. God gave Moses some "signs" by which to authenticate that his mission was from God.

So Moses began by going to the workers as soon as he arrived in Egypt, with his brother Aaron at his side to speak if he were stage-shy and to perform these magic "signs." Aaron was to turn a stick into a snake and back again, and to turn its skin scaly white and back again. These signs were typical of what Egyptian priests could do in celebration of the gods of Egypt (including Pharaoh himself). Aaron's ability to do them in the name of God convinced the enslaved community that God was on their side.

Then Moses went to ask Pharaoh for time off to celebrate a festival for three days in the wilderness. Pharaoh responded with contempt, and worse: he ordered the Israelite slaves to search out their own straw to make the bricks with which they were building storehouses for Pharaoh, as part of their forced labor. This edict meant it would take much more time to make the bricks, yet the required number of bricks was not reduced. The work would be much harder.

Making Things Worse

Robbed of the servile comforts of their regular work, the brickmakers lost all their newfound self-confidence. Their foremen went to plead with Pharaoh but found him obdurate: "You must have plenty of time on your hands, if you think you can take off three days to honor this 'God' that no one knows. So stop shirking and start working!" The foremen turned against Moses and Aaron for making life worse for the workers, not better. And Moses complained to *YHWH*.

This sequence—a thin confidence, followed by a setback, followed by a hunger for the comforts of servility, leading to an attack on Moses's bona fides, and then to Moses's own complaint to God—foreshadowed what would happen later, when the people had achieved some freedom and were journeying in the Wilderness. Over and over, Moses was unable to forge them into a focused and committed community.

Failing to achieve the worker solidarity that might have dared a strike, Moses abandoned grassroots organizing and turned back to the arena he knew best: the palace. Through ten disastrous "plagues," Moses suspended working directly with the groaning people while he connected with God and tried to force the Pharaoh's hand. He had come to understand the interconnection between oppressing people and distressing the earth, but he did not yet understand how to mobilize the people to resist.

What he was doing did, however, slowly instill them with new hope. According to the story, their outlying region on the edge of Egypt was immune to the growing storm of blood, frogs, locusts, hail—and perhaps that immunity fed their growing self-confidence, their growing trust that Moses, Aaron, and Miriam knew what they were doing.

Night fell upon the land, three "days" so filled with darkness that even more than see it, the people could feel its thickness press against their eyeballs—perhaps an enormous sandstorm. But once more, Pharaoh dithered.

Finally the moment came for explicit solidarity and resistance. On God's instructions, Moses told the people their deliverance was coming. At last they were to act on their own instead of depending on Moses's eloquence or Pharaoh's reluctant generosity. They were to act in what we might call a general strike.

First, each family was to buy itself a lamb—or if the family was too poor to afford one, to band together and share. This fulfilled two social functions:

On one hand, it was in itself a reaffirmation of the nomadic shepherd identity half-buried in Israelite awareness and an invitation for others to join in it. One might say it was like asking Americans who had no family connection and little cultural connection with the Mayflower to sing "My Country, 'Tis of Thee."

At the same time, it was a direct challenge to Egyptian religion and culture. For many Egyptians, sheep were sacred and prohibited to any but priests. For foreigners and slaves to be flaunting them was a violation of not only custom, not only law, but the structure of reality itself.

For four days the Israelites could look from house to house, seeing these tethered lambs, seeing that together they had dared to break all custom and all law. Together.

Sacrilege and Solidarity

And then, four days later, on the night of the New Moon of the month of Spring (*Aviv*), a time of birth in every sphere of nature, a time when their ancestral shepherds might have offered newborn lambs to the Nomad God of nomad fruitfulness, these lambs were to be slaughtered. Sacrilege!

All who were prepared to be reborn in freedom were to smear the doorposts of their houses with the blood of these lambs. As we have already seen, they were in this way to make each home a blood-encircled womb from which to be born anew.

And then as darkness lightened into morning, the wail of death arose from every household where the doorway had not been smeared with blood. Every family—even the most poverty-stricken slave girl in all Egypt—suffered the consequences of their Pharaoh's arrogance through the death of their firstborns.

As Moses had instructed them, the Israelites visited all their Egyptian neighbors to demand some gold and jewels. Call it "severance pay" for the unpaid past, or call it "reparations" for past cruelty, the

Egyptian households, overawed by the terror-filled events and stricken by the deaths of every firstborn, would deliver up their due. Or perhaps this treasure was a teaching for the future—to be ready for that later moment in the Wilderness when the Israelites learned that they might choose to use that gold for travesty or triumph—for the Golden Calf that embodied idolatry, or for the Golden *Mishkan*, the portable Shrine that carried God's own Presence.

And finally, they were to bake the hasty K rations of their day—the bread of the poor, barley flour and water with no yeast or flavoring; add a chunk of roasted lamb and a pungent vegetable, a "bitter herb" to flavor this thrown-together first meal outside their comfort zone. They were to throw on a pair of sandals, pick up a stick to help them through the rough spots on an unpaved road, get their bearings from the bright full moon. And run.

\W

12

Recalling the Past, Transforming the Future

Imagine that in the text of the American Declaration of Independence, one-third of the Declaration were a call for future generations to observe the Fourth of July as a sacred day of memory.

Imagine that these paragraphs, interspersed with the affirmation of "life, liberty, and the pursuit of happiness" and the condemnations of the king, included explicit commands to wear homespun clothing on that day, so as to honor the memory of those colonists who boycotted British wool; to explode fireworks; to eat corn on the cob and drink hot chocolate as indigenous American products; and of course to read aloud in families and congregations and public festivals the whole text of the Declaration of Independence.

That is what the biblical text about the Exodus does. The Bible calls urgently upon the people to prepare to leave slavery on the night so dark that the darkness could literally be touched, could physically be touched (Exod. 12:1–20).

They were to wear sandals and carry a staff.

They were to eat unleavened bread, because it was the bread of the poor and because they had to leave in such great haste that there was no time for the bread to leaven.

They were to smear blood on the doorposts of their houses, so that death would not visit the houses of those who were brave enough to smear the blood, even while death descended upon the firstborn in every Egyptian home that did not smear blood upon the doorposts.

And so they were to make their doorways like the doorway of a womb, through which every human being is born amid the blood into new birth.

And in the same breath that describes what they had to most urgently do in the most immediate present, the Bible insists that in every future generation they must tell the story of this momentous moment and must reenact their departure from slavery into freedom.

The text moves back and forth from the present to the future so seamlessly that many readers do not even notice the sliding through centuries and millennia of time.

The story even dips into the past. It mentions two different festivals long celebrated in many previous generations: one on the fourteenth, one on the fifteenth of the lunar month of Spring (*Aviv*)—both coming when the moon was full, yet one a shepherd's festival of newly birthing lambs, the other a farmer's festival of newly sprouted barley.

And then the story shifts into the future, when the people must celebrate a new festival that has emerged from this extraordinary historical moment, that has emerged from the melting of the shepherd's and the farmer's festivals into a new amalgam. This was a night of transformation so profound that it could absorb old festivals, heat them to the melting point, and create a whole new festival.

Here is where the Bible makes clear that telling the story and reenacting the action are just as important as walking into freedom in the first place, perhaps even more important.

Here is where the story makes clear that birthing happens not just once but again and again and again; that freedom happens not just once but again and again and again.

What is the darkness so thick it can be touched? It is easy to see this as a metaphor, a symbol, of Mystery so deep that at every moment—even though we cannot see into It—It is pressing into our eyes and lips, upon our tongues and hands and feet.

This Mystery is not even an inch away from us, let alone far up in heaven or across the seas. Though it touches us so intimately, there is no way for us to touch its depths.

It is also possible that this was a physical reality, that a sandstorm enveloped all of Egypt, darkening even the full moon of this spring month, and forced the people to stumble their way into a new reality.

Whatever else happened that night, whatever amalgam of grief and greed, fear and rage, relief and ecstasy, boiled in their innards, the memory was inserted in their souls.

Not only to remember, but to re-member. To reconnect the members of their bodies physical, their bodies politic. To reenact the surge, the wave of freedom as it moved to meet the surge, the waves, of Sea.

For in every generation, the storytellers knew, there is one who rises up to press us down, and in every generation there comes the moment for those pressed down to rise. Not to reenact the slavery upon others, but to follow the Cloud of Darkness, of Unknowing, into community and freedom.

13

The Sea of Ending and Beginning

The Torah calls the Sea of Transformation *Yam Suf*, "the Sea of Reeds." Or maybe the Torah had in mind *Yam Sof*, "the Sea of End." The end of one world, the beginning of another.

But for a couple of thousand years, and not just in English, where the shift from "reed" to "red" is obvious, many have called it "the Red Sea." Perhaps the image that flooded everybody's brain was Pharaoh's army, drowned. A sea of blood. Or—"My water has broken!" the birthing mother says. The end of one world, the beginning of another.

There are two tiny tales the ancient Rabbis read in the "white fire" between the letters of the *Yam Suf* story.

Their reading of the white fire of the Breaking of the Sea crystallized one of the great shifts from biblical to Rabbinic Judaism. The Torah says that at the edge of the Sea, with Pharaoh's chariots thundering behind and the waters of the Sea thundering before, Moses raised his staff and prayed. Then, says the Torah, God said to Moses, "Tell My people to move forward."

But the Rabbis heard a story in the silence: "Moses," said God, "there are times to pray at length, and there are times to pray briefly. My people are hemmed in, and you stand there piling prayer on prayer? Tell My people to move forward!"

The Rabbis were teaching that prayer should not substitute for action. And then they took one more step: The black fire of Torah says that the people "went into the Sea on the dry land" (Exod. 14:22), and then God split the waters. When the Rabbis read this line with deep attention, they thought it was peculiar. If it was sea, then it was not dry land; if dry land, it wasn't sea. What was it, then?

So they read another story in the white fire: As the people approached, the Sea flowed on, unmoving. The Pharaoh's army, all in chariots, their trumpets braying triumph, approached; the Sea flowed on, unmoving. The people stood there—unmoving, frozen.

Even after Moses told the people to "move forward," they were unwilling. The newly trapped Israelites began to wail. Still nothing happened.

Plunging into the Unknown

Then one man, moved by faith or fear, cowardice or courage, stumbled his way into the water. Up to his knees: he staggered from one rock to another. Up to his waist: he pushed himself against the waves. Up to his nose: he began to cough and choke.

And then the waters parted. Not till then.

Let's not forget his name. According to the Rabbis' midrash, it was Nachshon ben Amminadav. Not a great national hero before that moment; just a local leader of the tribe of Levi. A community organizer.

By seeing these stories hidden in the fire of the spaces, the Rabbis crossed their own *Yam Sof*, Sea of Transformation, an End and a Beginning. The God of miracle and magic gave way, at least a little, to the human pioneer. These stories meant that freedom lay in human hands and legs.

The path the Rabbis opened for action when they read the Torah two thousand years ago was still open for Rabbi David Einhorn in Baltimore in 1861. He chose to "pray" by calling for the abolition of slavery. When his own congregants in that slave-holding city threatened to tar and feather him, he prayed again—by using his legs in an Exodus of his own—fleeing Baltimore, crossing the Sea of Ending and Beginning called the Mason-Dixon Line, to lead a synagogue in the free city of Philadelphia.

The path the Rabbis opened for action when they read the Torah two thousand years ago was still open for Rabbi Abraham Joshua Heschel in 1965 when he marched alongside Dr. Martin Luther King Jr. in Selma, Alabama, to demand that the grandchildren of slaves be accorded the right to vote.

He came back home from that march to say, "I felt as if my legs were praying." Still another Nachshon ben Amminadav.

And having crossed that Sea of Ending and Beginning, Heschel was able to walk still further into freedom, even when that meant going beyond the civil rights activism that his supporters celebrated—into opposing the Vietnam War, an opposition that to many of his supporters seemed unwise, unpatriotic.

"Tell My people to move forward!"

PART IV

From the Sea to Sinai

Crossing the Sea was not the goal of the Freedom Journey, but only the end of the first step. On the other shore, the Children of Israel started out as a straggling single-file line of runaway slaves. Each kept in touch only with the two or three runaways ahead and two or three behind. There was no center, no unity of purpose.

No community.

But in the great sweep of history, at this very moment it was necessary to give birth to a new form of community. For Pharaoh's behavior took to extremes the necessary aspect of control in the world, and that overbearing element of hypercontrol cried out for balance and correction.

Indeed, whenever the powerful overpower the world, the dance of God between control and community falls out of balance. The world's leg of control keeps charging onward—stamping, stamping in its effort to move forward. The other leg, community, lags far behind. So the Body of God, reflected in the body of the earth and human earthlings, staggers, stumbles, with the two legs out of sync.

To heal themselves, to walk again, the human communities that have been overpowered must go beyond shaking off that overpowerment. They must shape a new form of community that can absorb and match the new forms of control, instead of being overpowered by them.

When Pharaoh overreached, his drowning in the Red Sea was not enough to heal society. There needed to be a new form of community.

And so came Sinai. Not till then did the straggle of runaway slaves become a community centered on a Center. Not till then could they begin the long journey in the Wilderness, working out the kinks in the new forms of community.

14

The Taste of Freedom

Moving forward into the Wilderness after the supernal experience of the Sea, the people began to run low on food and water, and the grumbling began. "Why did you bother taking us out of the Narrow Place we knew, into this broad and barren Wilderness?" they taunted Moses and Aaron. "The pangs of hunger now are as sharp and bitter as the whips before. Yes, we felt transported beyond ourselves when we saw what happened at the Sea, but now we feel like ill-fed ants creeping toward an ever-vanishing horizon! Weren't there graves enough in Egypt, that you had to bring us here to die?"

Moses reminded them, "It wasn't the two of us but the Breath of Life Itself, the Hurricane of change, whose wind blew back the Sea and carried you from slavery to freedom. Stop kvetching! Your nourishment will have to come not from the two of us but from that same Breath of Life!"

And indeed the Breath of Life brought nurture on Its wings, Its winds. Something the people had never see before began to rain upon them. They said *Mahn hu*—"What's that?—Watchamacallit" (Exod. 16:15), until the name stuck: *mahn*, manna. Moses told them it was the food that they were so badly wanting.

Every day, the manna fell. The people learned to gather just enough to meet their needs for one more day. Any surplus rotted away, began to stink of greed or fear.

Until this moment, for many human beings life was locked into the pattern of an even deeper, broader serfdom than had been true for the Israelites in Egypt. Everyone had worked day after day, every day, sweat pouring down their faces, to wring from the hostile earth barely enough food to survive. If often felt as if the earth would bring forth only thorns and thistles.

Lost Eden

This pattern of real life got encoded into the biblical legend of Eden, the Garden of Delight. Over and over, people had found themselves following the tragic trajectory that is given poetic shape in the Eden story. "Look around!" the universe had said again and again. "The earth is full of abundance beyond measure. But you must bring some measure to it. You must not gobble up all the life around you. For if you do, you will prosper in a big way for a short while. But then the abundance will wither—you yourself will cause it to wither—and you will find yourselves scrabbling to eat what little there is left. To prevent that happening, you must learn to put some gentle limits on your eating."

In the Bible, that is what God says—first at the beginning of the Eden idyll: "Of all the trees of the abundant garden you may eat, save only one you must refrain from eating" (Gen. 2:16–17); and then at the end: "Because you ate without attending to My warning, you have ruined My abundance. Now you must toil every day of your life, and the earth will be reluctant to feed you" (Gen. 3:17–19).

Again and again, history itself had taught this lesson. Again and again, the fear of running out of food had led to a greedy overreaching to amass it. But gathering all life energy into a few hands meant that there was too little left for other people and for other life-forms.

And then indeed the fountains of abundance had dried up. Work—which had degenerated from a joyful partnering with earth into a greedy effort to subdue it—degenerated still further as the abundance withered, into a desperate effort to subdue the earth.

Eden for a Moment—Once Again

That had been the experience of human history. Slavery under Pharaoh had simply been an accentuation of this reality. But now something new was coming into the world. Something profound had changed in this moment of the Pharaoh's fall. The Israelites had been offered a taste of Eden once again. The manna did not require sweat and toil to bring it forth from a hostile earth. Instead, it betokened a newly free and playful reconnection with the earth.

With this freely given food came an even deeper freedom: One day of every seven, the people did not even need to do the light and joyful work of gathering the manna. For on the sixth day, a double portion would appear. On that day, the extra did not rot away. It was the Sabbatical portion, to be eaten on the seventh day. And thus no longer did the community need work "all the days of [their] life" (Gen. 3:17) in order to eat. One-seventh of those days, they had been offered time to make a conscious Eden.

The coming of the manna was the first major experience the people had after their birthing through the breaking of the Red Sea waters. It was the milk of God's mothering for these newborns.

Indeed, this Shabbat-of-manna betokened the first stage of a peace agreement to end the primordial war between *adam* (human beings) and *adamah* (earth), the war that began as we left Eden. What started with a troubled act of eating is healed with a jubilant act of eating.

Eden's Failure as a Satire on Babylon

From what historical experience sprang these related myths of Eden and manna/Shabbat? Evan Eisenberg, in *The Ecology of Eden*, suggests that the Eden story is a sardonic critique of agro-imperial Sumeria and its breakthrough into feeding more people than hunter-gatherers or small farmers or shepherds could.

Through monocrop agriculture and irrigation canals, Sumeria invented a way of multiplying food. But the surplus did not add to the freedom of the people. Instead, the irrigation canals required an insistence on strict rules of ownership that had been foreign to the Western Semites. It required an army to enforce the rules of ownership, and it allowed the birthing of more people—a surplus to serve in the new army.

To the Western Semites, says Eisenberg, the new monocrop empire was a profound threat—not only political and military but economic, ecological, and spiritual. For the Western Semites had worshiped a God of fluidity, nomadry, small farms on rocky hillsides and the shepherds' wandering to new meadows.

How to deal with the new imperious economics? To imitate it meant to surrender precious values. To ignore it meant to be conquered. Either way, a culture shattered.

The Eden story was a critique: Human beings break through the harmonious rules of how to eat from a friendly earth. The result? Yes, more food, but at the cost of alienation between the earth and human earthlings. The cost of endless toil. The subjugation of women. More births, more labor pains.

Shabbat: Eat Your Cake and Have It Too

But critique is not enough. How could the Western Semites live their values, caught between the pressure of victorious agro-imperial Sumeria and the path of a grassroots God?

Shabbat, and the Sabbatical year and Jubilee that are its echoes, offered a creative resolution of the impossible dilemma. Through six days, six years, of ownership and accumulation, they could do what the Sumerians did. And then, through Shabbat and the Sabbatical year, they could reclaim their freedom and their intimacy with a God Who reminded them that no *adam* owns the *adamah*, no earthling owns the earth, no human owns the humus.

Shabbat is the world in which as hardworking grown-ups we can experience our childlike playfulness.

No wonder Shabbat came with a new kind of food—the food of a bounteous, unboundaried God. No wonder that Jewish tradition still teaches that Shabbat is not only an echo of Eden past, but the foretaste—truly a "taste"—of a higher, more conscious Eden of the future, a foretaste of messianic time.

The biblical mind placed this story in the context of an empire's fall. (Was the placement of that imperial collapse in Egypt a literary displacement of the confrontation with Sumeria?) The stern politics of "Put limits on the exercise of power! Control those who would control you!" is intertwined with the joyful politics of community: "Rest, reflect, celebrate!"

As we read the tales of Eden and of manna, we ruefully remember that not once alone, but over and over, individual human beings and the human race as a body have chosen to leap headlong forward in our desire to control and command. When we do, we find ourselves both more powerful, and more conflicted.

But there is one way to transform this future of greater power and sharper conflict. We can, like the Western Semites and like the story the Israelites told about their first step from the Narrow Space into the

Freedom Journey, enter into a deeper journey toward a broader community. We can learn to include more beings in our loving and learn to pause for more Being in our Doing.

Today, we—all humanity—face an imperial modernity that goes far beyond Sumeria or Pharaoh. More material food, more spiritual hunger. More food, less sharing. Can we invent new forms of community, can we heal the earth and ourselves, can we remind ourselves to rest and reflect, can we taste Eden, Messiah, Shabbat?

15

Before the Sinai Marriage

As the Israelites continued to stumble their weary way into the Wilderness, they met a family member of their leader.

Who was he? The Torah makes very sure we know: in the first twelve lines of Exodus 18, Yitro is referred to *seven times* as *choteyn Moshe*, "Moses's father-in-law" (vv. 1, 2, 5, 6, 7, 8, 12).

Not merely who he was, and not who his forebears were: who he was in relationship to Moses, again and again, as if one explanation, or even two, would not be enough to impress this in our consciousness.

Fathering Moses

We learn that Yitro was another name for the Reuel whose daughters Moses met at a wellspring in Midian. When he came to visit Moses at this pausing-place upon the epic journey in the Wilderness, Yitro brought along his daughter Tzipporah, Moses's wife, and their two sons.

Why did his name change? Forty years before, he had been "God's shepherd," watching over the seven ewe lambs of his daughters at a well that invited Moses to replay the roles of his forebear Abraham at the Well of Seven/Swearing and of his forebear Jacob, finding his wife at a wellspring. Now, he was "Remnant," "Leftover"—perhaps the last leftover of Moses's life before he became the leader/liberator. What could this Leftover have come to say?

And why would we need to know that Moses's relationship with his father-in-law and a visit with his family were foremost in his awareness in this time just before the people came to rest at the foot of the Mountain of God?

In retrospect, we know—and perhaps God and Moses knew ahead of time—that the people were about to receive what Hebrew calls *Aseret HaDibrot* (the Ten Words or Ten Utterances) and in English are called the Ten Commandments.

Many Torah commentators have seen the encounter at Sinai as the wedding ceremony between God and the Jewish people. As in every Jewish wedding, there had to be a written contract, the *ketubah*, explaining the obligations of both partners. For this ceremony, say the commentators, the Torah itself was the *ketubah*, making clear what the parties owed each other. Since one of the major aspects of a *ketubah* in an ordinary marriage is to specify what will happen in case there is a divorce, there is a foreboding tone to this comparison. Thinking about it, we may recall the many warnings in the Torah of the disastrous consequences that may follow if the Israelites failed to carry out the covenant.

The Marriage of God and Israel

Beyond whatever shadows may be cast by this prenuptial agreement, the ceremony itself is both solemn and joyful. Solemnity—of course, since each marriage looks toward future fruitfulness, toward the joining not only of bodies but of minds and hearts and spirits. And joy— the ceremonial prayers by ancient custom are not only recited but sung. "Dancing before the bride" is viewed by Rabbinic tradition as not just delightful but obligatory.

The solemn side of the event is emphasized by a custom of treating the day before the wedding like a mini–Yom Kippur. Often the partners about to be married fast from food and drink for the day. They focus all their attention on the day's holy purpose for generations and centuries to come—and not on such momentary distractions as physical nourishment.

Like Yom Kippur, it is a day of at-one-ment, a preparation for beginning a new way of life by reflecting on, forgiving, and asking forgiveness for relational misdeeds and hurts of the person's past. We notice that at Sinai there was a three-day pause for focusing intention and attention, before the mountain itself began to shake and dance, before the sky erupted in fireworks and thunder.

In ordinary marriages, this pause before the wedding may give time for the partnering couple to address what may be the most important of those hurts and misdeeds that need a resolution. These are likely to be those that arose in the families of their birth and rearing. Those families were probably the contexts for the most intense and intimate experience each partner had of love and anger, of work that fit the family's inclinations—and didn't; of work that met the family's needs—and didn't. Adults and siblings had strong effects on each other. So one major aspect of preparing for married life, for partnership, may be reflecting on and forgiving whatever missteps and misdeeds have arisen in the families where each partner grew up.

For each partner, hovering breathless on the edge of partnership, this is a crucial moment for gathering up the truth of each one's parents.

How was Moses to do this? He may have had a plethora of mothers. But he had had very sketchy fathering. Where could he turn to gather up the truth of his own parenting, as he hovered on the edge of this "wedding" where he would be representing the people Israel in the emerging partnership with God?

To his birth-father Amram? We know hardly anything about him besides the bare fact of biological ancestry. To Pharaoh, the father of the princess who drew Moses from the Nile and so became an extra mother for him? But Pharaoh had commanded he be killed. So we certainly can't expect that Pharaoh would have taken on any fathering or grandfathering role for Moses—the foundling who lived only because Bat-Yah disobeyed her father's will, and so saved the wretched baby's life.

The one man who had fathered Moses was his father-in-law—Yitro, priest of Midian, who through forty years of Moses's marriage to Tzipporah had watched and guided and counseled not only Moses but the partnering. Indeed, since we hear nothing at all about a wife to Yitro, his counseling may have been the nearest Moses came to a living model for his own marriage—and for the people's.

So it is important that Yitro arrived just as the people were ready for their "wedding." And it is important that the two men not only greeted each other warmly, but immediately went into a tent to talk in private. Moses told Yitro all that had happened since they had last seen each other—the Exodus from *Mitzrayyim*, the crossing of the Red Sea, the need for food and water, "all the hardships that have befallen the [people], and how *YHWH* has delivered them" (Exod. 18:8).

And in turn Yitro, Moses's father-in-law, did what every child (adult or young) wants of their parents: he listened carefully and took pleasure in what had happened. This is a first step in the healing of the relationship with parents in preparation for marriage: we speak from our hearts, unguarded, to our parents and find them listening openly, without interruption or advice, and responsive to what we have to say.

The next day, Moses continued his work adjudicating disputes between Israelites. There were so many people who needed to be heard and judged that people lined up from morning to night, waiting for Moses. Yitro, Moses's father-in-law, watched the process and then spoke honestly to Moses, as one leader to another and as a father to a son.

Yitro warned Moses that he would burn out, that it was too much work for one person to do, that it was unfair for people to have to stand around and wait all day for disputes to be settled. Yitro counseled Moses to appoint a cadre of judges who, because they were themselves capable, God-fearing, and trustworthy, could share the burden with Moses and settle all the minor disputes, bringing only the major ones to Moses.

And Moses, the mature son, did what all parents want of their children: he listened carefully and accepted the counsel of his father-in-law, acting on it without rejecting Yitro's advice as interfering or shaming or irrelevant.

This is a second step in the healing of the relationship between parents and children in preparation for marriage: we listen openly to what parents have to say and find wisdom for ourselves in their caring comments.

When parents and children are able to speak and listen openly to one another and find meaningful connection in the exchange, the children are better prepared for the challenges of being a loving partner and becoming a loving parent.

And so these conversations became the worthy backdrop for the covenantal "marriage" that began at Sinai. What seems like a "leftover" piece of Moses's past becomes a crucial guide into his future.

卐

16

The Wordless Torah of the Wordless Mountains

M oses was ready. Were the people?

Seven weeks they had been walking from the Narrows through the open Wilderness that is the Land of No One. In Hebrew, "wilderness" is *midbar*. It could be understood as *midaber*, "wording, speaking," or *m'devar/m'dibbur*, "away from word, without a word, beyond words."

Or both: "A speaking beyond words."

In our own generation, on many nights in *Midbar Sinai*, the Wilderness of Sinai, hundreds of pilgrims from many religions and from all around the world spend all night climbing the mountain that either is or isn't the mountain where the people Israel once upon a time assembled.

In their generation long ago, they too struggled over crags and crevices to hear the Teaching that was beyond words.

Yes, beyond words. Indeed, one teaching about the Teaching says no word at all was spoken—only an *aleph*, the first letter of the Ten Words that have come down to us.

The *aleph* is a letter with no sound of its own. Only the silent sound made by an open throat. From just the truth that the universe wants to speak with us, opens its throat to speak with us, comes all the rest, for us to figure out: Don't kill. Don't breathe without remembering that each breath is the Name of the One Breath. Don't take a useful part of the whole and carve it out from all the flow, make it an idol, rigidify it, and bow down to it. Don't steal from another's share of the great abundance, for then the abundance will wither.

All that wisdom, encoded in just the open throat of the world that wants to speak.

And when the many diverse pilgrims look out today at dawn just as those walkers in the Wilderness looked out so long ago at dawn, across millennia they join to sing and sob in joy, they look to the nearby mountains and see—the Tablets!

The mountains themselves, in their geological formations, looking like the conventional images of the Tablets that we see in our art and on many synagogues. Running across them are horizontal outcroppings, grooves, furrows, horizontal bands of rough out-jutting rock separated from each other by horizontal bands of smoothness. Layer on layer, the outcomes of convulsive wordless history.

Outcroppings that can *almost* be read. Beyond words.

The Tablets of the earth itself and the Utterances of the earth itself. Torah.

Now the people were ready.

17

Sinai

The Universe Says "I"

The Israelites stood at the foot of Sinai.

They gazed at the holy mountain but could not see its crags, its precipices. The clouds enfolded it in an enormous mirror. More than enormous: Infinite.

In that mirror each one saw a self and the entire people—saw all who had just trekked out of slavery, and ancient Sarah with her husband, Abraham, and many, many descendants, beyond the generation that had just fled slavery and on and on, to many centuries later.

And each one, looking, saw Egypt, Mother Egypt. And Babylon. And Rome. And India, and the Americas, and snowy plains of ice, and rolling oceans.

Saw the intricate web of human settlements, languages, cultures, dances; a hundred thousand foods, herbs, drinks of nourishment and ecstasy, the shimmering touch of hands and thighs and lips in delicate connection.

And the glaring sun. Spinning planets. Whole whirling galaxies.

And blood cells. One tiny red corpuscle. An atom of oxygen within it. Weightless positrons, dancing in nothing.

All the while each one, each "I" seeing, each "I" hearing. Infinite mirror, infinite echo—echoing a sound, a word: *Anokhi*, "I."

Time drops away. The past becomes an ever-present present. From all around each "I" and from within each "I," each self hears an overwhelming single word:

Anokhi,

"I!"

It comes like a drumbeat, again again: *Anokhi.*

This is my "I," my own self, but there is no "my," no possessing, no being possessed.

The "I" is the "I" that I am. I speak it, it rolls from my throat, I affirm it, I. *Anokhi.*

And the "I" is also the entire people. I speak *Anokhi* also as one voice of all the people. Again again again again, *Anokhi.* I.

At every moment—there is only one moment—there is I the person, I the people.

One I.

And, still in the same moment, the entire universe becomes *Anokhi,* "I."

My "I" is caught up in the "I" of the universe, the "I" of the universe is caught up in my "I."

This "I" is all there is; there is no "Thou," no "Other," no verb, no predicate. No past, no future, no present, no tense. Only the subject is the sentence, only "I."

I see the wilderness, I am the wilderness, the shimmering heat waves rising from its surface are my I, the spirals of time and history, the woven tapestries of art and custom, the patterned laws of science: world upon world, infinity upon infinity, all I.

I see myself, part of an unfathomable Whole, not facing it but integrated in it.

For an instant I am infinitesimal, a tiny, rhythmic, breathing, conscious cell in some vast, breathing, conscious ultra-human.

For an instant, I am infinite, containing in one enormous self all the worlds of fact and meaning.

These instants are themselves a single instant, infinitely unfolding; they last for just a flashing moment that stretches out for all eternity.

All time, all space whirls like a Möbius strip through a vast expanse curved in an unspeakable dimension—while it holds but one surface and one edge.

I tremble, topple, fall to ground that disappears beneath while its textures enter every inch of blazing, open skin.

I am the shaking earth, all my skin is quivering, unending one great quivering shudder.

Stop stop how can I stop forget how can forget, I need forget, how can forget?

I see too deep, I stand too big, I must forget, how to forget?

Our body quivers; I taste the world, the world is tasting me, is touching all my skin, and inside too: inside our mouths, my belly, every opening filled and every limb outreaching to fill whatever is empty in the world.

Back and forth, I am / we are All All There Is—*Anokhi*, "I"—and Everything is all there is, we are / I am part of everything and less than nothing,

Anokhi I a cell of great *Anokhi* of the world come conscious.

I stand *inside* God's skull, behind the face; I look out through God's eyes, my face in Face, I see myself, ourself. *Anokhi*.

And reeling, stunned, I fall, roll, stumble away from the Mirror in the Mountain, I close all eyes and shriek to see that I can still see Everything.

I close our ears, I hear the Voice still ringing in my bones, I back away and try to blot it out, forget. To not be "I" or "we" or anyone.

And gradually I can become a separate "thou." Gradually I can / we can / you can / they can begin to hear the "I" expand, contract, become—

"I *YHWH your* God Who brought *you* out ..."

I disentangle our selves, distinguish between the voice in their throats and the Voice in my ears. Gradually they/I distinguish me/us/themselves from the ground beneath, distinguish the pain in tightly clenched fists from pleasure in their open mouth, the breath within them from the wind around them,

Na'aseh, "We will do ... we / All There Is / will do," there is no Other.

Nishma, "We *will hear* ... the Other speak to us."

I

I–Thou.

I connect Thou, Thou connect I.

Connect.

An artery channels streams of blood, just I; but now organic unity is gone. "Connect" is necessary.

Gradually: connections and commandments. "You shall keep Shabat." "You shall not kill."

From organic into what is organized; replace harmonious wholeness with a plan, a patterning. Gradually distinguish what they are doing from what they should be doing.

Ruefully I linger, trying to remember the *Anokhi* and trying to forget it, relieved I have been able to escape and joyful I will never be able to escape, already wishing to re-create the moment and frightened that the moment will recur without my wishing, still tingling, touching the impossible I have just done, laughing, tasting an apple rolling on my tongue, each drop of juice as if I had just returned to Eden.

As the wandering people opened up to Sinai, for the moment of *Anokhi*—the first word of the Ten that came in lightning and in thunder—there was no distinction between the "mystical" and "secular." One Consciousness suffused / gave life to / became the life of all the infinite worlds / Is "God" / Is world.

In Mirrored Sinai, there is not God on the one side and the secular, the world, on the other. There is no way to leap out of the world in order to have a "mystical" experience—because the world is all there is, there is no "out" of it. And there is no way to turn away from God by turning toward the "secular" world. For God is all there is, there is no "away" from God.

It is the full experiencing of the secular world itself that is the mystical experience.

From this vision of utter wholeness the Israelites fled. Sent Moses into the Mountain's heart to live with I, *Anokhi*.

And still today, most human beings flee—into seeing "I" counterposed to "Thou," "God" counterposed to "the world." Once this separation, this duality, had been established, it became one of the great tasks of human living to hold both ends of the rope, so as neither to "ascend" into the utterly spiritual nor to "descend" into the purely material.

How do we hold both ends of the rope, conscious that it is a single rope?

For Jews, the connective rope is the *mitzvot*, commandments or connections; what other cultures may call ethics, precepts, relationships—the "Do" and "Do not" that bind our lives together. Making bonds, not bondage.

And those bonds created not only a new community, but a new kind of community, one already distinguished from the neighboring nations by their passion for the God Who is always becoming, always liberating, for the God Who breathes all life and is all life-breath, interweaving all; and by their commitment to the Shabbat, a time to celebrate not doing, not knowing, not controlling.

Part V

Encountering Wilderness, Creating Community

Sinai provided the straggling band of runaway slaves with a new spiritual center: God's word. But that was only a beckoning into community; it took the actual experience of living together to map a communal path ahead. The Wilderness was the nearest to an empty space in which the experimenting could begin without the sounds of foreign static that might interfere.

So the people faced the quandaries of a newborn beginning to crawl, seeking to walk, even to run. The moving was not only a physical journey from Sinai to and across the Jordan, but a spiritual, political, and cultural journey toward responsible adulthood.

God and the people tested each other at every step of the way. Many of the steps forward, following the Radiant Cloud of Mystery, were followed by steps backward. Yet even the awkward, backward steps taught the people something.

Sacred space, sacred time, and sacred personhood became for them the three dimensions of community.

For this new people, what delineated space? Unlike other peoples who lived in a land they intimately knew, this new people was attached to a land only in legend, imagination, and intention. So they built a space—a Shrine, a *Mishkan*, a place of God's Presence that was in a sense a movable Sinai. Its interior defined sacred space. When the Cloud of Mystery that rested on it moved, it led them through the space that was not their own, pausing to define each momentary encampment as a place that was for a moment their own.

How would this new people measure time? They defined sacred time: festivals that tracked the year of agricultural seasons they expected to live through after they entered a land that would need working to feed them, plus a time for restfulness that crosshatched the festivals—the seventh day, the seventh month, and the seventh year.

How could the new people define the sacredness of its own members? They distinguished the homeborn citizen from the sojourner, and within the people they distinguished several kinds of sacred personhood: hereditary priests and their Levitical assistants; the possibility that "ordinary" people could choose to live a sacred separate role; and the ways in which "ordinary" people could, through risky encounters with deaths and births and uncanny illnesses, shift from inclusion in communal holiness to living their holiness in seclusion.

These three aspects of shaping reality to make a peoplehood did not come to them in a simple "logical" order in the way we have just summed them up. They arose instead in moments of lived experience as they journeyed.

But for us, it will be easier to mark the people's journey through the Wilderness by exploring each of these three dimensions in order.

॥

18

Carrying the Sacred Space

As Moses entered the cloud upon the holy mountain, instructions began to pour into his head and heart. Many of them were the rules that make community possible: not only "Don't kill," "Don't steal," but more detailed instructions to govern work and food and sex.

And then a great outpouring of words about a sacred space. A portable Shrine, a *Mishkan*—the Hebrew that translates into "a Bearer of the Presence." (*Shekhinah* is the Immanent Presence of God in the world; *shikkun* in modern Hebrew is a neighborhood.)

Celebrating Freedom in Color, Scent, Texture

From the Voice that had beckoned Moses and the people to birth and freedom, they heard the Vision of a sacred space. Full of scarlet and purple and deep blue. Woven of cloth, fashioned of fur. Shaped in sections that could be grommeted together. Light enough to carry on their journey, place to place.

Moses said the instructions were so complex that the words left him confused; he needed a diagram, a picture. God showed him one. Then God named the artists who were to bring this blueprint into three-dimensional reality—the only people other than Moses and Aaron who were named in the cloud on Sinai. Words alone, rules alone, even with Miriam's songs and dances added, were not enough for a sacred journey into freedom. Color, space, shape, texture were also necessary. Artists and architects were as crucial as the prophet and the priest.

Why did this space need to be constructed and carried?

First of all, the writers tell us that the Cloud of Mystery felt attracted to this inner space. Even though the whole Wilderness was the Place of God, always speaking, always beyond words, God also needed a House more defined, more physically available. Or, as the Rabbis later put it, God understood that the people needed such a space. In the language of the psychology of art, they stretched themselves to celebrating God as "ground" and found they also needed God as "figure." The proof of this need was their hunger to build a Golden Calf when they felt bereft, abandoned in the Wild.

We will come back to the complex relationship between the *Mishkan* and the Calf, but for now we can focus on the need of the people for a focus. No more single-file running headlong into Wilderness; now the people were to have a center. Indeed, the instructions made the *Mishkan* physically and geographically central by naming which tribes were to march to its east, west, north, and south.

Second, the center had to be not only geographical, not only intellectual, but actual, built of the deeds of everyone. The entire community had to bring their gold, their jewels, their arms and hands, to make a Place for God.

And the story teaches us the importance, the holiness, of sensuality. No bare ascetic tent, the *Mishkan*. Savoring spices and perfumes; gazing on scarlet and purple; roasting beef, frying pancakes, baking bread; burning olive oil to light the inner path; feeling the proportions of space expansive and restricted—all were necessary for the Spirit to be present. And for the people to experience the Spirit's presence. For on occasion a Cloud of Mystery would descend when It wished, awesome and unbidden.

As the body is built of heart and liver, brain and foot, with the breath carried by the blood to every cell and organ, so this Place was to be infused with Spirit, soaking into each inch of stone and fur and wood and cloth. Connected in two ways at once: connected by the Spirit within each part of it, and connected by the grommets that held the parts together. Connected, dry bone to dry bone, dry cloth to dry stone.

The plans for the *Mishkan* are so important that they take up one-third of the book of Exodus. They appear in three different ways: once when Moses heard its description on the mountaintop, once when he explained it to the people, once when they actually built it. In the story—after Moses heard and saw the vision, before he communicated it to the people—there was an interruption: the people built a Golden Calf. The rhythm is like a poem in the form ABCBA. Somehow the story of the sacred *Mishkan* was shaped so as to point to the sacrilegious Calf.

One way to understand the relationship between the *Mishkan* and the Golden Calf is that, from watching the people build an idol, the bull-calf that had been a god in the Egypt they had fled, God ruefully accepted that the people needed a physical focus for their experience of God—and gave them the *Mishkan* in place of a calf.

If we understand the story this way, the order of events seems chronologically reversed. For God described the *Mishkan* while Moses was on the mountain; it was only when Moses returned to the people that he found them carousing 'round the Calf. But perhaps the poetic point of putting the Golden Calf at the heart of the story was more important to the writers than chronological order.

Was the *Mishkan* God's Golden Calf?

Still, suppose we accept both the centrality of the Golden Calf to the story and the chronology as it appears in the Torah: the plan for *Mishkan* first, the Calf second, the building of the *Mishkan* third. If we follow the story this way, perhaps we learn an additional lesson.

Why did the people need the Golden Calf anyway? Because, the Torah says, Moses's long absence frightened them. They felt their physical connection with God had disappeared. Forty days and nights upon the sacred mountain, the mountain they themselves were afraid to climb. (Why was the time of forty days prescribed for his sojourn on the mountaintop? Later in the story, why was forty years the length of time the people wandered in the Wilderness? Rabbi Jeff Roth suggested to me that since "forty weeks" is the average time of human pregnancy, every "forty" in the Bible means a pregnant pause as some process works its way to fruition.)

Perhaps, the people thought, this pregnant pause has failed, miscarried; perhaps Moses has died. So they regressed to wishing for the kind of god connection that they knew in Egypt—better a visible idol than a vanished prophet.

Why had Moses been away so long?

Look at the Torah's telling of what he heard upon the mountain, and we see that perhaps three-fourths of it is God's description of the

Mishkan! What if the description had been briefer, what if the rules for building a physical House for God had been as broad and sketchlike as the rules for how to shape an ethical space for God? Perhaps Moses could have come down the mountain after twenty days, not forty!

The people might never have become so frightened. They might never have needed to build the Golden Calf.

Why does the Torah describe God as taking so much time and space to describe the Divine Indwelling Place? Perhaps the *Mishkan* was, *k'v'yachol* (if we dared to be able to say it), God's own golden calf. God's own triumphalist idol.

Perhaps the Torah does dare to say it, albeit in a hidden, coded way. Perhaps it is hinting that even the God Who has all earth and heaven for a dwelling place can swell with pride at imagining the place where one small people will come to worship with the Presence.

And the people? Dimly, from the foot of the mountain, they heard the overtones, a blur: "Plenty of gold? Uh-huh. And—something about horns? Uh-huh. Must be a golden bull-calf!" So they built it.

It is not likely that the Torah was trying to instruct God in a richer spiritual path. But by the metaphor of hinting at God's misdeed, it might be trying to instruct humanity. For us as well as for God, the truth is firm: What you sow, that you shall reap. Or to put it in another way: certainly earth is spirit, but there needs to be a physical context for the spiritual path. (A "path" is very earthy.) But do not get addicted to the physicality, do not turn the earthen altar into golden splendor, do not become a "spiritual materialist" who piles up the golden moments of spiritual experiences as if they were gold, to be held tight, possessed, sought for their own sake.

If you need to make a house for God, take care to put less energy into that than into making society a sacred home for human beings! For if you do, the addiction—no matter how spiritual it may have been at the beginning, no matter how inspired by God—will degenerate into an atavistic idol.

And yet—and yet!—is there no value in this burst of art, of beauty, of human creativity and commitment? Even as we take into account the danger of idolizing beauty that does not serve love and justice, even as we take into account this delicate balance of Calf, *Mishkan*, and community, we might still ask: what was so crucial about this burst of artistic creativity so close to the time of liberation?

Freedom and Beauty

Perhaps we can learn to understand this aspect of the ancient story better by realizing its affinities with a story of our era. Once upon a time, not so long ago, soon after the gay community in America came out of its narrow closet, the community began to make a quilt.

Each square was made by the friends and family of one person who had suffered and died of AIDS—most of them young, full of excitement and energy and hope until the disease laid hold of them.

Thousands upon thousands of squares, enough to cover huge areas of the Mall in Washington, D.C., where all the squares were brought and tied together. Grommeted together.

A few of the squares were in dark and mournful colors. Many more were bright, crimson and purple and indigo, crocheted and knitted and embroidered with flowers and symbols and words and names. Each one a tombstone in cloth. There on the grass of the Mall in Washington, a whole graveyard in cloth.

Each square had been made with grommets so that it could be connected to the ones around it. Those who remembered each person who had died, those who had celebrated and remembered and memorialized each life, began to tie one grommet to another.

When the quilt was completed, it was ready to be carried from city to city, from country to country. A holy memorial to life much more than death, to hope much more than fear, to courage much more than pain.

A sacred work of art, the first public art made by a community that had been hidden in the narrow place of secrecy.

In the words of Torah that describe the *Mishkan*, we meet an ancient Quilt—woven three thousand years ago by a band of runaway slaves, carried three thousand years ago by a band of runaway slaves. The passages of Torah describe that portable place in which God's very Presence loved to hover.

The Children of Israel had been locked tight in a Narrow Place, Constricted Space, *Mitzrayyim*—a narrow-minded closet. Its prisoners had broken free, had turned the Narrow Space into a narrow birth canal.

And from the Voice that had beckoned them to birth and freedom, they heard the Vision of a sacred space. Full of scarlet and purple and deep blue. Light enough to carry on their journey, place to place.

Grief and Beauty

Was each earring tossed into the simmering pot of molten gold a gift in memory of some slave who had died sick and starving?

Was each curving wooden pole and pulley carved in memory of some boy-child bashed and beaten by the Pharaoh's bullies?

Like those just freed from Egypt, the newly free community of gay men and lesbians celebrated their first taste of freedom with a first act of communal responsibility—making sure that their dead were not forgotten. Making sure that the world turned its attention to ending this plague and curing its victims. Turning what the world called their "transgressions" into freedom and community.

Building. Creating. Sewing. Weaving. Carrying. Connecting.

The *Mishkan*: a Quilt. The Quilt: a *Mishkan*.

A *Mishkan* not only in the sense of a portable shrine.

A *Mishkan* in the sense of a place where the *Shekhinah* dwells, a place where God's Presence can be felt in our very midst.

For God dwells most deeply where the newly free remember their pain with tears, create their future in joy, and carry their vision into every journey of their lives.

19

The Green Menorah

One of the key elements of the sacred space of the *Mishkan* was a menorah—literally, a "light-bearer" shaped in gold.

This bearer of light was clearly meant to resemble a tree. It was to have a central stalk, holding six branches (three on one side of the central stalk, three on the other). On each branch there were to be three cups shaped like almond-blossoms, each with a calyx (the bundle of tight green leaves that hold a blossom) and petals.

Indeed, there is a plant native to the Land of Israel/Palestine, called a *moriah*, that usually has a central stalk from which grow three branches on each side, reaching diagonally upward. So it resembles the menorah described by the Torah and may have been the model for the Tree of Light.

The menorah's light came from olive oil held in each almond-blossom cup, and this oil was kept alight by burning.

Centuries later, after the replacement of the movable *Mishkan* with a rooted Temple in Jerusalem and after this stationary Temple had been destroyed by the Babylonian Empire, the prophet Zechariah began to imagine and describe a rebuilt Temple with a recast menorah.

He went beyond the Torah's description of the menorah as a Tree of Light. Next to the gold light-bearer he imagined two olive trees, one to the right of the bowl and one to its left, that feed their oil through two golden tubes straight into the menorah. No human intervention is necessary to press the olives or distill this oil, to make it sacred or feed it to the cups of light.

101

This is astonishing: the menorah has two olive trees that are actually a part of it, interwoven with the part made by human beings. The light of the menorah is actually fed and sustained by a continuous natural source of oil. The menorah, then, is a combination of "nature" and of human beings, shaped by both of them into an interwoven whole.

What a powerful image, the menorah becoming the embodiment of the close relationship we see between human beings and the rest of nature, as symbolized by the Creation story in which *adam* (human beings) are made out of *adamah* (earth).

The shared linguistic root implies an entire unity, an interrelatedness of human beings with all the rest of Creation. That Creation is not "us" versus "it," but rather one continuous whole, within which we have a crucial creative and destructive potential, a relationship and a responsibility.

In our generation, this tiny forest of three trees—one made by human hands and two growing from the earth—might be called a cyborg, a cybernetic organism that is interwoven from the fruitfulness both of *adamah* and *adam*. Just as earth and earthling were deeply intermingled in the biblical Creation story, so the Divine Light must interweave them once again, and again and again, every time the light is lit in the Holy Space.

So we see the wistful Israelites of a generation's journey, making a sacred space of earth-connecting light to carry toward their own connecting with farm and meadow and orchard. We see their vision lit again by the prophet, wistful in a generation's exile, trying to imagine a sacred space where once again the earth and earthling could be intertwined, where once again from their connection light could burst forth.

Does their wistfulness call forth our own, that anywhere we live we can reconnect with Mother Earth so fully that from our awareness of that weaving can spring our light, our true enlightenment?

20

Sacred Time

The Seventh Day

The teaching from Sinai expanded like a seed growing from invisibility to magnificence—in moments, not years.

Sinai began as the *aleph* alone, a soundless letter signifying that the universe speaks to us all, in every language, taste, and smell, that we can see the thunder and hear the lightning because the result and sign of freedom is that we can tune our ears to hear the silence as no-speech and all-speech.

And then the invisible, soundless seed grew into *Anokhi*—the expansive "I" not of an egotistical God swallowing up the universe, but of implanted sacred identity within each being in the universe, each being saying "I" as well as hearing the universe say "I."

And then the seed, now visible, grew into words. "I, Breath, liberating you from slavery in Tight and Narrow Places. Do not carve out a piece of this infinite entirety and make this carved-out piece your God. My Name is a Breath, do not breathe a single breath so empty-hearted, empty-minded that you forget each breathing is My Name, your name."

And then a series of ethical commands that are obvious to anyone who seeks to live in community, as all human beings must live to live at all: honoring parents; refusing to murder, to steal, to lie, to violate the holiness of sexual covenant, to covet.

Anyone applying reason to the structure of a peoplehood will nod a Yes to all these prohibitions.

And one surprising demand: To set aside each seventh day a time of restfulness not only for oneself but for all friends and family, for domestic animals, for foreigners sojourning amid this new people. To do this as a symbol of the covenant with All There Is.

Two Ways of Teaching Shabbat

Surprising for two reasons: First of all, this doesn't seem to be an obvious communal need the way "Don't murder" does. And second, didn't the people learn this just a few weeks earlier? When the manna came to feed them in the Wilderness, along with this strange food came Shabbat. Why does it come from Sinai too—indeed, the longest of all the Ten Teachings from the mountain?

Manna came as a kind of Mother's milk for the newborn people, and Shabbat was in the very practice of the manna. On the sixth day came a double portion of the manna, and on the seventh none. No one had to be commanded not to gather it on Shabbat; it wasn't there to gather. It's true that Moses gave a hasty explanation, but the words were much less important than the practice. Psychologists today call this kind of teaching "operant conditioning." Mythmakers might see in it the breast milk from the Mother God—it flows when it flows; it stops when it stops.

The same mythmakers might say that in thunder and lightning at the smoke-shrouded mountain, God spoke like a Father whose body cannot make a direct connection with the child and who must use words instead. Rational therapy.

And "rationality" needs reasons. Once the universe has taught this unexpected teaching, we need to know why. Not so with the others. No one needs to know "why" it would be a bad idea to murder, rob, or lie about your neighbor. But suppose someone had asked you, putting one tired foot in front of the other in your trek through the Wilderness, to specify an ethical constitution. Would this rule about the seventh day have occurred to you? Would you have thought it up from the get-go, like honoring your parents and not murdering your fellows?

Two Reasons for Shabbat

So there needed to be a reason. And here we face astonishment. For there are two versions of what happened at Sinai. One is in the narrative told by the Torah herself, as set forth in the book of Exodus (20:8–11). The other is the story retold by a storyteller, set forth in the book of Deuteronomy (5:12–15)—stories told by Moses thirty-nine years later, as he was facing his own death and the people were facing their crossover beyond the Jordan, entering the Land that Moses told them God had promised them.

The people who actually stood at Sinai had almost all died out. It is true that Moses turned the history upside down, saying, "Not with our forebears did *YHWH* cut this covenant but with us, yes, us, those here today, all of us alive!" (Deut. 5:3). But his very insistence on the immortal inner truth of Sinai beyond the generations bespoke the outer truth that the new generation could only hear the teaching from his lips.

So he told them the story, this tragic old man who knew that he would die before the fullness of his vision could become reality—and that only what he told them would survive to guide them in his absence. Almost all of what he told them is identical to what we read in Exodus. That's what you'd expect. Surely the Great Storyteller as his death approached would want to tell the next generation precisely, exactly, what actually happened at this supernal moment when God spoke.

But what is not identical is the reason for this unexpected part of the Instruction, the passage about the seventh day, the day for pausing, Shabbat. Far from identical.

First of all, the Deuteronomy passage begins with a different word, *Shamor*! "Guard!" or "Keep!" or "Carry out!" even though the text of Exodus says, *Zachor*! "Remember!" or "Keep in mind!"

All right. They were about to enter the Land. They were going at last to be sowing seed, pruning grapevines, guiding lambs. Because the need to feed themselves would be so great, they might fail to pause, to rest, to contemplate. Moses wanted to be sure they would act upon the Teaching, not just be mindful of it. In his anxiety, he changed a word. No big deal.

Shabbat: The Rest of Creation

But that's not all. According to the Exodus version of the Word that came from Sinai, the reason for Shabbat is cosmic. It is intended to affirm through human action (or inaction) that in the very creation of the universe, God paused, rested, on the seventh beat of time. Carved into the deepest recesses of reality is the need for a rhythm of Doing and Being. Death itself, we may surmise, is a given of the universe we live in: all beings cease from action. Even when human beings have no explicit information about it, rest is real. Sinai simply encoded it, and the act of pausing became a way of affirming connection—covenant-ing—with the God Who has implanted this reality in all.

Indeed, so crucial was Shabbat as a cosmic reality that God's description to Moses of how to build the *Mishkan* was completed with a repetition of the command to keep Shabbat, on pain of death.

Why? Perhaps Moses or the people might have thought that once they began such a sacred act as building a shelter for God's Presence, a miniature version of the universe in which God dwells, the building process would take precedence over Shabbat. But the text seems to be strongly suggesting just the opposite: the ultimate sacred act required restfulness, rather than preventing it.

Just as God made Shabbat after constructing the world—and per-haps could complete and fully hallow the building only by an act of "not building"—so the people Israel, constructing the microworld of the *Mishkan,* had to hallow the process of building by pausing for Shabbat. Just as not pausing for Shabbat might have brought death and disaster to the whole Creation, so refusing to pause for Shabbat would bring death upon whoever failed to stop.

In transmitting to the people God's command to build the *Mishkan,* Moses not only admonished them to observe the Shabbat but added a specific prohibition respecting work: "You shall kindle no fire throughout your settlements on the day of Shabbat" (Exod. 35:2–3). Kindling fire is often thought to have been the primal act of doing that distinguished humankind from other animals. It symbolizes and leads to every form of human technology. Prohibiting it is a pow-erful challenge to the assumption that we are *Homo laborans, Homo technicus, Homo economicus.* We are more.

The sense that this prohibition encompassed many other techno-logical acts became the basis for an expansion of the decree. During the Wilderness trek, the Israelites discovered someone gathering fire-wood on Shabbat. Though he had kindled no flame, he was brought for judgment before Moses, Aaron, and the community as a whole. God ordered Moses to put him to death, and it was done.

So all this in the book of Exodus reinforced the proclamation on Sinai that the practice of Shabbat by human beings was to be a way of affirming the cosmic truth that Shabbat is at the heart of reality. But that was not the way Moses explained Shabbat when he retold the story of Sinai.

Shabbat: The Rest of Freedom

According to Moses, speaking in the book of Deuteronomy near the end of his life, the Voice at Sinai had said that Shabbat was a way of making sure that even servants of the people Israel, as well as Israelites themselves and all their animals, could rest, could not be reduced to utter toilsome slavery. For this people had been utterly enslaved, and having won its freedom must make sure it did not enslave others or fall into slavery itself. Not the Creation, not the cosmos, but the Liberation, the political and economic society, was the reason for Shabbat.

Puzzling over this seeming contradiction, we might begin by saying that the people who physically stood at Sinai, the people who just a few months earlier had been freed from slavery to Pharaoh, did not need reminders about it—but thirty-nine years later, their sons and daughters did.

We might turn to modern scholars who insist that the text of the book of Deuteronomy, its style and language, reflect a Hebrew centuries later—a Hebrew of the monarchy in the Land of Israel, where social conflict was high and the call for social justice intense, where prophets were using the kind of language, in style and content, that Deuteronomy uses.

The Bible itself (2 Kings 22; 2 Chronicles 34) tells the story of a scroll that was found in a little-used corner of the Temple, about twenty-seven hundred years ago, when King Josiah had ordered the building to be repaired and renovated. Its content electrified the king and the people, who realized that it called for a new society with protections for the poor and limits on the powers of a king. But the scroll did not seem to them a new demand but an old one—invoking the ancient authority of Moses.

King Josiah sent for the prophetess Huldah (2 Kings 22:14–20) to interpret and explain it. Did this scroll bear the text of Deuteronomy? Some modern scholars suggest that Huldah may actually have written much or all of the scroll that became public. Though written in the Hebrew of the time, did it claim Moses's ancient authority because some contemporary prophet—perhaps Huldah herself—thought that would carry more weight with the king and the people? Or perhaps part of the text may be rooted in oral traditions of Moses's teaching, with later wisdom grafted onto those passages.

From that perspective, Deuteronomy was perhaps the first reworking of the Exodus story in the light of the needs of a later era—the first effort to do what early Christianity did with stories of Passover week as a time of resistance to Caesar; what the Puritan Revolution in England did with Exodus as a model for resistance to King Charles; what Black Americans did by calling Harriet Tubman "Moses" when she led slaves to freedom and by singing "Go Tell It on the Mountain" as an Exodus song of their own liberation.

Regardless of who we think wrote the book of Deuteronomy and when, it clearly redefined Shabbat. In the course of calling for justice throughout society, it singled out Shabbat as a special sign and symbol of that justice, insisting that Israel's covenant with God is a covenantal affirmation of human freedom, justice, and equality.

We can practically hear the voice of some prophet of King Josiah's day: "You think we are supposed to 'remember' that Shabbat is a cosmic truth? Yeah, yeah, if that's the way philosophers want to understand the world, that's fine. But the point is to *do* something real: every human being, every animal, deserves a day off, a day when everyone is free, a day when everyone is equal because nobody is the boss, a day of love and sharing. Don't just remember it—*do* it!"

Whoever edited several different narratives into what we know as the Five Books of Moses, the Torah, knew full well that any reader would be shocked that stories of the Sinai event, so central to the identity of the people, could contain such a contradiction about Shabbat, so central to the practice of the people. Would not this kind of contradiction undermine belief in any version of the Sinai story? Whoever did the editing could have edited out the seeming contradiction. Why not?

Is there any value in teaching both that Shabbat is cosmic reality and that Shabbat is a political commitment?

In the sixteenth century CE, more than a millennium after Deuteronomy appeared, Jewish mystics in the little town of Safed in the northern reaches of the Land of Israel wrote a song to welcome Shabbat each Friday night. It spread throughout the Jewish world, and is sung today in synagogues everywhere. One of its verses reads:

"Shamor" v'"Zachor" b'dibbur echad;
Hishmianu El ha'meuchad.

"Keep" and "Remember" within one word:
God Who is One made our Teaching heard.

The *shamor* and *zachor* to which it is referring are of course the two words at the beginnings of the two versions of Shabbat at Sinai. By mentioning the initial words, the kabbalists were referring to both versions of the reasons for Shabbat.

But these Kabbalists were not just affirming two different aspects of Shabbat. *B'dibbur echad*, "within *one* word," they said. For us to hear the Oneness of God, we must grow into a place where the cosmic and the political are deeply the same truth.

Try it on for size: All life, all being, lives through a rhythm of Doing and Being. For the universe to exist, it must have at its core not only constant action to keep it going, but constant pause to let it be. Rabbinic midrash (*Bereshit Rabbah* 3:7, 9:2; *Kohelet Rabbah* 3:11) says God created other worlds before this one, but they crashed into chaos again and again. We can extend this teaching: Those were worlds without Shabbat. God tried to pile on more and more creation, more and more action, more and more doing. The structures of those universes grew taller and taller, heavier and heavier, until they could not bear their own weight—and collapsed.

Only a universe in which restfulness, reflectiveness, inwardness were woven into every being, large or small, could live from moment to moment and eon to eon. Each mountain must crumble for a new continent to emerge. Each life-form must die for life as a whole to be renewed.

One of those kabbalists in the sixteenth-century town of Safed was a young man named Isaac Luria, nicknamed by his followers "the Lion." Even before the universe itself, according to Luria, this truth prevailed. What began as *Eyn Sof*, Infinite—the unbounded original undifferentiated universal thing-less Holiness—needed to contract inward for there to be enough ontological space for a thingy universe to emerge alongside a version of God that needed to be boundaried so that a universe could happen. And *Eyn Sof* "preferred" this self-limitation to the Onliness and Loneliness of utter Holiness. Better an imperfect partner to love than Perfection Itself.

All right. We grok this much. Now stretch our minds and hearts a little more: This very truth about the cosmos embodies the truth about the freedom of humanity. Only a society that knows to pause, to play, to meditate and dance and sing and make love, to reflect on its life and thus experience its collective consciousness, is in accord with the cosmic truth.

And it is not just that the cosmic leads to the political. The political leads to the cosmic. Only a society that knows to pause can intuit and celebrate the cosmic truth of a universe of pause and rhythm. It may even be true that if the human race were to abandon this truth in our behavior, we would bring disaster and destruction upon our planet, our own local aspect of the cosmos.

Of course the seventh day is not the only avenue for pausing. In some cultures, time is set aside for prayer and meditation as the path of pause. Judaism itself treasures the many moments throughout a day when people pause in a moment of awe to bless the One who has brought forth bread from the earth, made the blossoms bud, shaken the world with thunder, elevated seers to wisdom and rulers to seeming majesty.

The Sacredness of Seven

Why then did the Israelites choose to experience the cosmic truth of rest, of being, through the rhythm of the seventh day? If a specific day at all, why not the tenth, or fiftieth?

Perhaps there is a connection between the way they experienced sacred space at the most personal level and their sense of sacred time.

One of the characteristic forms of ancient Israel's sacred approach to God was the "wave offering," in which an earthy object—it might be a cluster of branches of some native trees or the thighbone of a sheep—was shaken in the six directions of the universe: left and right, front and back, up and down. In each case, the shaking reached out in that direction—and then the sacred object was brought inward to touch the heart.

Inward: as Rabbi Shefa Gold has taught us, the seventh direction.

Perhaps the sense of sacred space was transmuted into sacred time: six dimensions of active time, reaching out to do and make the world; and then an inward dimension, the seventh dimension, Shabbat.

〜

21

Sacred Time

The Seventh Year

According to our saga of runaway slaves becoming a community of freedom, the Shabbat of the seventh day became a guide toward enriching the Freedom Journey with plans for an entire year of Shabbat.

Still living in the aura of the Ten Great Words from Sinai, the people learned that workers who had failed financially and so had had to sell themselves into indentured servitude must be freed in the seventh year of their service. Unlike the weekly Shabbat, this provision applied to individuals, so that some might be released in one year and others in another—not everyone at once, as with the seventh day.

Could the community imagine a yearlong Shabbat that applied to everyone at the same time—an astonishing vision of social transformation? Yes. Already looking forward to the role of farmers in the land beyond the Jordan, Exodus (23:11) commanded that every seventh year from the moment when Israel crossed into the Land, the land must be free of cultivation and both the poor and the wildlife of the land would have free access to its freely growing produce.

Just as Deuteronomy describes Shabbat as a time of social liberation, it adds an element of social justice—the annulment of debt—to the practice of the seventh year (Deut. 15:1–6), and it names the year *shemittah*— "freedom," "release," "nonattachment," "relinquishment," "letting go," "letting be." So both the Wilderness voice looking toward agricultural abundance in the land across the Jordan and the voice of social justice in the Land call for a pause.

More surprisingly, so does Leviticus—a handbook for priests that focuses on how to keep the land and the people holy. In Leviticus (25:1–6), this seventh year is called a time of *shabbat shabbaton*—utter restfulness, deep pause. *B'Har Sinai*, the passage starts (Lev. 25:1), "On Mount Sinai," as if to point out that Sinai's teachings were not exhausted in the book of Exodus. As if to say, "What we priests are about to learn and teach is just as important as the Ten Great Words and the pattern of the *Mishkan* that the prophet Moses taught."

The priestly handbook connected Shabbat of the seventh day with the longer rhythms of natural time. It was here that the seventh month and the seventh year, as well as the seventh day, were made not only *shemittah* but Shabbat.

The people had already learned to count the time from setting to setting of the sun and to mark as sacred the seventh in the rhythm. Now they learned to count the time between the glimmering and vanishing of the moon—each "moonth"—as also holy and to mark the seventh in that rhythm as especially sacred.

How did they learn to know and practice this? They learned that the month of Spring (*Aviv*) in which their liberation started was for them the first of months, and they learned that counting from then, the seventh month was to be marked out with special holy days. The first, tenth, fifteenth, and twenty-second days—new moon, waxing moon, full moon, waning moon (corresponding to the festivals we now know as Rosh Hashanah, Yom Kippur, Sukkot, and *Shemini Atzeret*)—were each to be observed as *shabbaton*, and of these, Yom Kippur was described even more intensely as *shabbat shabbaton*.

The Earth Must Get to Rest

And then this whirling spiral took off into another level. Beyond even the seventh year, there hovered the plan for a sacred seventh cycle: after a "week" of Sabbatical years—that is, seven times seven years, plus one—in the fiftieth year, there would be a year that in most translations is called the "Jubilee." Since this word is more a Westernization of the Hebrew *yovel* than it is a translation, one translator—Everett Fox—searched out what he believed was the original meaning of *yovel*: the note shepherds blew on the ram's horn to signal the flock of sheep to head home in the evening. Thus, he said, the year of "Home-bringing."[1]

In this year of "Home-bringing" the land was to rest yet again, and each piece of it was to be returned to its original lease-holding family, which at least in theory had been allotted its fair share of land when the people Israel entered the Land of Israel. "Lease-holding" because no human being, no family, no nation, owned the land. For, said God, "the land is Mine—and you are only temporary resident-sojourners with Me" (Lev. 25:23).

These Levitical provisions reinforced the sense that Shabbat is both embedded by the Creator in the cosmic rhythms of time and embedded by the Liberator in the rhythms of freedom and justice. The Creator connection is obvious: just as the earth in its daily rotation around the sun marks Shabbat at the seventh turning, so the moon marks "Shabbat" in its seventh renewing, and the earth again in its seventh annual revolution around the sun.

The Earth *Does* Rest

These sacred turnings affirm that the land itself has an independent sacred relationship with God. If we did not let the earth follow this pattern of seventh-year rest, Leviticus asserts, the earth would rest anyway—through famine, drought, and exile. The earth needed to rest, whether we joined it in joy or rejected it and suffered. Indeed, the very end of the Hebrew Scriptures, 2 Chronicles, claims that this was exactly what happened—that the people were forced to live in the Babylonian Exile as many years as they had prevented the land from making Shabbat.

This sounds like an ecologist's warning of today: poison the earth, and it will poison you and inflict upon you asthma and cancers; overwork it by pouring too much carbon dioxide into the air, and it will overheat and create global scorching.

The restful rhythm of the God-created cosmos is like the law of gravity. We can use it to dance with grace and joy—or ignore it and fall hundreds of feet to squash on the rocks of reality.

The Liberator connection with Shabbat, *shemittah*, and Jubilee became obvious when the runaway slaves on the Freedom Journey learned how to observe and carry out these holy times. One of these was the provision for restoration of equality in landholding, to be accomplished every fifty years by restoring to those who had become poor their family's equal share in the land—and conversely, by withdrawing from those who have become wealthy the surplus land that was not originally in their family's possession. The other is the provision for the freeing of all slaves in the Jubilee year.

Deuteronomy also strengthened this political-historical aspect of Shabbat by providing that in the seventh year, the year of freeing the land from cultivation, all debts must be annulled. Thus all were restored to their equal station—no matter whether improvidence, bad luck, laziness, or generosity had reduced them to borrowing from their neighbors. And Deuteronomy strengthened the provision for the seventh-year release of individual servants by providing that their liberation must include severance pay in the form of grain, oil, and animals of the flock.

In the sixth century BCE, the people of Israel faced subjugation to another pharaoh: imperial Babylonia. Jeremiah, scorned by the public during his lifetime, was after his death acclaimed as a prophet because he called for action to prevent subjugation to Babylonia in a new, nonmilitary way—by enacting the provisions for a Jubilee. It was as if Jeremiah remembered that the first liberating response to freedom from the Egyptian Pharaoh long before had been the practice of Shabbat and manna; so facing a new pharaoh from a different empire, he saw that somehow the ultimate Shabbat of Jubilee would save the people. Even though he failed to persuade them, or in a sense because he failed and afterwards they recognized his insight, his writings and speeches were canonized.

This is what Jeremiah did at the moment of deep crisis (Jer. 34:8–22):

As the Babylonian army besieged Jerusalem, Jeremiah invoked the Jubilee tradition of the *dror*, "release" or "liberation," of all slaves and called for all who held in thrall an Israelite slave to free them at once.

The Israelite masters, struck with fear and galvanized by the emergency, agreed and freed their slaves. For whatever reason, the Babylonians retreated.

The masters then in great relief revoked their *dror*—took back their slaves. So Jeremiah proclaimed a *dror*, a release, of war and famine. On behalf of God, he pronounced that war and famine would be allowed to "run free" in the land. If the people would not free their slaves, they would all become slaves. If they would not allow their land the Jubilee rest to which it was entitled, they would lose the Land.

And so it was: the Babylonian army returned, captured the city, burned the Temple, and carried off to captivity most of the leading elite of the kingdom. Not till the exile had "paid off" the years of failure to make Shabbat were the people able to return and share the land.

What moderns might call social justice was, in this biblical outlook, treated as one form of rest—as social repose or social renewal. Institutional structures of domination and control were themselves seen as a kind of work, not only because of the economic work they do, but also because of the "work" they are—simply by existing, simply by dominating and controlling. The structures themselves, not only the economic work they do, must be periodically dissolved for Shabbat. The social-political and the cosmic fused.

To rest meant to return to a state of nature, which was seen as loving, not "red in tooth and claw." (Tennyson himself, though he coined that phrase, insisted in the same quatrain that "Love [is] Creation's final law.") For the Bible, nature was where the earth grows peacefully as it wishes, without economic coercion, and the human community grows peacefully in natural clans and families, without institutional coercion. In this state of repose, the land and the community are directly in touch with each other: the land freely feeds the people without intervention by owners, masters, employers, or creditors, and the people freely "feed" the land without sowers, dressers, cultivators, or harvesters.

The Rhythm of Sustainability

Is it irresponsible for a society to insist that land is returned to the original landholders, even if they had lost it through laziness and lack of care? What kind of society would insist that moneylenders continue to lend to those in need, even if they knew that the borrower would be unable to pay the money back by the seventh year?

If God owns the earth, then it is not irresponsible to insist that someone who has purchased land from someone who has fallen into difficulty and must sell it, must return that land to the original owner—so that once a generation, there is equal ownership of land again.

Whether some people had lost land because they were unlucky in rainfall, or lazy in work, or "too generous" in helping others—they got their original holding back. This is a different moral outlook from that of many moderns, who would condition getting help on the morals and efforts of the down-and-out person. Here the criterion is the health and holiness of the whole society, which is best affirmed by a periodic return to equality and dissolution of hierarchy. The slate gets wiped clean.

The Jubilee is a "karma stopper"—whatever bad baggage you brought in, you get a fresh chance. Thus the society as a whole starts fresh as well. That is why the Jubilee year was to begin not on Rosh Hashanah when the year began, but ten days later on Yom Kippur—when after ten days of repentance and forgiveness, the slate was clean.

Annulling debts only seems "unjust" if one starts from a place in which property is really, and is intended to be, "private." That is, "Shimon," for example, really does own his money. But that is not the Torah's sense of justice. For the Torah, God owns Shimon's money. God has lent it to Shimon. So if Shimon hangs on to it when God wants to lend it to "Reuven," Shimon is stealing God's money.

This was not a system aimed at "economic development"—at least not the kind of explosive development the world has seen in the last hundred or two hundred years. It aimed at much slower growth, as pausing for one whole year out of every seven would suggest.

The main value was not the rapid expansion of wealth—it was the *balancing* of work and rest, wealth and sharing.

This system rested on Shabbat. It re-created the Shabbat of the beginning, the Shabbat that sealed and forever seals the Creation, because at that Shabbat all was and is free, loving, and in the state of plenitude, sharing, and repose. For human beings and the earth to act in this way is most fully to honor and imitate the Creator. And indeed for the Creator to act again in this way—as in the liberation from Egypt and from every slavery—is most fully to repeat the act of Creation.

22

Transforming Our Festivals and Our Lives

It is not enough for a people to become free just once, any more than it is enough for the grain to sprout or the lambs to be born just once. Over and over, year after year, rebirth, regrowth must come again.

So says Leviticus 23:5–6, "In the first month [literally, "renewing" of the moon for a true lunar "moonth," as the English word reminds us], on the fourteenth day of the month, at twilight, there shall be a *pesach* [lamb-offering] for *YHWH*. And on the fifteenth after this day of renewing is the circle-dance festival of *matzot* [unleavened bread] to *YHWH*. For seven days, *matzot* are you to eat!"

As we have already noticed, there are two distinct celebrations named here: the shepherd's *pesach* offering of roasted lamb, and the barley farmer's special primitive bread without yeast or flavoring. Here they are connected, happening on successive evenings at the full moon of the "first month."

God as Stumbling Lamb and Dancing Shepherd

The word *pesach* comes to mean "pass over." In Exodus 12:27, the Torah says that God made a *pesach*—passed over—the houses of the Israelites to spare them from the doom of the firstborns of the Tight and Narrow Place on the night of the Exodus. Many modern scholars think the word originally described the awkward walk of newborn lambs, who "skip over" as they learn to walk. And then it became the name of a shepherd's ritual dance that at the time of lambing imitated this skipping walk.

How amazing!—to think that the Torah is describing God's protection of the Israelites both as a lamb's early awkward skipping-over
steps, and as the shepherd's playful and profound imitation of the
lambs that the shepherd must protect! God's own Self, newborn at
this moment of Self-transformation, still awkward and uncertain,
dancing in the earthquake as the earth quakes in upheaval. And God's
own Self as Shepherd, imitating and honoring the newborn people
that is just learning how to walk on its own.

But notice that we have already assumed and absorbed the sense
that this double festival of *pesach* and *matzot* is also our single festival
of liberation from *Mitzrayyim*, from the Tight and Narrow Place.
Between the priestly earth-oriented double festival described in Leviticus and the single historical-political-spiritual festival described in the
book of Exodus, what is the connection?

There seem to be three steps in this dance of shaping the full moon
festival of the "first moonth."

The first step was that shepherds and farmers each separately created their celebration of crucial springtime events.

For farmers, this celebration focused not just on the current
springtime, but on the "springtime of agrarian springtimes," the earliest remembered experiments with turning grain into bread. For
instead of using the starter yeast from the year before, the starter yeast
that they had learned to use in making leavened bread, farmers harked
back to their very earliest remembered version of agrarian life, eating
the simplest agrarian food that human hands could shape, using fire
to turn a barley paste into a flat and simple bread.

Meanwhile, shepherds were slaughtering some of the newborn lambs,
roasting them whole, perhaps dancing their skipping *pesach* walk around
the fire, eating their meat—again the simplest meat that human hands
could cook by using fire, harking back to the earliest days of shepherding.

The second step in this dance of celebration was to connect the
festivals of shepherds and barley farmers. Leviticus is saying that the
whole community of Israel must celebrate them both. Shepherds must
honor the farmers' festival, and farmers must honor the shepherds'
festival. Both are festivals for *YHWH*, the Breath of Life. Both must
honor the fullness of the moon in this moonth of beginnings.

And the third step in the dance was to subsume these two festivals
into the birthing of a people, from the narrow birth canal of the Tight

and Narrow Place. And not just the birth of a new ethnicity, but the birth of a new ethic—freedom.

Springing into Freedom

Freedom itself, at the level of society, means what biological birthing means: the emergence of new and unpredictable possibility. For just as the entrance into the world of a new generation of lambs, a new barley crop, a new spring means something unpredictable has come to life, so freedom means that new possibilities are opening in society and politics.

So the newborn people Israel chose to keep celebrating the drowning of despotic Pharaoh's army in the life-giving waters, the breaking waters of their own birthing—the birthing of their ability to choose freedom and rebirth themselves again and again from whatever Tight and Narrow Place might once have been a sheltering womb until they grew too large in body and soul to stay therein.

In the histories of Rabbinic Judaism and of Christianity after the era of biblical Israel, this spring festival has been transformed again. As Michael Walzer has shown in his book *Exodus and Revolution*, the biblical version that focuses on freedom has indeed shaped the thoughts and lives of many peoples.

What can we learn from this deep process in which the very celebration of birthing has been reborn again and again?

Today we might be asking:

Are the pangs of the earthquake of our planet and the human race, of *adamah* and *adam*, the labor pains of a new rebirth? Painful as they are, are they calling us to birth ourselves anew from our own Tight and Narrow Place into new shapes for all our peoplehoods?

How might our springtime celebrations begin to reflect such birthing? Celebrations, rituals, festivals, are sparkling crystals of a broader, deeper pattern in our lives. Like the birthing koan of the chicken and the egg, can a new direction in our celebration both give birth to and be born from a new direction in our culture as a whole?

Does the emergence of the "Freedom Seder," of the "Seder of the Children of Abraham, Hagar, and Sarah," and of many other versions of the Passover "telling"—*haggadot*—signal a new need to express both the emergence of new forms of Judaism and the need for new rituals of connection between different cultures and peoples in their linked yet distinctive efforts toward a "new birth of freedom" (as Lincoln called it)?

Should we be celebrating the connection between earth and earthling as did the earliest versions of the first full moon festival? Is the birth of Earth Day—and its relative weakness in our culture so far—pointing to a need so far not well fulfilled?

\\\///

23

In the Dangerous Doorways

Twice in the Torah—twice in Moses's retelling of the Freedom Journey—we are taught to place upon our doorways (for which the Hebrew is *mezuzot*) some words that "I [God] command you this day." These words are also to appear between our eyes, upon our hands, and upon our gates.

What are the words? After centuries of experiment and difference, the Jewish people settled on the two passages that are themselves the sources of the commandment: Deuteronomy 6:4–9 and 11:13–21.

Sh-sh-sh

These passages begin with the *Sh'ma*. At first hearing, the *Sh'ma* itself, the six bare words, may seem to be simply an assertion of the unity of *YHWH*. "*Sh'ma Yisrael, YHWH Elohenu, YHWH Echad*: Listen, God-wrestler—the Breath of Life is our Divine Creative Power; the Breath of Life is One" (Deut. 6:4). But if we pause to listen to the word that says "Listen," the word *sh'ma* is itself an imperative, a command, "to listen," "to hearken." Perhaps it is no accident that the word begins with "*Sh-sh-sh*," the sound of "shush," the inner quiet that must open the heart as well as the ears to listen. (And perhaps it is no accident that the words *Shabbat* and *shalom* begin with the same sound; both restfulness and peaceful harmony must begin with the same inner quiet.)

After the six words there comes a command to love *YHWH*, the Breath of Life; a command to write out these very words in the everyday places of our doors, our eyes, our hands, our gates; and a warning to act in accord with God's Teachings so that the earth's fertility is ensured. For, we are told, if we prostitute ourselves to "other gods" or "afterthought gods," the heavens will close and the rain will halt and the earth will not feed us.

To these two paragraphs, Rabbinic tradition has added a third—about wearing bud-like fringes, *tzitzit*, on the corners of our clothing (Num. 15:37–41). The *Sh'ma* itself and these three paragraphs are to be read three times a day. If the nineteen blessings of the standing prayer, the *Amidah*, are the vertebrae of the service, making up the spine, the *Sh'ma* and its three paragraphs are perhaps the head, resting on the spine.

Uniting In/Out, Up/Down

In the nineteenth century, many rationalist Jews cited ancient texts, including the Talmud, to show that *mezuzot*—the capsules carrying these passages that were to sit on every doorway—were merely magical amulets to lessen the magical danger that the superstitious may feel hovering at doorways and so were inconsistent with the nobility and spirituality of monotheism, the very Unity that the *Sh'ma* proclaims. So these "amulets" were abandoned by many of the people, only to return to the doorways of almost all Jews—even the marginally connected—by the end of the twentieth century.

But the questions of meaning remain: Is there any way to reunite these "magical amulets" with the sense of Unity and the hope of earth's fertility? Why were these words to be placed where the Torah commands?

The doorway, the gate, the eyes and hands, the corners of our clothing—all are marginal. Spaces in between. So are the special times the Torah also mentions when these words are to be spoken—between sleep and wakefulness, between the generations ("Teach them to your children ..."). These are times and places when and where we might easily feel ourselves falling from one world into an utterly different one.

Inside my house: family, familiar; outside: scary. Or inside: boring; outside: adventurous. Beyond the gates of my city: a strange barbarian people; those folks don't speak my language. Dreams or reality: two utterly different worlds. Those beings beyond all human settlements—rivers, clouds, the ozone layer—that do not even speak at all: utterly different from humanity. The danger of these thresholds is not magical. What is dangerous is the temptation not only to distinguish but to separate, to denigrate—as if these others, the outsiders, were not also part of the One.

And so precisely at these boundaries we remember to remind ourselves: *Echad*, the Unity.

What if we carried this sense of the meaning of these texts back into the liturgical chanting of the *Sh'ma*? Is there a way to get "Israel"—the Jewish people—actually to hear, to hearken, to listen to this assertion of the Unity?

Imagine pausing after reciting the *Sh'ma* to ask a congregation: See yourselves caught in the doorway between home and unfamiliar turf—and then softly chant the *Sh'ma* again; between our own culture and a foreign one—pause, and then softly chant the *Sh'ma* again.

> See yourself
> between the horrified eye that sees the broken bodies
> of the terror victims, and the doer's hand that aims
> the bomb to blast an enemy neighborhood,
> and pause;
> between the sleeper's hopeful dream, and the wakeful
> sense of constricted possibility,
> and pause;
> between the wordless global-scorching hurricane and
> the wordy politician tuned to the purr of Big Oil's
> automobile commercials,
> and pause;
> and at each perilous threshold, pause to softly chant
> the *Sh'ma* again.

For the *Sh'ma* is saying: "Listen!" Listen, you Israelites, "our" God is not a tribal figure; "our" God is the very Breath of Life, the One Who brings being into being, the One Who transcends past and future, the One Who breathes into tree and ozone layer the breath that we breathe out, Who breathes the wisdom of the other cultures into us; "our" God is not our property, "our" God is One!

Can we dare to hear the *Sh'ma* as somewhere between a rebuke and a reminder?

24

Sacred Clothing, Holy Body, Naked Torah

Peep inside the holy ark in synagogues today: we see the tailored jackets, woven of dark and bright and many-colored cloth, embroidered with gold and silver threads, bearing glowing breastplates of gems and gold and silver—all to act as protection, celebration, for the Torah.

Holy ornaments. Yet the Torah scroll is holiest not clothed but naked—laid bare with only letters showing. The letters glowing amid the still more naked white space on the parchment, inviting readers to weave new meaning from the strands of blankness.

The Torah is taken out, carried from person to person around the room. We cradle the scroll like a baby, kiss the cover, lay it gently on a waiting table, undress it, and finally read its naked teaching. Just short of the erotic.

And find there a tale of cloth and fur and color, gold and silver. A tale of crimson, purple, blue. Of clothing. The ornamental clothing of the priest.

God told Moses how to make the High Priest's sacred clothing, and Oholiav the son of Ahisamach, couturier extraordinaire, wove scarlet and purple and violet, linen and silver and gold. The place of God's Presence could not be made holy unless the High Priest had donned special clothing (Exodus 39).

Is there a spiritual discipline in what we wear? Does clothing screen us from God's awesome, overwhelming presence—or does some clothing bring us closer, like the priest's? Did nakedness in Eden represent a closer spiritual contact with God? As Eden disappeared, was the first set of clothing that Eve and Adam made for themselves a screen against God out of fear? Was the second set, the clothing God made for them, a tender mesh of reconnection?

Why did the Shrine itself have at its center two *keruvim* (usually rendered "cherubim," but that is just a transliteration; they were sphinxes), "their faces, each toward the other" (Exod. 37:9), so that the Talmud (*Baba Batra* 99a; *Yoma* 54a) teaches that they were actually in sexual embrace? And why then did the High Priest wear beneath his finery a pair of linen underpants, lest by accident his naked body be uncovered?

How did the priests see and feel this presence of the *keruvim*, embracing, while they themselves were always clothed?

Once, in a Shabbat discussion of the High Priest's clothing, we heard a davener report, "Last summer I spent a week on a beach of naked people. Those days felt drenched with sexuality, but something else as well: community. Since we were utterly open—unable to conceal our bodies, our fears, our embarrassments, our attractions, our desires—I suppose we could have responded voraciously, as prey or predator.

"But in fact we responded not by devouring each other but by caring for each other, worrying for each other's sakes about our skin, our sunburn, our dignity. We became a community."

Hearing her, the gathering of prayer and Torah study glowed. She had shown that the message could be the medium, the clothing could be the naked body. As she had bared her skin there, here she bared her feelings: first her desires, then her fears, then her growing confidence, finally her trust.

And the gathering responded to her spiritual nakedness as the bathers had responded to physical nakedness: by forming a community.

For biblical Judaism, the body—offerings of food, hereditary priests enclothed in crimson, silver Shrines—was holy. For Rabbinic Judaism, the naked word was much more holy, with the body much more veiled.

Today, modernity has emptied both the bodies and the words of sacred Spirit.

Today, modernity has shriveled our words into commercials and the earth into an object of commerce, no more holy than the ones and zeroes strung together in computers.

But as we have already noticed in the dance of Miriam's heirs, some synthesis of word and body is beginning. Dance is reentering prayer. The conscious Breath, YyyyHhhhWwwwHhhh, is reentering prayer. Silent breathing, walking meditation, are transforming what it means to pray. The word "eco-kosher" has lifted up the possibility of renewing and creating new sacred relationships with earth—so that "eating" coal, oil, plastics, as well as food can be done in a sacred way, so that we can restrain ourselves not in fear but in joy at leaving some resources for the communities and ecosystems that nourish us.

Blessed is the One Who clothes the naked, Who frees the captive body, Who guides the footsteps of the brave, Who renews the body and transcends the word.

25

Two Kinds of Holy Light

Though the people journeys through the Wilderness in community, there are moments when the bands of community stretch thin—moments when some members of the assembly must step apart for a period of time. So the Torah creates categories for connection and distance, and we confront two difficult concepts: *tahor* and *tamei*.

In many English translations, those words have been translated as "pure" and "impure," or "clean" and "unclean," signifying that one is all good and one is all bad. Understood that way, the Torah has seemed to be condemning menstrual blood, semen, the birthing process as impure. For many years I, Phyllis, felt horrified, offended, every single time I came across the words.

But when the Torah applies these categories to a birth-giver, it teaches me—a birth-giver—a new way to understand the words.

What happens when a woman has given birth to a male or a female child? She is to be separated from the community as *tamei*, before she rejoins the community as *tahor*. But the length of time she is to be *tamei* depends upon whether it is a boy or a girl she has birthed (Lev. 12:1–6).

The Laser Beam of Inward-Looking Holiness

Out of my experience as a mother, I remember very clearly that indeed there is a period of time right after you've given birth that you want and need to be separated from the community. Your community narrows down to the baby right in your arms and at your breast, and there isn't, for some period of time, another world except for that child.

Then I began to think about other moments in our lives when that kind of close focused attention happens as well: when we're lucky enough to fall in love; when we're taken over by the *ruach hakodesh* (holy spirit); when we're utterly captivated by a creative process.

So I began to think that indeed there are two different kinds of holiness. There is the holiness of such complete concentration and narrow focus—like a laser beam of light—that we can't look out into the larger world, and there is the holiness where we are so at balance that we can see out into a much broader world, handle multiple worlds simultaneously.

Then I began to understand a little bit more about these words *tahor* and *tamei*. I began to think that *tahor* refers to those holy times in our lives when the focus is broad, when we can see the whole picture, and *tamei* is about that holy time when the focus is narrow and we can see only the immediate concern that's right at hand for us.

During the biblical era, people became *tamei*—narrowly focused—through contact with a dead body, through sexual coupling, during menstruation, through birthing, and with certain skin diseases—the subject of the rest of this Torah portion. In actual practice, becoming *tamei* meant that the person did not enter the Shrine or Temple area, the most communal and collective of all holy spaces, until going through a ritual of transmutation.

The Tug of Community

Then I was troubled: why is it that for a girl child we take sixty-six days and two more weeks, a total of eighty days, and for a boy child we take thirty-three days and one more week, a total of forty days, to separate ourselves from the community?

In my own mothering experience, eighty days with a new child, regardless of the gender of my newborn, was about what I needed—perhaps what most mothers need—to make that bonding happen without feeling the obligations, the responsibilities, of the world at large.

But I wonder what happened in the nervousness of the male community when a male child was born—whether perhaps women were forced back into the broader community more quickly with the male child than might have been their natural rhythm, so that the male child would not be long separated from the world of his fathers.

Commentators on this passage have conventionally assumed that the normal time of separation was the forty days after birth of a boy and have tried to explain the departure from normal after birth of a girl. But out of my new understanding of *tahor* and *tamei*, I saw that perhaps the real question was not why the isolation with a girl-child is so long, but why the isolation with a boy-child is so short. Not whether eighty days of separation is a punishment or even a recognition of some special uncanniness arising from the birth of a birth-giver, a female child—but rather, whether forty days of separation is an abridgement of the more natural time of separation.

Notice that to reframe the question in this way not only requires being able to see female experience as normative experience, but also requires drawing on the life experience of giving birth.

And let us notice that from this new perspective we can more broadly reassess how in our own day to celebrate the sacred times that are *tamei*, as well as those that are *tahor*.

26

Food, Our Innards, and God's Inwardness

As the story of the Wilderness journey continues, the story focuses on what is to happen in the Holy Shrine, to bring the people close to God. Food becomes the crucial connection.

We often hear the words "sacrificial cult" used to describe the process of making offerings to God in the Shrine. But this phrase is so vague, bloodless, and theoretical that it screens from us the truth: mutton, beef, barley, wheat, bread leavened and unleavened, various fruits, pancakes. (Yes, pancakes! "Take fine flour, mix it with oil and spices, turn it to smoke upon the Altar": a pancake! [Lev. 6:8].)

All food.

Just as the story of the moment of Exodus is fused with the ceremonies of the future that will remember it, so the story of the traveling Wilderness Shrine is fused with the future of shepherds and farms and orchard folk once they have settled in the Land of Israel. So it is with the foods of the Land of Israel that are to be brought to the Shrine. They are brought in the awareness that human beings alone did not create this food, nor sun alone nor seed alone nor soil alone nor rain alone—but all of them together, united by a Life Force that infuses all the universe with holiness and mystery.

Often we dismiss the "sacrificial cult" with contempt—today we use words, not foods, to worship—but this process took earth and body seriously. We have lost, as well as gained, by severing ourselves from earthiness.

Nearer, Our God, to You

The Hebrew word that the Bible most often uses for these offerings of food, *korbanot*, means "that which is brought near." A closely related Hebrew word means "innards," as in "guts" or "intestines." *Korbanot* are what bring the inwardness of God near to the innards of humans.

In English today, the word most often used as a translation for *korbanot* is "sacrifices." Literally, that word means "making sacred"; in practice, it has taken on the somewhat ascetic flavor of "giving away." "Offering" or "gift" gives more of the taste of intimacy that the Hebrew implies, but even these words sound more like "sending away" than like "bringing close."

To get really close to the Hebrew meaning, we would have to turn into nouns such English words as "nearing" or "innering" or perhaps "endearing": Israelites brought "innerings" to the Temple.

By using the word *korbanot*, the Bible puts every human speaker, every human reader, not only in the position of giving food away, but in the position of receiving it. But at the Shrine, who is receiving food? God. So every human who brings food to the Shrine thereby stands in the place of God—receiving food. The face of everyone who brings the food is a face of the God Who savors the food. And a great deal of the food is given to the poor, the landless who cannot grow food on their own.

God is not left to hunger in loneliness, not left to weep unfed. And therefore, neither are the people.

〰

27

Strange Fire, All-Consuming Commitment

The "nearing" of food to the nearness of God is filled with awe and danger. Two sons of the High Priest Aaron bring "strange fire" as an offering to God and are consumed in an instant, as if they themselves had become the burnt offering (Lev. 10:1–2).

Most traditional commentators focus on what Nadav ("Gift") and Abihu ("That One Is My Father") did "wrong" in offering "strange fire" that caused them to be consumed. But we might go in a completely different direction.

Think about "strange": whatever is unfamiliar or unknown, like a "stranger" or an idea before it's become popular. Innovators—in science, in spirituality, in music and art, in loving—are ahead of their time, inspired by and absorbed by what most others might consider "strange." Especially when we are creative, we can become totally consumed by the creative process.

Each of us desires to live fully, well used. Some people are fortunate to live each moment in that way. Though we pray that everyone has a "full" life, it may be that "full" has more to do with quality than with longevity. "Longevity has its place," said Martin Luther King Jr. "But I'm not concerned about that now. I just want to do God's will.... I'm happy, tonight.... Mine eyes have seen the glory of the coming of the Lord." And the next day, he was killed. Consumed by the fire, the passion, the glorious commitment he brought into the world.

Perhaps that's why Aaron was "silent" after the death of his sons (Lev. 10:3). Perhaps there were no words to speak that mixture of utterly bitter grief for the loss of his sons and utterly sweet joy for the richness of their lives—so blessed with meaning and with passion.

28

The Emerging Torah of Same-Sex Sexuality

Just as the portable Shrine, the *Mishkan*, moved forward in the Freedom Journey at the heart and center of the people on the move, the book of Leviticus, the delineation of priestly ritual and purity, stands at the center of the story of the journey. It is the third book, the middle book, of what we call the Five Books of Moses.

The same book of Leviticus that celebrates the earth through the "food nearings" that embrace God takes up the earthy questions of sexuality. It forbids (Lev. 18:6–18) various sexual relationships within a family—incest—and then we find what in our lives today are perhaps the most controversial verses of the Bible—condemning the act of a "male lying with a male as with a woman" as an abomination subject to the death penalty (Lev. 18:22, 20:13).

Why?

The sexual ethic of Levitical Judaism was rooted in a broader biblical sexual ethic that professed three basic rules for proper sexual ethics:

1. Have as many children as possible: "Be fruitful, multiply, fill up the earth, and subdue it" (Gen. 1:28).

2. Men were to be in charge: God said to Eve, "Your desire shall be for your husband, and he shall rule over you" (Gen. 3:16).

3. Sex was delightful and sacred (Song of Songs, throughout). Celibacy was almost unheard of and almost always strongly discouraged.

134

How did these rules affect attitudes toward homosexuality?

"Be fruitful and multiply, fill up the earth and subdue it" worked against homosexuality, since having children was presumably impossible.

What were the effects of "He shall rule over you"? If a man had to be in charge in a sexual relationship, there was no way to deal with a relationship of two men. Neither one could be subordinated—"as with a woman." Today, if we were to use a modern metaphor to express this ancient worldview, it might be to say that such a relationship would blow out all the circuits. Conversely, in the same metaphor, a relationship between two "subordinate" women would not even turn the power on—and so it was ignored in biblical tradition.

Is this statement of male supremacy as one of the consequences of Eden intended by Torah to persist forever? No more than the twin statement that human beings (or at least men) shall "toil in the sweat of their brow" (Gen. 3:17–19), wringing a livelihood from a hostile earth. Do we think Torah commands us to eschew the machines that make our labor easier?

Like this statement about unremitting toil and like "Be fruitful and multiply," the overlordship of men was not an edict to be obeyed but the description of a sad oncoming history that Torah wants us to transcend.

Some have argued that Torah prohibits male homosexuality for sure and perhaps lesbian sexuality as well. Others have argued that "You shall not lie with a man as with a woman" is ambiguous, leaving open to question what the text really means. (Is this physically possible? Was it only about casual or ritual homosexuality, not committed relationships? Was it only about anal sex?)

And some have argued that in any case, privacy is of such high value as to prevent governmental or even religious-institutional interference in specific sexual behavior by specific couples. They cite the Rabbinic teaching that what Balaam found to be *mah tovu*, "so good" in the tents of the House of Jacob (Num. 24:5) was precisely that they were pitched at angles to each other so that each household preserved its privacy—probably especially its sexual privacy.

But we think that we need to go beyond these historical or midrashic quibbles, to look more deeply into Torah.

Does Torah look forward to its own transformation? If so, under what circumstances?

For guidance to the process of transforming Torah, we might look to a wise and powerful teaching in the passage of Talmud (*Baba Kama* 79b–80a) that cautions against raising goats and sheep in the Land of Israel. Since our forebears Abraham and Sarah, Isaac and Rivkah, did precisely that, how could the Talmud have the chutzpah to oppose it?

The Rabbis knew the world had changed. They knew that the numbers of goats and sheep, and of the human population, would denude and ruin the Land if these animals were bred there.

The world had changed, and so did Jewish holy practice.

So then we must ask ourselves, as the Rabbis of the Talmud understood that in their new world they must oppose raising sheep and goats as their forebears did, what must we change in our new world?

In a world filled and subdued by the human race, multiplying our numbers may actually contravene God's intention. In a world where men are not required to be dominant nor women to be subordinate, a relationship of two men or two women need not be either destructive or irrelevant.

So we are evolving past these two rules that underlay the opposition to gay and lesbian relationships and marriages.

Torah for a New Era?

What then shall we do today, in a generation when the earth is full, over-full, of human beings? When the sheer number of humans is putting impossible burdens on our global ecosystem? When our biological multiplication is plunging into extinction thousands of the species that God commanded in the story of the Flood we must not allow to die?

Indeed, the biblical injunction to multiply at the biological and numerical level has not only been accomplished, but has become perversely self-defeating.

The third basic rule—that sex is delightful and sacred—still stands. The biblical Song of Songs embodies it, and the Song—far from being outdated—may point beyond the Eden of the past, beyond our history of adolescent sexual shame and hierarchy, toward an Eden of the future: "Eden for grown-ups," for a grown-up human race and for newly mature individual human beings.

Though the drama of the Song is on its face heterosexual, it describes the kind of sensual pleasure beyond the rules that has characterized some aspects of gay and lesbian desire, especially since marriage was forbidden.

So we now have the opportunity to open heterosexual relationships and marriages to the kind of joy the Song embodies, while opening gay and lesbian life to the more planned structure that marriage makes possible.

From a legal standpoint, some of the secular courts and legislatures of the United States, Canada, and several European countries have begun opening the way to enhancing, not destroying, marriage. (Some of them have even cited the spiritual value of marriage as a reason to take this legal step.) They have opened the gates; but only spiritual communities can fully enter.

Today we need to encourage, not forbid, forms of sexuality that avoid biological multiplication. We might now read the command as teaching us to be fruitful and expansive emotionally, intellectually, and spiritually rather than biologically.

Modernity has transformed the world we live in. The modernity that eases our work and makes women and men equal and brings the human race to fill up and subdue the earth may well be what God intended as a step forward in the maturation of humanity.

Like most maturations, it also brings problems—like the danger that our continuing to enforce immature rules as we wield adult tools will destroy the planet that nurtures us. It is up to us to discern what rules from our collective youth must be transformed as we grow up.

🝊

PART VI

Death, Rebellion, and War

Three dimensions of a sacred life—sacred space, sacred time, sacred personhood—made up the life-giving boundaries of Israelite community. But hovering on the edges of this lively body were death and its most deadly form: death by violence.

How could the community deal with rebellion within, attacks from outside, its own aggressive violence, the encroachments of individual disease and widespread epidemics, and the fear, awe, and repugnance that might often accompany the touch of death?

No community can live a fully sacred, fully life-filled life unless it learns to deal with the ever-present reality of death and the ever-present danger of deadly violence.

The forty years of journey in the Wilderness were a pregnant pause, preparing the people for another birth across the waters of the Jordan as they had been born across the waters of the Sea. But this pregnancy did not provide a magical surcease from knowing death, grokking death.

〜

29

Into the Earth

As the band of runaway Israelite slaves wandered in their search for freedom, again and again they grew rebellious. In the greatest of these rebellions, a Levite named Korach criticized Moses, claiming, "The whole community is holy—all of them! Why do you, Moses and Aaron, raise yourselves above them?" (Num. 16:3).

God was evidently not happy with this challenge to Moses; Korach was swallowed up by the earth.

Martin Buber in his book *Moses* does some interesting work with this. He starts: So what's wrong with Korach's position? Don't we—indeed we!—want the whole people to be holy and not have to depend on an elite?

But then Buber says: Korach thought the whole people was holy regardless of how it acted. A kind of racial, even racist, holiness. It could kill, or worship gold, or rape the earth—it could do anything, thought Korach, and still be holy.

Moses understood that the people had to become holy, always and over and over—had to act to make holiness out of ordinary life.

If we see Moses this way, his view of holiness seems more truthful than Korach's. Perhaps Korach (whose name means "frozen") had become frozen into resisting any leader as if every leader were Pharaoh. But that does not mean he was totally wrong. He spoke for what we—and Moses, and Buber—desire even if it is not yet true: that the whole people *become* holy, even though—and because—it was not then ready to be altogether and seamlessly holy. (Still isn't.)

Become. Grow. That is our goal.

141

What we want to grow toward is the day when Korach will be not frozen but fluid, growthful; the day when the whole people will indeed have learned to become holy.

And perhaps that casts new light on what it means for Korach to have been swallowed up by the earth. Since the Torah and Prophets almost always see a "punishment" as springing intrinsically from the misdeed, *middah k'neged middah*, "measure for measure," "reaping what you sow," what do we learn about his misdeed from its result?

Thawing What's Frozen into Growth

Imagine that when God had heard Korach out, God said, "Korach, you are right—but only in potential, only as a seed. You think the people's holiness already is full-grown, fully fruitful. It is not. It is a tiny seed, and it needs time to germinate and grow, time in the womb of Mother Earth. Korach, what you need to learn is what it means to become seed deep in the earth, waiting for the season of your sprouting.

"Korach, you are as your name: frozen. You do not yet understand growth, thawing, all the wisdom a seed learns through the winter as the earth thaws and the seed sprouts.

"Into the earth, Korach. Learn to be seed!"

So that is why the earth swallowed Korach.

And that is why, a little later in the story (Num. 17:23), God and Moses tried a new approach to teaching the people to grow along with their leaders, rather than against them. They had the different tribes each plant a barren stick into the earth. One stick sprouted and flowered: it was the Levites' stick, the stick of Korach's family. Korach's family did learn to thaw and grow.

And so did God, for God learned that the people could be more fully convinced by hope and promise, the flowering stick, than by plagues and fires and earthquakes, threats of death.

God grew into a teacher of growth.

How could humanity today grow into the beloved community, a sacred society, a multicultured holy peoplehood? One way to grow is to reconnect with the earth that we have been poisoning and oppressing. Rabbi Abraham Joshua Heschel spoke of learning to pray with his legs—by marching alongside Martin Luther King Jr. in a civil rights demonstration. We could learn to pray with our legs by walking consciously on the springy earth. By lying down for an hour of simply breathing, not on a "meditation mat" but on the naked earth, buzzing with grasshoppers and grass seeds.

By letting the earth "swallow up" our minds, attuning our politics not only to human justice but to the seasons and the interbreathing of the trees and animals.

If we do this fully, this is not just a private personal experience. We learn to share the earth instead of trying to gobble it up. We learn that no one of us, no nation among us, no corporation we have invented, owns the abundance in which we live. This is not apolitical but a new kind of politics, deeply rooted. Our earth connection could give birth to justice, to peace, to a fuller freedom than Korach—or even Moses—learned from the Exodus. It could give birth to a holy people.

30

Staring Death in the Face

In their Freedom Journey, again and again the people faced death: death from plague, death from war, death from the dearth of food and water.

How should they have looked upon this prospect? A series of teachings and stories taught them literally about "looking" upon death, letting it appear before their eyes.

First we are told that direct physical contact with the dead made a person become *tamei* ("taboo" or "uncanny" or "laser-beam focused" or "obsessed") in a way that separated that person from the communal experience of holiness. In order to restore the *tamei* person to the community, the ashes of a burnt red heifer that had been stored away were mixed with water and sprinkled on the *tamei* person (Numbers 19).

From Blood-Red to Grass-Green

Crucial to this process was the preparation of the heifer. A totally red heifer with not a single hair of any other color was slaughtered and then burned in red fire with red cedar wood, red spice, and red dye in a great cloud of red smoke *for/before the eyes* of the priest.

The burning cow became literally a spectacle of redness for the priest to stare at hard. *Look hard at all this red, then quickly shut your eyes: You will see a flash of green, a field of green. Green grass, green growth, green Tree of Life, green Garden.*

If you fix your gaze intensely upon the color of death—and then release your eyes by blinking—you will live.

Then the ashes of the burnt heifer were mixed with water, to sprinkle over anyone who had touched the dead body of any human being. This sprinkling took away the uncanniness of that touch, and it had to be done before the person could enter the Temple area.

But the priest who killed the heifer and the one who burned the heifer's body and even the one who gathered up the ashes were all made *tamei*/uncanny by the process. They had to be purified.

Paradox upon paradox. Death purified from death, but the process of purification itself made for impurity. Yet the "paradox" seems not so strange to physicians, clergy, therapists, or chaplains who take on the task of dealing with the deep uncanniness of a person who is mortally ill, or emotionally bereft, or morally distraught. The healer becomes wounded in the very process of healing and needs release.

After this teaching in the Bible sequence comes what seems at first a totally different story: When the people were desperately athirst, God told Moses to speak to a rock so that, *for/before the eyes* of the people, it would turn to water. If they stared hard at hardness, dryness, deadliness, unchangeableness, it would turn to flow, to giving life (Num. 20:1–13).

Moses did not do quite what he was told. Rather than speak to the rock as if it were a person, he struck it. The water flowed, the people looked, their lives were saved. But his success was also a failure. For he failed to realize that even the earth must be addressed, persuaded, not coerced. So he was sentenced to die without entering the Land of Promise when the people would, lest the spark of coerciveness within him become a raging fire of tyranny over the people and the earth itself.

Twice now the Freedom Journey has shown us how shamanic power can free from death, even when it endangers the shaman. Now Moses's own past has risen up before him in a dangerous rage. His first shamanic act had been to turn his staff into a snake. Now a plague of fiery snakes came burning into the bodies, hearts, and souls of the people.

Copper Viper, Super-Serpent

God told Moses to cure the people of these fiery serpents. How? By raising before them a special kind of serpent—a *n'chash n'choshet* for them to stare at. What does this Hebrew phrase mean? According to the dictionary, "a brass or copper serpent." But if we listen not only to the dictionary meaning of the words but also to their sound, we might hear "a copper copperhead," a "serpenty serpent," a "super-serpent" (Num. 21:6–9).

What cures us from serpents? The cure is a serpent that we call forth for ourselves, even more deeply "serpenty" in its essence than the deadly living snakes.

And what do we do with these super-serpents? Look hard into their faces. Stare hard at death, the face of fear, and you will be freed to life.

Stare hard at death—and blink. Shut your eyes tight. Stare, and stop staring. Then the colors of life will appear.

And for us, we who still shudder from our brush with death at Auschwitz, our brush with death in the H-bomb doomsday system, our brushes with death in the cancers of our friends and lovers, what does this mean? For us who choke on the dryness of our lives, us who fear the burning serpents that writhe their way into our very souls, what does this mean?

Stare these dangers in the face before we blink. Look—and do not be addicted to the looking. Without looking, there is no gift of life. But to be mesmerized by the looking is also to reject the gift of life.

The Freedom Journey requires these shamanic acts. We need physicians, therapists, chaplains, clergy who can both draw on empirical knowledge and rational judgment and go beyond them to invoke shamanic truth: to guide their fearful folk into staring straight at death and then freeing their gaze. What is even harder, we need politicians who can do this for societies as a whole. Where are the politicians who can free the Jewish people from nightmares of the Holocaust, free Palestinians from the nightmare of the Naqba, free America from the collective posttraumatic stress of moral and military failure in Vietnam, Iraq, Afghanistan?

Without the shamanic power of a Moses, these terrors recur and recur, poisoning the life of the community, as these terrors recurred and recurred in the ancient Wilderness.

31

Meeting Brings Disaster, and a Cure

As the Israelites were marching in the Wilderness, they met another people. There was risk in this meeting. There may have been danger; there may have been benefit. There might even have been delight. But among at least one of the peoples, the leadership was frightened and forbade all contact.

But there was contact anyway. Some of it was literal, physical contact: sexual relationships. But even traveling, buying, selling across old boundaries may have brought together maladies that had hardened one people but never been known by the other. As a result, as such diseases leaped the boundaries, Reality Itself, the very Winds of Change, may have brought on a plague of death.

In the ancient story, *YHWH*, the Breath of Life, the Hurricane of Change, blew on Its wings a plague, a pestilence. People began to die—thousands of them.

Is this just uncanny, a miracle of punishment? In a much more recent story, just five hundred years ago, we hear of a canny, scientifically explicable disaster that bears marks of similarity: When the age-old barriers of ocean were torn apart in the sixteenth century, two cultures came together that had never met. One result: measles decimated the Native Americans; syphilis, the Europeans.

Was this because their intimate connection was in itself a "sin"? Or was it because the rush of new connection outran the care necessary to make the connection holy?

And what if the plague is perhaps even worse than a bacteriological disease? What if it is a plague of arrogance and dominance—on one side, cannons; on the other, spears?

When the Sea splits or ghetto walls fall, best make sure that as the boundaries that had been sharp and high between you become newly fuzzy, you tie sacred *tzitzit*—conscious fuzzy fringes—to mark the contact points. Take care!

But what about those who do not take sufficient care?

Zealotry, Jealousy

The Torah's story of Pinchas is one of our sharpest tests. The Israelites made friends with the people of Moab, joining with them sexually and celebrating their gods. God—that is, Reality Itself—sent a plague upon them. The Breath of Life, the Wind of Change, became a zealous, deadly hurricane.

The peoples met each other unprepared. The Wind of Change blew across their unprepared and unprotected boundaries, blowing into them a plague, a pestilence (Num. 25:1–9). Lethal measles. Lethal syphilis.

Then Pinchas, a priest and one of Aaron's sons, saw an Israelite and a Midianite having sex. In rage he flung his lance at them, transfixed and killed them both. The plague of violence ended the plague of sickness. And the Torah continues:

> YHWH so worded it through Moses, saying:
> "Pinchas has turned back my hot wrath from upon the Children of Israel by expressing zealously My zeal [*b'kano et-kinati*] amidst them. And so I did not finish off the Children of Israel in My zealotry [*b'kinati*].
> "Therefore say: Here! I give him my covenant of *shalom* [peace]; it shall be for him and his seed after him a covenant of priesthood forever, because of / replacing [*tachat*] his zealotry for his God, through which he made atonement for the Children of Israel."
>
> NUMBERS 25:10–13

Most readers have taken this to mean that God was pleased with Pinchas. But try reading God's words this way:

In a blind rage, consumed with jealousy/zealotry, I began killing
My people with the plague. Then Pinchas imitated Me: in his own
blind and jealous rage, he turned his hand to killing.

His jealous/zealous act opened my eyes, shocked me into shame at
what I Myself was doing. That is why I stopped the plague; that is
why I made with Pinchas my covenant of *shalom*/peace.

In this reading, God did a turnaround, a *"tshuvah."* God grew.
The God Who began by bringing a plague upon the people ended by
making a covenant of peace. The God Who was horrified by Pinchas
also saw in Pinchas's face one facet of God's own Face.

The Dance of I–It, I–Thou

But if we mean by "God" not a white-bearded old man in the sky but
rather the Breath of Life; if we mean that God who is within us, among
us, beyond us—then what does it mean for that God to do *tshuvah?*

What do we mean when we say "God" brought on the plague and
halted it, ordered a genocide and made a covenant of peace?

We mean that the deep processes of the universe, the Very Breath
of Life Itself, *Ehyeh Asher Ehyeh*, the Name that means "I Will Be
Who I Will Be," the Name that is a spiral process of Becoming—those
processes themselves act in subterranean ways to bring on genocides
and plagues, and also to call forth human intervention to prevent, to
soften, and to heal them.

Sometimes we imagine this Deep Process as a double spiral or
helix of I–It and I–Thou—both of them, divine attributes that arise in
the very process of the arousal of the universe: one devotedly pursuing
more and more self-reflectiveness in order to become more efficient;
the other devotedly pursuing more and more self-reflectiveness in
order to become more loving.

One I–It, one I–Thou. Both, aspects of One God, perhaps more
satisfying and more accurate than the classic (kabbalistic) sense of
male and female aspects of God.

Alone, I–It consumes everything around us, everything we grow
from, ultimately ourselves. Alone, I-Thou dissolves us into an
unboundaried pool of smug complacency. When the one leaps forward or the other hunkers down, the universe must "do *tshuvah*,"
make a crucial turn on the spiral of sacred history, in order to mirror
the Infinite God more fully.

And what does it mean for us today? A surge of I–It power within both the Jewish and Palestinian peoples has given each of them a political strength and toughness that neither had one century ago. And that surge of volcanic energy has thrown them into conflict with each other as they erupt in each other's faces in the one land they both call home.

Affirming the Covenant of Peace

Out of this I–It collision, each people has already given birth to more than one Pinchas: zealous murderers, zealous home demolishers, zealous wielders of asphalt to bury farmland and divide communities. What we need is a new surge of I–Thou, a new covenant of peace.

For Jews, that means not only making sure that every Pinchas among us abides by God's covenant of peace. Not only repudiating all efforts to justify murder today in the name of Pinchas. Not only undertaking a public, clear, explicit, and vigorous effort to reeducate all Jews to see that God learned from Pinchas to repudiate such acts of zealotry.

It also means that we must shape our contacts with other peoples in as much mindfulness as the weaver shapes the fuzzy, intricate boundaries of *tzitzit*.

When Palestinians and Israelis, or Americans and Iraqis, or Jews and Muslims and Christians join with each other to mourn those who have died at each other's hands, that weaves a sacred fringe between us.

When our peoples join in a "Seder of the Children of Abraham, Hagar, and Sarah," remembering our ancient loving family, the conflicts that erupted between us, and the peace that Ishmael and Isaac created at their father's grave, that Seder weaves a sacred fringe between us.

When Israelis and Palestinians work together to rebuild the homes destroyed by order of the Israeli government, when they work together to substitute nonviolence for suicide bombers, that weaves a sacred fringe between us.

And on an even larger scene—our planet, filled with hurricanes of change—it is not only Israelis and Palestinians who must learn to make the careful fringes of covenant.

Who must?

Americans who sing "from sea to shining sea" as if those seas were impervious boundaries that give us safety. Americans who sing of the "alabaster cities undimmed by human tears"—but ignore the city that was drowned in not only water but indifference, drowning in its own tears. Americans who think we meet others only to convince them our ways are best—or if they say No, to civilize 'em with a bomb.

Muslims who dream of the uncorrupted Territory of the Faithful and are enraged by the fuzzy truths of other cultures, nations, dotted in their midst. Muslims who respond to outrageous attacks on their own self-determination with outrageous attacks on the peoples, the civilians, of those domineering governments.

Those Americans, and those Muslims, who see "America" and "Islam" as brutal enemies to be brutally attacked, who gobble oil and slobber blood as they seek a wider, longer, fuller war against the Other.

Here too we must mourn together, pray together, act together to bring each other and all the life-forms on our planet into a new covenant of peace.

When together we rebuild a house in New Orleans; when together we erect a windmill for the sake of decarbonated energy; when together we lobby to subtract subsidies from Big Oil and Big Auto and offer them instead to wind power, to solar energy, to the railroads— these will be the common ceremonies, the common tasks, we can weave onto the corners of our peoplehoods and species so as to create a covenant of peace, to become true priests of the Breath of Life.

〰

32

To Remember, to Blot Out

As the Israelites moved forward in their zigzag journey toward freedom in community, they were assaulted in a way that scarred their memories. Or—maybe they were scarred so badly that they could not bear to remember? Or—?

So they wrote a memorandum to themselves:

> Remember what Amalek did to you on the road as you came forth from *Mitzrayyim*, the Narrows: how he met you on the road and smashed the stragglers among you, all who were enfeebled in your rear, when you were faint and weary. For he did not revere the Divine Creative Power.
>
> When *YHWH* your God has given you safety from all your enemies that surround you, in the land that *YHWH* gives you for an inheritance to possess it, you shall blot out the memory of Amalek from under heaven. Do not forget!
>
> DEUTERONOMY 25:17–19

It is easy to see this paragraph as a bed of paradoxes: "Remember! Blot out the memory! Don't forget!" Is there any way to make sense of it? Is it only a bit of Jewish historical experience? Or can it teach us—all of us, any of us—how to deal with atrocious attacks and their perpetrators? Does it apply only to whole nations as perpetrators or as victims, or can individuals learn from it as well?

Remembering and Blurring Memory

In the generation after the Nazi Holocaust, this archetypal myth of disaster bit home with intense cruelty and fear. Suddenly, Jews for whom the Amalek mythos had become somewhat quiescent became attuned to it.

And then, once that nerve of stark terror had been plucked, it would not stop quivering. For some Holocaust survivors and their children, it was hard to distinguish Nazi perpetrators from the whole German people, even from the whole Polish people. Many refused to set foot in Germany or Poland or to buy their products.

As the memory of the Holocaust became intense ritual and literature, powerful museums and agonizing music, the memory turned, as the story of the Passover liberation teaches, into repeated experience. "In every generation, one rises up to destroy us," as the Passover Haggadah says.

In more recent generations, for some Jews it was the Arabs, and especially the Palestinians, who became Amalek. Some Palestinians are terrorists? Some Palestinians call publicly for the State of Israel to be shattered? And some Lebanese, organized in Hezbollah? Iranians, whose president pooh-poohs the Holocaust? For some, the archetypes of fear slide into place: For some, all Palestinians are Amalek. And for some, Hezbollah. And for some, Iran. And for some, all Arabs. All Muslims.

For members of other communities, some other version of "Amalek" resides in their own personal memories:

For some Palestinians, it may be Israel. For some Americans since 9/11, it may be "jihadis" or "radical Islamists." Or even all Muslims.

For some Iraqis, it may be America. For some Americans—especially some soldiers stretched beyond their limits by repetitive calls to duty in an endless war—it may be Iraqis, any and all of them.

For people who have been abused as children, it may be a terrifying vision of all priests. Or of all men. Or of the entire world.

Victim/Victimizer

And what happens when abused children grow into powerful grown-ups? For some, the need to prevent abuse and the tug to reenact it fuse into becoming preemptive abusers. The vengeful fantasies of the powerless become the oppressive actions of the powerful.

For one of the most dangerous stances in the world is thinking you are a powerless victim when you actually have great power. Even if you are also vulnerable, as well as powerful, forgetting your power and remembering only your weakness endangers yourself and everyone else.

We live in a generation when Jews have great power but are also vulnerable. Bombs in a pizzeria, rockets landing on Haifa remind Jews that we are vulnerable even when we have enough power to smash another nation.

That is the condition not only of newly powerful Jews, but of all the powerful. The America that could destroy the world and has indeed ruined Iraq was, and still is, vulnerable to a terrorist attack.

So each people must reimagine how to deal with its own Amalek, how to deal with those who would destroy us if they could and who have the power to wound us.

So let us go back to Torah. What does it mean to blot out the memory of Amalek? The key command has three parts: First, "Remember what Amalek did to you." Then, "When *YHWH* your God has given you safety ... in the land ... you shall blot out the memory of Amalek." Finally, "Do not forget."

So let us go forward to Torah. Dr. Barbara Breitman, a psychotherapist and spiritual director who teaches pastoral counseling at the Reconstructionist Rabbinical College, sees these three separate moments in the command about Amalek as parallel to the process of recovery from abuse.

She explained in a letter to me that when people move through a process of healing from childhood abuse:

- First, the victim needs to acknowledge there has been a history of victimization and abuse and move through a process of recovering and working through memories in the body and the mind.
- But then, when the survivor is no longer weak and powerless but safe in a good place, it is necessary to let go of an obsession with the abuser in order to shift identification from victim to survivor; for it is when people cling to a sense of self as victim and/or harbor unrealistic and obsessive fears and rage about the abuser that they place themselves in positions to be re-victimized or become abusers themselves.
- Finally, the survivor must learn to hold all this in exquisite balance. Remember that evil does exist in the world. Don't forget to

keep making conscious choices. Even when the perpetrator is weak or dead, even when the victim is now safe, someone who has been touched by evil must not become unconscious about the human capacity for evil. Only by remembering can we begin to blot out the lingering poison within us.

So: Do not forget! This is what you must do or Amalek will continue to have power over you through the generations!

And Rabbi Tirzah Firestone pointed out to me that Amalek was a descendant of Esau, that grandson of Abraham who was cheated out of the birthright and the blessing that would have let him follow in Abraham's footsteps. So Amalek is part of our own family—the residue of rage that sprang from the grief and anger Esau felt.

Amalek is always a possibility within us, as well as in others. The Torah teaches that we must blot out every urge to become Amalek—our own as well as others'—by remembering what the dangers are and by turning those urges toward both safety and compassion.

Jews have long demanded that Christians and Muslims face the ways in which their traditions have been used to justify the murder of Jews. Now Jews as well—Jews alongside Muslims and Christians—must look inward.

Bloody Strands in All Traditions

We must all face, understand, and transcend the bloody streaks in each of our own different religious traditions that lead to the dehumanization and murder of others. If we pretend they are not there, we are ignoring the wisdom of the first and third teachings of this interlinked commandment.

And having faced the truth about each other, all our peoples and all our individual selves must affirm that we are connected to each other like conjoined twins. If I assault my twin, I am wounding myself. In our generation, it is clear that the "connective tissue" we all share is the earth itself. So each of us has a positive need and goal not only to keep "myself" healthy, but also my twin.

Our peoples and every human being must face the always recurring "Amalek urge" within ourselves and act to prevent the urge from turning into action.

For nations, how do we translate such a new vision into public policy?

Shaking Loose the Paralyzing Memories

When we create security for our own community, we must also reach out to create the maximum degree of self-government and security for the other side that is consonant with our own basic security, not the minimum we can get away with.

And we must take a step not only in political policy, but in public psychospiritual cleansing. Rituals to remember the abuse must also go forward to celebrate the liberation. The bitter herb of Passover must not consume the meal; there must also be the joy of communal song and wine. The danger of "remembering" what Amalek did without taking the next step to "blot out" or blur that memory is, for Jews, the danger that the Holocaust might take over Jewish identity.

Just as biblical Judaism followed the mournful memory of the destruction of the Temple with a day of public dance and joyful marriage; just as Rabbinic Judaism followed the same mournful anniversary with seven weeks of prophetic consolation leading to renewal of the year and the soul—so must the Jews of our generation create the celebratory forms that go beyond the Holocaust, for otherwise we are doomed only to reexperience it.

And so for other peoples too: remembering their varied times of suffering, they must also remember celebration. Re-member, reconnect.

And for individual human beings? We must do our best to provide a safe place for each one of us, because each one of us has suffered some abuses—a safe place where first our suffering is remembered and then is allowed to blur at the edges as we realize we are safe. Safe to become witnesses of our suffering, rather than its victims. Safe to celebrate our bodies, our lives.

Do not forget!

॥ﾉﾉ

33

From Genocide to Purification

Moses—who himself had married a Midianite woman, lived forty years in a Midianite household, and learned wisdom from his Midianite father-in-law—heard the Breath of Life calling on him to exact retribution upon the Midianite community.

Retribution for what? For seducing—so the Torah says—the Israelites into idolatry.

When the Israelite army killed every Midianite male and returned triumphantly to Moses, he was angry that they had spared the women and children and the flocks and herds. He demanded that they kill every woman who was not a virgin, and every boy-child (Num. 31:14–18).

What we would call genocide.

Was this what *YHWH* had commanded? It's not clear. Perhaps Moses went beyond what God had had in mind. He might have had good reason to be overwrought: God had taken this very moment to tell him that after taking retribution on the Midianites, he would be "gathered to his kinfolk"—that is, he would die (Num. 31:2).

Think how ironic the warning, how fraught the emotion: "Kill your kinfolk, and then be gathered to them—die!"

Or perhaps: "I know that you will not be able to bear killing these kinfolk of yours. Do it anyway, and then, in guilt and horror—die."

Must we accept either God's demand for retribution on a whole people or Moses's escalation of the command into genocide as sacred teachings to inform our behavior today?

Most of us cannot, will not, must not accept the notion of genocide as a sacred act. Then why do we keep treating this passage as a sacred text?

The Sacred Family Argument

First of all, we can see our texts as records of family arguments among all sorts of people who are seeking God. It is the conversation, not every specific outlook, that is sacred.

We can choose to identify with and strengthen the strands of the conversation that speak of a compassionate God by living that way in our own world.

Following this model, none of us needs to celebrate a genocidal text or walk a genocidal path just because some people may quote Scripture as a warrant. We can engage in the conversation, even the argument, just as whoever wrote the story of the midwives nonviolently resisting Pharaoh and whoever wrote the story of Moses commanding genocide joined the argument.

Secondly, we can also affirm a God Who grows, Who becomes, and we can affirm a God-hearing community that grows and evolves as well.

Sword and Plowshare in Three Jewish Eras

The first two great eras of Jewish history looked quite differently on war; the third era, our own, is struggling toward its own approach.

The biblical model was the use of war to protect and advance what Israelites thought was the decent, holy society. They were convinced they stood alone as a culture; there were no allies to share their values. Today we might have compassion for their fear of being corrupted by the societies around them, without endorsing their way to protect themselves from corruption. This biblical model of war for self-affirmation was shattered by the Roman legions, when they decimated the Jewish population after the Great Rebellion of 135 CE.

The Rabbinic model (and early Christianity, until the deal with Emperor Constantine) was to avoid violence while preserving the decent, holy society through nonviolent resistance—often passive resistance. The model included Jews' giving up the effort to change the rest of the world and recognizing there would be many moments of suffering through pogroms and expulsions. Here too the assumption was that Jews stood alone; no allies shared their values.

This pattern worked for almost eighteen hundred years. But the Holocaust created a crisis even more profound than its own mass murders. A pogrom is one thing; the industrialized sadism that murdered one-third of the Jewish people, quite another. Though some nations, and some resistance movements, fought against Hitler, many Jews felt that "the others" had fought for their own interests alone and had left the Jews on their own once more.

After the war—but only then—the horror of the Holocaust was absorbed into shaping the values of non-Jewish peoples and codified into international laws against genocide and torture.

So out of this complex event came a complex of responses. One response was the State of Israel's insistence on the use of military force to defend itself, and on some occasions in more aggressive ways. Another—the movement to free Soviet Jewry—used such assertive tactics of nonviolent resistance as marches, sit-ins, and boycotts. Some Jews, like Rabbis for Human Rights in Israel, are even using nonviolence against some violent actions of the Israeli government. In all three responses, there have been allies from outside the Jewish community.

So as we wrestle with this ancient genocidal passage in the Torah's story of the Wilderness journey, we can ask: is it possible today to mobilize active, assertive nonviolence and—at long last with allies who share our values—work to change the world, to halt oppression rather than simply to suffer it?

Purifying the Distraught Veterans

Meanwhile, as the Torah's story of the genocide concludes, something unexpected happened: Moses commanded every soldier who had slain a person or touched a corpse to remain outside the camp for seven days and to undergo purgation from this death encounter (Num. 31:19–24).

On the third and on the seventh days, they had to plunge themselves, their clothing, and their tools into water, so as to clarify and purify their lives. Contact with death may have turned them inward, obsessed with death, so consumed with their own demons as to make them unable to turn toward others, unfit for taking part in a sacred community. To reenter communal space, they had to be reborn through immersion in the waters of rebirth.

What might this say about how we deal today with posttraumatic stress disorder and with other hangovers from violence?

For example, if breaking your heart is one way of opening it, then take the risk of reading Penny Coleman's book *Flashback*. She reports in vivid language her painful research into the truths of those who have returned with wounded souls from the wars of the last 150 years. And between each chapter there are a few pages from an interview with one or another woman whose Vietnam-veteran husband, beset with the nightmares that do not end in daytime, has killed himself.

As Coleman's book reported, the rates of PTSD from Iraq have already doubled the rates from Vietnam and are almost certain to climb. For posttraumatic stress often took five to eight years after service in Vietnam to manifest, whereas the rates are already higher for veterans of the Iraq War—after a maximum of four and a half years of service, and usually less.[1]

As part of the politicized effort to treat Iraq like a diversion, not a terrible disaster, these cases have until very recently been ignored or hidden by the government and the press. (So has the high rate of disastrous wounding—brain damage and the losses of arms, legs, eyes, and genitals.)

What to do with these soul-damaged soldiers? There is some evidence that for some, the usual sorts of psychotherapy may not work. For many, the therapy of recovering the past may stimulate more flashbacks.

Treatment of the body and mind may not be enough, if it is the soul that is damaged. But our social system is not set up to recognize the existence of souls, let alone treat their woundedness. That is almost as true about our religious communities as it is about the Veterans Administration.

The Bible, however, knows that there is something unholy about carrying on even a "holy war." It prescribes some steps to take to restore wounded souls. Perhaps the specific steps it requires were at an early level of "spiritual technology," just as its careful medical treatment of skin disease was ignorant of bacteria and viruses. Perhaps we need to do a great deal more.

But perhaps the Bible points the way. Its requirement of ritual immersion in a body of water—what today Jews call the *mikveh* and some Christians call baptism—points toward the need for a whole rebirthing of the wounded person.

Today immersion is seen by some religious communities as an important step in entry into a new and different religious reality—a new way of conceiving one's relationship with God. It deals not necessarily with the healing of damaged souls but with the transformation of the souls of seekers, those in spiritual search.

The utterly physical act of return to the womb, the origin of every mammal's life, and to the ocean, origin of all life, when infused with sacred intention and surrounded by the words and hopes of the community, may work this miracle of transformation.

Could we encourage our religious and spiritual communities to assist in the rebirthing of these soul-damaged soldiers?

34

Dying Leader, Dying Generation

As the Torah tells the story of the Freedom Journey, there comes a moment when the story itself becomes a story. Moses has learned that he was soon to die, that he would see the culmination of his life-work from afar, but would not himself enter the Land that God had promised to the people.

After almost forty years in the Wilderness, there were very few folks left who remembered crossing the Red Sea—so Moses decided to tell the people the story of the journey as he remembered it, complete with his own ideas of what it all meant. And he added his own ideas about how they should act when he would no longer be around for them to consult. (What's the point of telling fables, factual or fictional, unless you get to tell the listeners the "moral" at the end?)

So the Torah explains this is how we get the book that is known in the West as "Deuteronomy," or "Second Telling."

The death sentence upon Moses that was voiced by God's own Self, his life breath coming shorter and shorter as the distance from the Jordan grew shorter and shorter, may surely seem unfair. Moses thought so; he begged to cross the river. And several times he grouchily told the people that it was their fault he had to die so soon. But God reminded him: he had failed God when he was to bring forth water from a rock.

Smash or Speak?

Moses failed God because he smote the rock with his staff, instead of speaking to it. It did gush water; what was the problem, then?

Several thoughts: including, most poignantly, from a ten-year-old who didn't like being spanked: "God wanted Moses to speak to the rock, like a person. Even rocks can understand, especially rocks that are ready to give water. But Moses hit it—just as the overseers in Egypt beat the slaves. Moses forgot that he didn't like what the overseer did—or maybe he remembered that he himself hit the overseer so hard it killed him. Anyway, he hit. And God didn't want even that last little bit of Egyptian overseer in Moses to be in the leader when they crossed into the new land."

Another thought: Thirty-some years before, early in the journey, God had told Moses to hit another rock so that it would gush forth water. Moses did; the rock cracked open, and the water gushed. Now God had called for a new approach, but Moses was still stuck in the old pattern. He wasn't flexible enough to change. And God wanted a leader in the new land who was open to new possibilities, new actions.

Meanwhile, not only the leader but the people who had known *Mitzrayyim* were dying off. According to the Torah, this was also the result of disobeying God. Much earlier in the journey, Moses had thought the people might be ready to enter the Land. So God had arranged for Moses to send twelve tribal notables to scout out the territory. Ten of them had come back so frightened at the power of its inhabitants that the Israelites, hearing them whine and quaver, had refused God's command to move forward.

Some might say that the enthusiastic spirit had sunk so low in them that the very winds of change that had carried them so far were deadened—and so they died before taking the decisive step. In the Torah's version of the process, *YHWH*, the Breath/Wind/Hurricane of Life, exasperated, said that the whole generation of Israelites who had thus refused to take a chance would lose the chance: they would all die before anyone crossed the Jordan. Only their children would enter the Land of Promise. There would be but two exceptions: Joshua and Caleb, the two scouts who had rejected fear and urged the people to take heart (Num. 14:26–34).

Freeing Mind as well as Body

Yet there are other ways to understand the need for a whole new generation that had never known slavery under Pharaoh to shape a new society. Two interpretations, also by ten-year-olds:

The only kind of country that the older generation knew was Egypt, with a Pharaoh and slaves. If they had created the new country on the other side of the Jordan, they would have automatically set it up the same way, with a Pharaoh and slaves. God didn't want that!

And—

The older folks had been so badly treated as slaves in Egypt that they hated Egypt. If they had set up a new country, they would have set up everything to take revenge on Egypt. God didn't want that!

(All these ten-year-olds were themselves, of course, a new generation. They were old enough to think for themselves, not yet rigidified into the patterns of their parents, and not yet so shaken by the changes their own bodies would soon be going through that they would be afraid to take a chance on "weird" ideas. They didn't really know the "old" country and were free to come up with new approaches. No wonder they understood the younger generation in the Wilderness.)

The whole outlook on Deuteronomy that we have been describing assumes that it is indeed the "last will and testament of Moses." But modern scholars say its style and language are radically different from the earlier books of Torah and much more like the Hebrew of the kingly period.

They suggest that when Deuteronomy seems to be looking forward prophetically to imagine the problems that might arise across the Jordan as the people settle into farming, shepherding, keeping cattle, and tending orchards, it is really speaking from the very midst of the new situation, speaking especially from the very midst of the social conflicts and the ecological tensions that arose from centuries of dealing with wealth and poverty, kings tyrannical and kings compassionate.

As we have seen, perhaps these hints from style and substance of the text of Deuteronomy fit into the story told in 2 Kings about the hidden scroll of Torah that stirred King Josiah to reform Judean society.

The book as we have it has a double vision of life in the Land. On the one hand, Moses said to his successor Joshua, "Be strong and resolute! [Deut. 31:7, 31:23]. God will be with you and with the people as you enter this land that *YHWH* promised to your forebears, and the peoples who live there now will quail before your power, physical and moral. You will get to enjoy the extraordinary abundance of this extraordinary land."

Yet in practically the same breath he said, repeating the words of the One Who Breathes In-Out, "I know you all will soon take this abundance for granted. You will start thinking you invented it all yourselves, and you will forget Me, instead inventing gods that have no meaning. When you face away from Me, I will hide My face from you. Then your enemies and the land itself will turn upon you and make you suffer. You will moan and groan that I have abandoned you, but the truth will be that you have abandoned Me" (Deut. 31:16–21, 31:27–29).

What message can we hear in this mélange of "Be strong and resolute!" with "You will abandon truth, and then be stuck in suffering"?

We might hear it this way: "The future will be a mess. Many of the people will betray the Breath of Life and bring disaster on the whole community. Therefore, be strong and resolute! Seek always those remaining—they may be few at any given moment—who will preserve the teaching and will live by it."

Land of Soured Milk and Honey

To a generation that had seen the pharaohs fall, courage may have seemed so obvious, so endemic, that no one needed to wail and shriek demanding it. The outcry would become urgent when new pharaohs rose and claimed to be new gods. The call for courage would become urgent when an apathetic community obeyed these gods for the greedy sake of overflowing leeks and onions.

Telling the story, retelling the past, was not enough. If the people were not ready to feed themselves, govern themselves, defend themselves, it would all be for nothing. They were approaching the Jordan, whose name means "River of Judgment." They had to show good judgment, or harsh judgment would fall upon them. And it might have! They might have turned abundance into arrogance. They might have turned freedom into anarchy, or justice into tyranny. They might have turned defense into aggression. In any of these ways, they might have frozen the Breath of Life into an idol.

So Moses the Waterborn, Moses the Survivor, Moses the Shepherd, Moses the Liberator, Moses the Storyteller, Moses the Shaman, had to become Moses the Teacher—Moshe Rabbenu, as the tradition calls him ever afterward.

Across millennia into our own day, we ourselves have seen moments of hope and transformation turn to greed and apathy. So the poignant story of the lonely Moses standing on a mountaintop to glimpse the future that he could not live to shape has lasted, filled with hope and sorrow, to our own generations.

It was on April 3, 1968, that Martin Luther King Jr. stood in Memphis to call forth this ancient story of the lonely prophet. He knew that as he confronted ever more sharply the injustices of war and poverty, threats to kill him had been multiplying.

So he spoke about those injustices. He named the practical actions people must take to change the world, beginning with the garbage workers of Memphis. And then he ended:

> Well, I don't know what will happen now. We've got some difficult days ahead. But it doesn't matter with me now. Because I've been to the mountaintop. And I don't mind.
>
> Like anybody, I would like to live a long life. Longevity has its place. But I'm not concerned about that now. I just want to do God's will.
>
> And He's allowed me to go up to the mountain. And I've looked over. And I've seen the promised land. I may not get there with you. But I want you to know tonight, that we, as a people, will get to the promised land.
>
> And I'm happy, tonight. I'm not worried about anything. I'm not fearing any man. Mine eyes have seen the glory of the coming of the Lord.

The next day, he was murdered.

And we have not yet reached the promised land. Or we have betrayed it.

"Be strong and resolute!" the echo sounds.

PART VII

Across the River

Throughout the journey in the Wilderness, the people and their leaders kept in mind that they were hoping to cross the Jordan River into the Land to which their own family histories connected them: Canaan.

So there were questions to address: What other communities would they be facing? If they were hostile, could they depend on God to aid the band of runaway slaves? If war seemed necessary, how could they mobilize a dependable army? Might any of the neighboring peoples be won over to an Israelite worldview? What kinds of farming and shepherding should the Israelites be planning? Might their own government fall into a pharaonic pattern? How could they prevent such a disaster?

The Journey Is the Destination

The most sacred texts of Judaism, called in Hebrew the *Chumash* ("Five") and often in English the "Five Books of Moses," stop on the banks of the Jordan River, leaving entry into the Land for the books of the "early prophets," beginning with the book of Joshua—Moses's successor. That way of defining the most sacred texts has left a deep imprint on Jewish culture: the journey itself, we learn, is almost the entire destination. Perhaps this decision made it culturally and religiously easier for many generations of Jews to feel it was authentically Jewish for them to live in Diaspora, even while—or especially while—

167

like their forebears in the Wilderness they yearned and prayed to "cross the Jordan" yet again.

Centuries after this decision to define the heart of Torah as these five books, still other Jews reshaped how to read the story in a year-long stretch of time. They taught that immediately upon reading about Moses's death (Deut. 34:1–12), the readers should turn back to the very beginning, the Torah tales of the creation of the entire world (Gen. 1:1).

By keeping the most sacred version of the story in a scroll, a rollable parchment rather than a linear book, they made it physically possible to unroll the scroll into a circle in which the end was followed immediately by the beginning. And its end—a death—led at once to the ultimate birth, the ultimate beginning. By leaving the crossing of the Jordan River at a lower level of sacred text, Jewish culture taught that the journey itself was more important than the destination. By moving straight from Moses's death to the world's creation, Jewish culture taught that a death can lead to rebirth and renewal.

And yet, for this retelling of the story we have walked just a step or two into the Land of Promise. We begin this section with a tale of edges, of living on the edge both geographically and culturally. We end the section with an uncanny encounter with God's own military captain, who makes clear that the Breath of Life lives on the edges of each peoplehood, not committed to one community against another. And between these edgy fringes of the story, we gather in the plans for the central body of communal life. No community without the warp and woof, the woven fabric of a daily life; no sacred community without the edgy fringes.

35

Living on the Edge

The stories of the Freedom Journey do two things that we conventionally, today, might not think religiously "proper": they often use puns and wordplays to make a deep religious and spiritual point, and they sometimes treat sexuality not with prudish reserve but with relish, again to teach a spiritual point.

When Moses sent twelve scouts across the Jordan to tour (in Hebrew, *latur*) the Land, ten of them came back scared by the "giants," seemingly impregnable, they found there. From their panic came almost forty more years of wandering in the Wilderness (Numbers 13–14).

The bilingual Hebrew-English pun of *latur* and "tour" helps us to see *latur* as indeed a touristy kind of visit, in which the "tourists" merely glance here and there, never deeply gazing, never getting intimately connected with the Land they glance at. (To this very day, the Israeli Ministry of Tourism uses as its symbol the picture of two ancient Israelites, the scouts Moses sent into the Land, carrying between them a gigantic cluster of grapes, just as the Torah describes them [Num. 13:25].)

Latur is also used in the final verses of the same Torah portion about the *tzitzit* (fringes) we are to tie on the edges of our four-cornered clothing (Num. 15:37–41). There too the verb is used about the danger of just glancing around hither and thither at the world, not really deeply seeing—and thereby whoring (*zonim*) ourselves after trifles that we erect into false gods (Num. 15:39). Somehow, gazing at these fringes is to teach us to look deeply into the world, not casually like tourists.

Perhaps the Rabbis who chose how to divide up the weekly Torah portions chose to connect this passage about *tzitzit* with the one about the scouts precisely because they wanted to connect and highlight *latur* (Num. 15:39).

The Rabbis also assigned as the haftarah (prophetic passage) to be read with this Torah portion a report on the scouts whom Joshua sent into the Land thirty-eight years later, as the marching Israelites approached the city of Jericho—a high-walled Canaanite redoubt (Josh. 2:1–24).

These scouts found themselves in the house of a Jerichoan woman named Rachav, whose name means "broad." Think of Psalm 118:5:

> *Min hameytzar karati Yah;*
> *anani bamerchav Yah.*

> From the narrow place I called to God;
> God answered me with broad open spaces [*merchav*,
>   from the same root as *rachav*].

And note that *meytzar*, "narrow" echoes the word *Mitzrayyim*, that Tight and Narrow Place of slavery, that Egypt from which the Israelites were still escaping. It was a broad and opened woman who opens the Land to them.

And Rachav is specifically called a whore (*zonah* [Josh. 2:1]). She lived really on the edge—for she entertained guests at the very edge of the wall of Jericho.

But there was something different about this *zonah*, different from the *zonim* that the Torah portion warns us against, telling us to focus on the fringes of the edges of our garments.

Rachav the Broad, who out of all Jericho was by far the most broad-minded, the most wide-open to new possibility, welcomed the two Israelite scouts. She helped the scouts scope out the city. For this whore had fallen in love with *YHWH*, the Breath of all life, the God who had led the Godwrestlers out of slavery.

She knew the Godwrestlers would win because God had already turned history upside down to free these miserable slaves from the imperial Pharaoh. Now this band of runaway slaves was bringing their revolutionary vision into Canaan, facing a city famous for its walls. She expected the world to be turned upside down—or right-side up—again.

Seven Times around the Walls

Rachav the Broad asked the scouts she had befriended, "*Hishavu-na ... b' YHWH*—Make an oath, please, by *YHWH*, that just as I have shown loving-kindness to you, you will show loving-kindness to my family when you take the city" (Josh. 2:12).

But the words for "oath" and "seven" are the same. So *Hishavu-na*, "Make an oath, please!" could also be "Make a seven, please!"

"Make a 'seven' *b'YHWH*"—make the seven creative days for God, the seven days that culminate in Shabbat, the day of open possibility, the day when we do not make or do but simply be. This "seven" of restful self-reflection is what brings down the walls that make our lives narrow, the walls that block our way to a future full of open possibility.

No wonder that when the Godwrestlers did approach the walls of Jericho, they took the advice Rachav had given the scouting party. They made a "seven" for God. They danced seven dances around the walls of Jericho.

No wonder the walls fell.

Rachav the Broad, the whore, knew this wisdom because she lived on the edge like the *tzitzit*, the fringes on our clothing.

And not only geographically, on the edge of the edge—the edge of the city wall. She was a whore, a "broad." Broad-minded. Open to visitors, open to the people that itself lived always on the edge.

The Bible is not simplemindedly affirming sexual promiscuity for its own sake. But it is affirming that Rachav had learned from prostitution how to turn the openness of whoring into a far deeper kind of spiritual openness. She had learned to open herself when it came to ultimate issues—to open her life to the God of open possibility. She teaches us how to see the deepest truth embodied in the fringy *tzitzit*, instead of—as the Torah portion warns us—touring and whoring after the false gods of walls, giants, towers, arrogance.

Rachav stands with the Bible's group of "outsiders," "transgressive" women who have a healing impact on the future (e.g., Lot's daughter, Tamar, Ruth). Most of biblical tradition is dominated by men and is strongly committed to "insiders" and boundaries. These women were not only transgressive in their own time; their stories continue to be subversive across time, into our own time.

Can we lift up these women in new ways? What would it mean to have a Judaism, a Christianity, an Islam in which they were really models?

Gazing Deep

The scouts brought tragedy upon the people by looking merely at the surface of the land, like tourists. Can we look deeply at the land and at the earth, instead of seeing merely surfaces? Can we look deeply enough to heal the earth and air and water, instead of poisoning them to feed our giant appetites for wealth and power?

And can we look at ourselves and ask, are we still committed to that God of fringiness, the God who lives on edges, or have we built towers and walls around ourselves, do we preen ourselves on being giants in the land, impregnable—while God is getting ready to turn the world upside down on behalf of runaway slaves?

Puns and wordplays are themselves a kind of fringiness, breaking down the conventional walls and barriers we place between our words to make connections that are unexpected, funny. So from the wordplays of this story can we also learn to pause and laugh at the rigidity we often impose on ourselves in the very name of religion?

W

36

Wind, Rain, Sun, Soil, Seed Are One

As the journey moved closer to crossing the Jordan, Moses grew ever more insistent on teaching what the people would have to do once they began to farm the land, for they would no longer be able to depend on the manna, "Whatsit," of the Wilderness. So he explained the role that human beings play in bringing forth abundance—or destroying it.

What he taught was so powerful that in traditional prayer books, it is treated as the second paragraph that comes just after the *Sh'ma*—the affirmation/reminder of God's unity.

Moses taught:

If you hear, yes, fully hear [*shamoa tishm'u*] the commandments/connections [*mitzvot*] that today I command you / connect you to, to love *YHWH* / the Breath of Life your God and to serve Him with all your heart and every breath, then I will rain upon the earth in its right-time autumn rain that falls like an arrow and the soaking rains of winter, and you will gather in your grain, your wine, and your olive oil. I will give grass in your fields for your cattle. And you will eat and be satisfied.

Take care lest you twist your heart, turn aside, and become serfs to afterthought gods, bowing down to them. Then the Breath of Life will choke till the Face of *YHWH* will blaze, He will close up the heavens, there will be no more rain, and earth will not give forth its fullness. Swiftly you will be forced off the good earth that *YHWH* gives to you. [In Hebrew, the words translated "serf" and "force" are a wordplay, both sounding the same—*avad*—though spelled with different vowels. The closest we could come in English was to use "serf" and—the same sound backwards—"force." If you act like a serf to afterthought gods, your abundance will be reversed and you will be forced off the land where you acted serflike. If you abandon forethought, following mere afterthought gods, the God of truthful forethought, reversing reality, will reverse you.]

So place these words/deeds upon your heart and in your every breath, and bind them as a sign upon your hands, so they will be reminders between your eyes. Teach them to your children, to say them over and over, when you sit in your houses, when you walk on your roads, when you lie down, and when you rise up. Write them on the doorposts of your houses and on your city gates.

So that your days and the days of your children be expanded, upon the earth that *YHWH* sevenfold swore to your forebears to give them, as days like heaven upon the earth.

DEUTERONOMY 11:13–21

Some people have objected to this passage on the grounds that it seems to promise direct rewards for good behavior and punishment for bad behavior and thus is belied by our life experience. Indeed, it has been dropped from a number of contemporary prayer books or downgraded to an "alternative" status.

And even in synagogues where it survives, it is usually muttered in an undertone. The same congregations that say the first paragraph after the *Sh'ma* with vigor and attention, and that focus on the fringes mentioned in the third paragraph with strong intentionality, race through the second paragraph so that few worshippers actually experience its meaning.

Renewing the *Sh'ma*

Can we learn anew from this passage?

First of all, we make many problems for ourselves if we insist on translating *YHWH* as "*Adonai*/Lord"—which it surely does not mean—and thus treat *YHWH* as some power utterly separate from, above, and beyond us. To credit such an all-powerful King/Lord/Judge with punishing our every transgression and rewarding our every act of goodness certainly does not accord with what we know happens in our lives.

If we draw, instead, on the deep sense of *YHWH* as the In-Breath/Out-Breath that connects all life and being, the passage takes on a richer meaning. On the one hand, at the level of individuals it is certainly true that the life process in which we walk and breathe often does not let us reap from life what we sow. The universe may have some bias in that direction—that is, individuals who put out love and justice into the world are somewhat more likely to receive love and justice back than those who put out anger, hatred, or fear. But it is certainly not a one-to-one certainty, as the book of Job and the Holocaust remind us.

At the level of societies as a whole, there is much more truth to the second paragraph of the *Sh'ma* (and it is directed to whole communities; the pronouns are second person plural, unlike those in the first paragraph).

Most Jews are no longer "farmers" in the literal sense, and perhaps that is why the paragraph no longer made good sense to modern Jews. Yet all Jews and the whole human race still take part in the great flow of rain, sun, earth, seed that make up the rhythms of earth. And those rhythms are (a) crucial, (b) in crisis, and (c) responsive to human behavior.

So in our generation, this second paragraph is vital—literally, offers us the choice of life or death—and should be read with great devotion and attention. We might read the *Sh'ma* and its second paragraph as saying:

> Listen, you Godwrestlers! *YHWH*, Yahh, the Interbreathing of all life, is the Name of our God—and the Breath of Life is ONE.
>
> If you listen, *really* listen to the teachings of *YHWH*, the Breath of Life, especially the teaching that there is unity in the world and interconnection among all its parts, then the rains will fall as they should, the rivers will run, the heavens will smile, and the good earth and all its creatures will feed you and each other.
>
> *But* if you shatter the harmony of life, if you chop the world up into parts and choose one or a few to worship—like gods of wealth and power, greed, the addiction to do and make and produce without pausing to be and make Shabbat—then the Breath of Life will come as a hurricane to shatter your harmony.

For if you pour poison into earth and air and water, then it will be poison that you eat and drink and breathe. The rain won't fall, or it will turn to acid; the rivers won't run, or they will flood your cities because you have left no earth where the rain can soak in; and the heavens themselves will become your enemy: the ozone layer will stop shielding you, the carbon dioxide you pour into the air will scorch your planet. So you will perish from the good earth that the Breath of Life gives you.

So, therefore, set these words/deeds in your heart and in every breath, carry them in every act toward which you put your hands, and make them the pattern through which you see the world. Teach them to your children, to repeat them to their children; stay aware of them when you sit in your houses, when you travel on your roads, when you lie down to dream and when you rise up to act. Write them on the thresholds where you cross from world to world—the doorposts of your houses and your city gates.

So that your days and the days of your children grow more, grow deeper, grow higher, upon the earth that the Breath of Life swore to your forebears to give them—

So that as *shamayyim*, heaven, is where *eysh* and *mayyim*, fire and water, can live in harmony together, you can make the earth a harmonious haven, can live upon the earth days that are as filled with harmony as heaven.

May our human communities renew the deep forethought, the deep breath, that honors all the breathing life of earth.

☙

37

The Land Shall Not
Become *Mitzrayyim*

Perhaps Deuteronomy bespeaks Moses preparing the people for his death, for crossing the Jordan, and for making a living in the new society. Or perhaps it bespeaks Huldah channeling Moses to revitalize the call for justice in a time of social conflict. Either way, the story over and over again links concerns for the worker and the poor in the new Israelite society with the memory of slavery in Egypt: "You must bear in mind that a serf were you in the land of Egypt, and *YHWH* your God redeemed you; therefore I command you this word today!" (Deut. 15:15; see also 16:12, 24:18, and 24:22).

- The worker had to be paid by sundown of the day he worked.
- Even if a loan was not repaid on time, the lender could not invade the house of his neighbor to redeem his pledge, and if the borrower was poverty-stricken, the lender might not have been able to hold the pledge at all.
- No landholder could harvest for his own benefit all that his fields produced; he had to leave what the official gleaners missed and what grew in the corners of the field to be picked up by the poor and the landless.

Not only specific laws for protection of the poor but the basic constitution of the nation were explicitly guided by the memory of Pharaoh and of liberation. For about three centuries after escaping from slavery,

says the Bible, Israelites governed themselves in the most counter-
pharaonic way imaginable—without a central ruler, tribe by tribe or in
shifting tribal alliances.

Do We Need an Earthly King?

Then they had an intense debate. The people had wearied of defending themselves by slinging together guerrilla bands and emergency
resistance against foreign kings and their professional military. They
demanded to have a king "like all the other nations" (1 Sam. 8:5). The
prophet Samuel reminded them that they had a King in heaven. He
warned them first on theological grounds: An earthly king—a new
Pharaoh—would subvert their loyalty to God as King—might even,
like Pharaoh, demand homage to himself as God.

When they shrugged off this warning, he explained that an earthly
king would enslave the people. The men he would conscript to his
army, the women to his kitchen work. But the people insisted. God
finally told Samuel to give in (1 Sam. 8:4–22).

Constitutional Monarchy

The upshot of this intense debate over whether to have a king at all
was that the Israelites set up a constitutional monarchy. Its outlines
are sketched in Deuteronomy:

The king could not amass "horses"—that is, cavalry, the ancient
analogue in Pharaoh's army of tanks and helicopters to carry on
aggressive war. The king could not amass gold and silver, nor the
many wives that might bankrupt his people and turn away the king's
heart from public policy for the public good, and might well entangle
him in foreign alliances. He could not send the people back into
Mitzrayyim—the slavery and forced labor of narrow Egypt—in order
to pay for an imperial cavalry like that of Pharaoh.

And he had to sit day by day with the texts of these teachings—the
protections owed to the poor and the limits imposed on his own
power—and not only read the passages again and again, but write
them out with his own hand.

Notice that writing the text means a deep and muscular connection with it, far more than reading it, especially since he was writing
with a handmade quill and handmade ink on handmade parchment.

He had to do this in the presence of the Levites and priests, so that they could make sure he knew the Constitution and could make sure he was obeying it (Deut. 17:14–20).

Try imagining an American president today meeting even once a month with, say, the board of the American Civil Liberties Union, recopying the Bill of Rights with his own hand (let's give him a fountain pen), and listening to the ACLU challenge whether an executive order he has signed will violate its prohibitions. What else might flow from such a change?

38

Soldier, Go Home!

With kings come wars, and just as when the people settled in the Land there had to be rules to govern wealth and power and the treatment of the earth, so there had to be rules to govern war.

Not wars of God-commanded genocide, but more "ordinary" wars of defense and offense. Limited wars.

One limit that the Torah put on wars was that the fruit trees of the enemy were not to be destroyed. No scorched-earth strategy. For, as the writer of Deuteronomy demanded, "Is the tree of the field human, that you should make war against it?" (Deut. 20:19). (Or, as some read the sentence, "The tree of the field is human!" Do not destroy the future with the present.)

From this prohibition the Rabbis later concluded: If we must not cut down fruit trees even in time of war, then we must all the more protect them in peacetime—and not them alone: we must not waste what God has given us, but restrain our use of it to what we for certain need (*Baba Kama* 91b–92a; *Shabbat* 67b, 129a, 140b; *Kiddushin* 32a).

Conscience and the Conscript

Not only fruit trees, but even soldiers themselves were to be protected from the ravages of war. The Torah teaches:

Then the officials shall address the troops:

"Is there anyone who has built a new home but not yet dedicated it? Let him go back to his home, lest he die in battle and another dedicate it.

"Is there anyone who has planted a vineyard but has never harvested it? Let him go back to his home, lest he die in battle and another eat from it.

"Is there anyone who has paid the bride-price for a wife, but who has not yet married her? Let him return to his home, lest he die in battle and another marry her."

The officials shall go on addressing the troops and say, "Is there anyone afraid or *rack halevav* [gentle-hearted, disheartened, fainthearted, softhearted]? Let him go back to his home, lest he melt the heart of his brothers, like his heart!"

DEUTERONOMY 20:5–8

First Maccabees—a book not held by Jews to be part of the Hebrew Scriptures—was preserved as a history of the Maccabean rebellion against a Hellenistic emperor from Syria. It reports that even when the land was under imperial occupation by Antiochus, even when the Temple had been desecrated, even when those who refused to worship idols were being executed—the most extreme imaginable moment, when presumably no one would have been exempted from military service to fight against this conqueror—Judah Maccabee applied this passage of Torah. He ordered back to their homes the newly married, the new home builders, the new vine planters, and those who were frightened or gentle-hearted.

Fear of Dying, Fear of Killing

About three centuries later, Rabbi Akiba commented, "Why does the verse [after specifying 'afraid'] then say 'or disheartened'? To teach that even the mightiest and strongest of men, if he is compassionate [*rachaman*: womb-like, motherly], should turn back" (*Tosefta Sotah* 7:22). So both those who are afraid to be killed and those who are afraid lest they become killers must be exempted.

Perhaps this provision operated as a rough public check and balance, to measure whether the people really believed a specific war was worth dying for and worth killing for. If a king or a council of middle-aged men sent the young to kill and die in a worthless war, the young still had a way out. If a large number were reluctant to kill or to die, perhaps the war could not be fought.

The provisions limiting royal power and those limiting military power may have been intertwined in the Torah's mind with *Tzedek tzedek tirdof*, "Seek to achieve justice by just means" (Deut. 16:20).

Today, Would Armies Vanish?

What would happen to modern nation-states, military forces, and wars—including our own—if these passages of Torah were our model or even just our teaching?

Would we deny our national leaders the offensive weapons that are the "horse chariots" of today? Would our armies send home exactly the young who now make up the bulk of them—first-time home-owners, the newly married, those just entering a first career? Would fear of being killed, rather than being scorned as cowardice, become a reason for exemption? Would simply claiming "conscientious" objection be sufficient reason for exemption—rather than being surrounded by suspicion and demands for proof?

Today, even in armed forces filled by enlistment rather than conscription, enlisting is not exactly a "free choice" for those who have done poorly in school, for those who have no hope of finding a decent job, or for those who are "undocumented" even though they grew from childhood in the society that calls them "illegal immigrants." For them, the army may seem the only choice. If there were sacred teachers reviewing them as if the Bible mattered, would this priesthood say, "Go home"?

And beyond such individual choices—would present and projected wars meet the standard of public approval and soldierly compliance if the choices were fully free instead of coerced and if the fear to die for empty goals were affirmed instead of punished?

〰

39

Moses as Prophetic Model

L imiting war, limiting the power of the rich, and limiting the power of the king were connected with the emergence of what was then a uniquely Israelite institution: the anti-institutional prophets, speaking on behalf of God their passionate critiques of those in power.

The greatest of the prophets, in biblical tradition, was Moses—and he was the prototype, the first great challenger of arrogant and unaccountable power. All those prophets who challenged the powerful and wealthy of Israel and Judah drew upon the model of Moses's successful challenge to Pharaoh, followed by his partially successful effort to train an entire people to embody social justice and to keep striving for it.

When Amos and Hosea denounced betrayals of God, they were focusing not on mistakes or failures in celebrating the sacred rhythms of the Temple offerings but on the luxury and arrogance of the rich, coupled with their contempt for the poor. To most of the prophets, this outcry was precisely the way to channel God's politics into the body politic.

Several of the prophets saw a connection between internal Israelite corruption and the external danger from imperial Babylonia. This was not the Sumerian civilization of five hundred years or more before, but a fully developed empire. After years of threatening the two Jewish states, the Babylonian army under Nebuchadnezzar besieged and in 586 BCE conquered Jerusalem and destroyed the Temple.

Free Your Serfs or Suffer Serfdom

One of the best examples of this form of prophetic action was what Jeremiah did when he demanded that the people stave off the Babylonian

183

army by making a radical internal reform, a special Jubilee, a *dror*—releasing all their slaves (Jer. 34:8–22). We have already looked at these events as an aspect of the deep truth of the teaching that the earth and the poor must be allowed a rhythm of restfulness and respite. Now let us look at it as an example of the prophetic approach to life.

At first the people did release these serfs, and the Babylonian menace retreated. But then, thinking themselves safe, the people reversed their decision and took back their serfs. So Jeremiah prophesied an irremediable disaster: a *dror*—free rein—"to the sword, to pestilence, and famine" (Jer. 34:17). He invoked the pun on the word *dror* to announce that God would enact a terrifying "pun" in four-dimensional history: If the people would accord freedom to their own serfs, they would be able to remain free. But if they would not release their slaves, they would all become slaves; if they would not let the land rest, they would lose it so that through their exile it could rest. If the Israelites insisted on their own tyranny, they would become subjects of the Babylonian tyrant.

This teaching is not at first glance "reasonable": How could the internal reform of a small people stave off the overwhelming power of a Babylonian army? Why would Nebuchadnezzar have pulled back when slaves were freed, and conquered when they were again reduced to slavery?

Jeremiah's analysis depended on a deep version of realpolitik, wiser and more accurate than the shortsighted calculations of most politicians, because it was rooted in his sense of how a just universe works out in practice. He knew the story of the Great Liberation from the Egyptian Empire. Pharaoh fell and abject slaves were freed. What if the people were once again to share with each other as members of a compassionate community? Then perhaps the new pharaoh would remember Pharaoh's fate, would realize that a people united can never be defeated, would know that his only chance to enslave this people would come if they were already enslaving each other—only if the rich and powerful among them were already enslaving the poor.

But if Nebuchadnezzar remembered the fall of Pharaoh, the people did not remember their own Passover. And so they sold themselves into *Mitzrayyim*—this time in Babylonia.

40

Joshua Meets God's General

To this point, we have drawn chiefly on the tales of the Freedom Journey and of Wilderness that say of themselves that they were told on the outer side of Jordan—though some may actually have been written or radically edited later.

But there is one story about a moment of profound encounter once the people had crossed the Jordan River that is so unexpected, it cries out for us to pay attention (Josh. 5:13–15).

Joshua had inherited leadership of the Israelite people after the death of Moses. He had led the people in crossing the Jordan. He seemed to have every reason to think God wanted the Israelites to conquer the land of Canaan.

And then he met an awesome figure in full battle dress.

He called out to this figure, "Are you for us or for our enemies?"

Surely he was thinking: If this figure is a Canaanite soldier, he must be ready to support our enemies. And if he comes from God, everything Moses told us means he is sure to be supporting us.

But the awesome figure answers, "No!"

Think for a moment about that "No!"

We hear it to mean, "I am not here to support either one of you in your war against each other, nor do I support the conflict itself."

And now the awesome figure continues, "For I am a captain in the army of YHWH, the Interbreathing of all life."

The Power of a "No!"

To the extent that in our lives we can clumsily try to walk the path of serving only in God's army, the Infinite Host of that One Whose breathing gives life to all beings, we might understand this to mean:

We must not blindly support our own government—or its enemies—when they clash in unjust conflict with each other.

Not the U.S. government when it attacks half a dozen Muslim countries.

Nor al Qaeda when it attacks America.

In God's own army, we must not give blind support to the government of Israel or those Americans (Jews or others) who bow to its policies—nor may we support those who demonize Israeli society and try to bring disaster on its people.

We may be hungry to hear the trumpet blast of triumph.

But instead we hear the wailing, weeping, quavering ram's horn calling forth peace that is rooted in justice, the shofar that calls out, "Sleepers, awake!"

"Awake—for you must become the troops of God's own army."

The Infinite cannot be cramped into "us" or "our enemies."

The front-line service that we owe the One is to bring about not victories for these or those, but the wholeness that comes from weaving difference, the joy that comes from fitting together the pieces in the puzzle.

PART VIII
Across Millennia

We do not cross the Sea just once or open our eyes and ears but once to Sinai's earthquake. We do not settle only once in a land of promise. Again and again, our Freedom Journey itself carries us into a time of earthquake and a wilderness of uncertainty. Again and again, facing what seems to be overwhelming power, we must reshape community, make new connections. The two-step dance of God goes onward, but the dance floor changes.

Centuries after the time the Torah seems to be describing, new forms of Pharaoh—known as Caesar—loomed over the people whose liberation struggle lived at the heart of their identity. They had to reinvent themselves as the long-ago Hebrews had, and the Exodus and Sinai came alive again in their responses: Rabbinic Judaism and Christianity.

More centuries later, these stories told by Jews and Christians in a far-off country opened the ears of an Arab-speaking businessman to a new revelation from God, in which the story of the Exodus played a major part.

Leap more than a thousand years beyond, and an enslaved community in a continent Moses could never have imagined—newly introduced to the stories of Pharaoh and freedom—recognized themselves and built a large part of their identity out of the Exodus. And still later, as the great round earth began in agony to feel the plagues that had shaken ancient Egypt, the story rose again with new meaning, new momentum.

That pathway across millennia is told in the stories remaining in this book. We ourselves have told the stories of how the Rabbis remade

187

three aspects of the tales of Exodus and Wilderness. They sought a new version of liberation when outright rebellion against the Roman Empire failed; they taught a new understanding of the Torah that was revealed on Sinai; and they introduced an entirely new element, the erotic Song of Songs, into the epic tale of love between God and Israel.

For three other stories of the retelling of the Freedom Journey, we have turned to teachers and activists of those traditions. Two Christian theologian-activists explore how the Christian Gospel of Mark draws on and transforms the Exodus story in the life and death of Jesus. A Muslim scholar enfolds the similarities and differences between the Exodus tale as it was revealed to Muhammad and the Torah's telling (and retelling). And an activist/sage of the civil rights movement of the 1960s, a friend and co-worker of Dr. Martin Luther King Jr. and of the student activists, unfolds with passion the way in which African Americans in song and story have drawn on and reenacted the biblical tale of liberation.

And then, in the final chapter, we ourselves look at the beginnings of new ways of retelling and reenacting Exodus, Sinai, and Wilderness that have arisen among Jews and others in our own generation. The same kind of intense heat of social crisis that millennia ago melted the separate spring festivals of shepherds and farmers into the festival we know as Pesach, Passover—that same intensity seems to be gathering all around the planet today. New forms of control have enriched the human race, shattered many of its ancient forms of community, and endangered the earth that nurtures us. In God's two-step dance of control and community, the control step has far outstripped its other leg. So there have arisen experiments in new ways of resisting or absorbing or transforming new versions of Pharaoh. And there have arisen experiments in new ways of deepening and broadening community.

It may take another century for us to know whether any of these experiments will help restore God's dance and revitalize our planet— and if so, which experiments will work, which fail. In our last chapter of this book, we seek to bring together what we have learned from our rereading of the different generations of the Freedom Journey. We begin to name the ways in which the retelling of the ancient Freedom Journey can contribute to the journey in our lifetimes.

41

The Rabbis Cross
Their Own Red Sea

Rabbinic Judaism emerged out of a wrenching collision between Second Temple Judaism and the Roman Empire, which embodied not only political and military power but Hellenistic civilization.

Rome's domination was much broader than that of previous imperial powers. The empire not only invaded but absorbed the Land of Israel, the minds of many of its people, and their livelihoods.

What had been a Judaism focused entirely on the Land of Israel fell into crisis as hundreds of thousands of Jews moved to major cities of the Mediterranean basin, like Alexandria and Rome itself. Egypt, under Roman suzerainty, became the breadbasket of the whole region, undercutting the local economy of Jewish farmers and shepherds. Rome both absorbed and to some extent vulgarized Greek literature and philosophy, and then Roman power carried Hellenistic philosophy and science far and wide. It attracted many Jews, and Greek became a major language of intellectual discussion.

Though local Maccabean guerrilla fighters had been able to defeat the earlier Hellenistic armies of Antiochus, the Roman legions overawed the Middle East, and the outward forms of Jewish self-government became more and more a puppet state of the Roman Empire.

Freedom from Rome?

Although most of the community probably accepted Rome's domination as a given of everyday life, some resistance groups emerged that were convinced Rome was a new kind of *Mitzrayyim*/Egypt, with its successive Caesars as reenactments of Pharaoh, even to demanding worship as gods.

So the obvious question arose: was it possible for the Jewish people to win its freedom from Roman domination as it had from Pharaoh long ago—and if so, how?

If even a small number of Jews held such opinions, Rome and its local puppets could easily have feared the annual Passover pilgrimage of very large numbers of people to Jerusalem, the local capital of the empire's political machinery, to celebrate the overthrow of an ancient Pharaoh. Numbers in the millions by their very presence in the capital made up a massive "demonstration"; given the content of their pilgrimage, officials might have thought Pesach itself was a subversive danger to the state.

What was actually happening in this annual Passover pilgrimage?

On the tenth of the springtime month of Nisan, each family acquired a lamb—or, if the family was too small or too poor to deal with a whole lamb of its own, it shared with neighbors to make a tiny fellowship or co-op. Bringing these lambs with them, the people converged on Jerusalem in enormous multitudes—more than three million strong in the year 65 CE. (The Roman legions destroyed the Temple just five years later, in putting down a rebellion against their rule.)

The pilgrim multitudes would sacrifice their lambs as the day of the fourteenth of Nisan turned into dusk and moved toward the evening of the fifteenth. Until midnight they would roast and eat the *pesach* lamb, with bitter herbs to remember the bitterness of slavery, and with *matzah*—unleavened bread—to recall the haste of liberation.

For a week they would stay in Jerusalem, eating only *matzah*, telling the tales of freedom, gathering again on the seventh day for another solemn day of dedication. Sometime during the week they would begin to wave before God's altar an *omer* of the earliest ripened barley, starting the count of forty-nine days of awaiting the crop from different fields throughout the Land of Israel as the barley ripened—a count that itself would ripen on the festival of Shavuot. And after the seventh day they would return to their homes.

But many Jews lived too far away—even beyond the seas—to join together in Jerusalem, and even those who came wanted to eat and celebrate in the family groups or fellowships that had brought a lamb together.

In that atmosphere, there began to emerge a pattern for a Passover meal that would both tell the ancient story and physically embody in the very foods to be eaten its feelings—bitterness, haste, joy. It has continued to be the basic model to this day, with many additions and amendments across the centuries.

Can Questions Turn the World Around?

The Mishnah—a compilation of Jewish practice edited by about 200 CE—described the basic order (in Hebrew, *Seder*) of this meal. It reported and mandated the practice in which children would ask four questions and the Seder, or *Haggadah* ("The Telling"), would answer them with words from the biblical story of the Exodus and many interpretive midrashim that read between the biblical lines of text.

This "Seder" was an extraordinary amalgam of Jewish teaching infused into a Hellenistic literary form.

The carefully ordered meal borrowed from the pattern of the Greek and Roman *symposion*, which literally means "drinking together," a philosophical banquet. The best-known example of this kind of banquet takes place in Plato's *Symposium*.

As in the classic Hellenistic symposium, the guests drank four cups of wine—two before and two after the meal. As in Roman custom, where free citizens would recline to eat a formal dinner while servants stood or sat alert to serve them, the Seder participants reclined throughout the meal, as an expression of their freedom.

In regard to the most profound aspect of the symposium, the process of learning, the Seder drew on the symposium but in an ironic, satirical way. The Seder turned the symposium upside down.

For the Hellenistic philosophers, the crucial element was that the sage—in the most famous case, Socrates—would ask a series of questions of his followers and students. As he questioned, the shape of the questions would force the answers into a particular philosophical pattern—his own teaching.

The Seder, however, turned this pattern around. Here the children were to ask the questions. Their openness and curiosity freed the Seder from the rigidities of the Hellenistic symposium. No longer were the answers predetermined by the questions.

What were the ancient proto-Rabbis doing? They had begun to realize that no military miracle was likely to free them from the

Roman Empire. They might well have to live in the nooks and crannies of Roman civilization. And yet they wanted, needed, to celebrate
and reenact their freedom—especially in the moment of Passover
memories.

Can Words, Not Weapons, Free the People?

So the Rabbis of the Mishnah created a form of celebration that
would affirm their freedom in the very nook and cranny of the Hellenistic dinner. The medium would be the message. God was not likely
to come and sweep away the Roman legions as the Breath of Life, the
Wind of Change, had blown away the chariots of Pharaoh. So they
needed to cross their own Red Sea in a new way.

All this did not happen in a moment. It took more than a century
for the new understanding of Passover and of liberation to reshape
and be reshaped by the new paradigm of Jewish life.

Indeed, we can see the changes through two historic moments in
celebration of Passover.

The first of these is reported in the Christian Gospels (with some
differences in detail and nuance among them)—that is, in Jewish
memories of an extraordinary Passover time that slowly metamor-
phosed into the tradition of a new religion. As it took on its new
shape, Christianity still preserved its origins as a macro-midrash on
biblical Judaism—analogous to, though of course different from, its
sister macro-midrash, Rabbinic Judaism.

According to these tellings, followers of a young and radical rabbi
from the Galilee—Yeshua, or in the Greek tongue Jesus—gathered at
Passover time in Jerusalem, the local capital of the world empire, in a
year sometime between 26 and 36 CE. They publicly demonstrated
against Rome in a march bearing palm branches, as modern demon-
strators might carry signs and banners.

Then they gathered in private to share the Passover meal and discuss the ancient tales of liberation, though their secrecy may have
been compromised by an underground police agent or provocateur in
their midst. (Some modern scholars have suggested that this meal may
have taken place on a date that, translated into the modern Gregorian
calendar, was April 3 in the year 33 CE.)

That group was probably only one of a number of such rebellious
gatherings. It—or at least its leader—may have been committed to

nonviolence. Others may have been prepared to use violence against the empire. In any case, the Roman procurator of Judea, Pontius Pilate, evidently saw this one as a threat to Roman stability. He had its leader tortured and executed by the means the Romans used against thousands of common criminals and subversives: crucifixion.

The other Pesach Seder that became (not quite so) famous was held about a century later. Its story was inserted into the evolving Haggadah for Passover after the failure of the Great Rebellion against Rome in 135 CE. By this time, the Temple itself had been destroyed by the Roman legions in 70 CE, and its site had become a wasteland. The annual mass pilgrimages for Pesach were impossible, and the intimate Seder had become the norm for celebration of Passover.

The story preserved in the Haggadah is that the great rabbi Akiba and four other rabbis gathered for the Pesach Seder in the town of B'nai Brak and celebrated the Seder so long that their students came to tell them dawn was breaking and they must do the morning prayers.

There is also a tradition, passed on by word of mouth alone until our own day, that this Seder was actually the occasion for discussing and planning an uprising against the imperial power and that the students were actually warning the rabbis of the approach of Roman troops.

The background to this second level of the story is that Akiba did support the Great Rebellion, asserting that its leader, Bar Kochba, was indeed the long-awaited Messiah.

Others among the five rabbis doubted that the rebellion could succeed and denied that Bar Kochba was the Messiah.

The rebellion not only failed but brought on a brutal Roman crackdown that decimated the Jewish community in the Land of Israel / Palestine. So many Jews were sold as slaves that the price of slaves dropped all across the Roman Empire.

For the next eighteen hundred years, there was not even the semblance of Jewish self-government in the Land—and often, very few Jewish inhabitants. Why then did the editors of the Haggadah include this story?

Irony: The Sword of Truth

One possibility is that this story was precisely a sardonic warning: Those who thought freedom could be achieved again as it had been long ago in *Mitzrayyim*, in the way celebrated in the text of the Haggadah, must pay more attention to recent history. Only the Seder, where the Rabbis could freely discuss the issue, speaking freely in the very nooks and crannies of Roman rule, was the way to be free under Rome. Akiba was right in what he actually performed, wrong in what he promised and predicted. Any attempt to challenge Roman rule head-on with weapons instead of words would result in the destruction of freedom, not its triumph.

And so the Rabbis, facing their own Red Sea, passionately seeking to bring about the rebirth of the Jewish people from the Tight and Narrow Space of Roman domination, pointed the way in a new direction.

The "Sea of the Talmud"—an ocean of words in which the Rabbis debated and dialogued about what Torah meant, an ocean constantly being re-created by new streams of thought, in which indeed, without the label "Talmud," Jews continue to debate and dialogue—would be the waters of rebirth.

42

The Rabbis Climb
Their Own Mount Sinai

Just as the community-birthing event of Sinai was a necessary correction to the overpowering actions of Pharaoh, in order to rebalance the two legs of control and community in the dance of God, so the overpowering behavior of the Roman Empire called for a similar rebirthing of community.

In fact, there were two such rebirths—new sibling communities born almost simultaneously in the very midst of the empire: Christianity and Rabbinic Judaism.

Hardly surprising that just as both, in very different ways, drew on the memory of the Exodus and the festival of Passover, so both, again in very different ways, drew on the memory of Sinai and what became its memorial festival, Shavuot.

It was the Rabbis who played with the dates of Sinai and of the biblical agrarian festival of Shavuot to make them coincide. Biblically, Shavuot—which means "Weeks" in Hebrew—came seven weeks and a day after some unclear time during Passover. It celebrated the fulfillment of the spring barley harvest and the success of the spring wheat harvest in the Land of Israel.

Meanwhile, the Torah gave a vague timing "in the third month" after the Exodus for the revelation of Torah on Mount Sinai.

The ancient Rabbis, after decades of bitter argument with other branches of Jewish leadership (the Pharisees, the Qumran community) decided to fix the date of Shavuot and define it as the time of the giving of the Torah.

Oral Torah for an Oral People

Why? Because they, unlike the priestly Pharisees, were committed to the notion that ongoing study of the words of Torah and ongoing midrash on the words of Torah were the ways to give birth to a new word-centered Judaism. Somehow, from the pregnant body of biblical body-Judaism, through the wracking labor pains of responding to Hellenistic civilization and the Roman Empire, must come a new form of community.

Just as Passover gave every Jew the opportunity to take part in the Exodus and the crossing of the Sea, so every Jew needed a time to stand at Sinai.

Even more important, the ancient Rabbis invented the notion that a Torah "through the power of the mouth" was given at Sinai along with the Written Torah. They even told a story—a profound story that was also a conscious, deliberate, and serious joke—to give life to this philosophical idea.

In this Talmudic story (*Menachot* 29b), Moses is joyfully discussing Torah with God—the Torah that God had given him on Sinai. It occurs to Moses to ask God, "What are the people doing nowadays with the Torah that You gave me on Sinai?" God tells him to turn around, and Moses sees a class of rabbis learning from Akiba. Moses listens for a while to the class discussion and turns back to God in puzzlement. "I don't understand a word that they are saying," says Moses. "How can this be the Torah that I received from You on Sinai?" God says, "Turn around again." So Moses turns around, and this time hears one of the students asking Akiba, "How do we know that what you are teaching is the Torah God gave Moses on Mount Sinai?"

Akiba answers, "In the Written Torah God gave Moses, many of the letters had little flames and thorns encoded in the letters, on their tops. By word-of-mouth through all the centuries, we have decoded what these squiggles mean, and that is what I am teaching you today: by word of mouth, a second level of the Torah that Moses learned from God on Sinai."

Moses turns back to God. "Wonderful how they are learning now the Torah that You taught me on Sinai!" he says.

So the Rabbis knew full well that the Torah they were learning and teaching would have been unintelligible to Moses. They knew they were creating new rules for their community, born of necessity as they lived their lives in a new world. But they also knew that they were doing what Moses had done on the mountaintop: learning not just new rules, but learning to create a whole new structure of community. The content would be different, but the process was the same. So they knew that Moses and God would approve.

And the Rabbis end the story by having Moses turn to God once more and ask, "What is the reward for such an extraordinary Torah teacher?" God says once more, "Turn around," and Moses turns to see Akiba's flesh torn from his bones by Roman torturers.

Just as the Rabbis did with the story of Akiba's Passover Seder, they once more used a tale of Akiba to assert that Caesar might dominate with weapons, but the new community would be created by the sharing, the teaching, of words of Torah. The violent revolution that Akiba had supported would fail in the face of the Roman legions, but Akiba's nonviolent words would succeed.

As for the Festival of Weeks, Shavuot, they made it into the supernal celebration of the Oral Torah. They turned the mouths that had connected with God by eating food into mouths that would connect with God by speaking words.

The Seventy Nations as a New Community

And when for the followers of Jesus came the moment to turn their loose-linked network into a new kind of community that could reach beyond all the barriers of language and of culture in the Roman world, they too found the moment on Shavuot. They told the story of how when they gathered after seven weeks of seven days—on the fiftieth day, or "Pentecost" in Greek—they began to speak in all the seventy tongues of all the seventy nations of the world, and they could understand each other. The Holy Spirit, the Holy Breath, the wordless Breathing that unites all languages, united them.

And so two new communities set out upon their separate pathways in the world. In different ways, they rebalanced the overpowering power of the Roman Caesar. They made it possible for the dance of God to begin again, in balance on both legs.

43

The Rabbis Sing the Song of Songs

Love as Freedom

The same Akiba who thought the Great Rebellion of 135 CE heralded the messianic days, the same Akiba who kept a Passover Seder going all night, thirsting for the great redemption from the Roman "Pharaoh," the same Akiba who taught his students that the Oral Torah came with the written one from Sinai—that same Akiba also convinced the highest Jewish legal body in his generation that the Song of Songs should be included among the sacred books of what we call the Bible.

And the connection between Akiba's passion for Passover and his passion for the Song of Songs is no mere accident. For Rabbinic tradition taught that the Song should be chanted during Passover—either at the end of the Seder or on the Shabbat during Passover.

Why? What is the deep connection between Passover and this profoundly erotic poetry about the passionate love between the human-earthling and the earthy-humus, and the passionate love between two human beings?

That the Song was holy was certainly not a foregone conclusion. The Song is quite unlike any other book or passage of the Bible.

It never mentions God's Name and barely mentions the people of Israel. It focuses almost entirely on the tastes and smells and sights and songs of earth and on the delights of love and sex. Alone in all the Bible it celebrates the throat and breasts and thighs of a woman, the brow and belly and legs of a man.

Even more astonishing, the Song of Songs does not describe a world ruled by men, though it mentions men who try to rule the world—and fail. Nor does it describe a sexual relationship that is governed by men or a man. The woman or women who lead in most of these poems seem to be shaping their own reality, erotic and otherwise. The Song is the easiest book of the Bible to imagine having been written or edited by a woman.

The only anxieties put forward in the Song are those arising in and from the men who try to control or forbid the sexual expressions of the woman who is the leading figure.

There are no anxieties over procreation; for the Song, children are not the main point of sex. Loving, joyous pleasure is the point—or rather, the process, for the Song does not arrive at any climax, any point.

There are no anxieties, as in much of Torah, over the flow of sexual fluids. Instead, the Song takes joy in the flow and fluidity of love itself and of love's story. Is there a single story to the Song, or is it a gathering of tales and poems? We cannot tell; the Song wants not to tell us; the story gushes, trickles, vanishes, again wells up. It flows, and no one needs to call, "*Tamei*, taboo!"

"Do not rouse or wake love until it please" is a recurring refrain in the Song (2:7, 3:5, 8:4). Its sense of time is fluid and interpersonal, not measured by the sun or moon or calendar as time is in most of Torah (and especially in the Telling of the Exodus).

Just as the story of manna and the discovery of Shabbat just after the fall of Pharaoh came as an opening to a world of Eden renewed, a world where food comes joyfully from the earth and human beings learn to rest instead of toiling every day—so the Song of Songs evokes Eden renewed: a Garden, now, for grown-ups; Eden for a grown-up human race.

No longer are the protagonists children bursting into rebellious adolescence and resisting Papa/Mama God, no longer are they at war with the earth or with each other—but a woman and a man who now are grown-ups. The Name of God is no longer outside them but integrated wholly within, holy within.

So the deep content of the Song, its subversion of all authority and domination, evokes a teaching at the root of God's freedom in overthrowing Pharaoh. And the Song evokes the tastes and smells and colors of spring—the time when the people rose up against Pharaoh, when the flowers rise up against winter.

Not only its content but the process by which the Song was adopted as part of the Hebrew Bible may have felt like a liberating Pesach moment to the Rabbis. The Sanhedrin, seventy-one sages who comprised the highest judicial and legislative authority of the Jewish people, voted on such questions. The day when they voted on the Song of Songs was perhaps the most remarkable in the history of the Sanhedrin (Babylonian Talmud, *Brachot* 27b–28a; *Sanhedrin* 11a; Jerusalem Talmud, *Sanhedrin* 1:19a).

It was approximately the year 90 CE. Early in the day, the president of the Sanhedrin, Rabban Gamaliel, had once again displayed enormous arrogance toward one of its most respected and popular members, Joshua ben Hananiah—forcing Joshua to remain standing while Gamaliel, seated, poured contempt on Joshua's interpretation of a point of law.

The members of the Sanhedrin rebelled. They chanted "Stop!" until the proceedings were forced to stop, and they decided to depose Gamaliel as president and appoint a new one.

The new president permitted several hundred students of Torah who had been barred by Gamaliel because he deemed them insufficiently learned to enter the House of Study.

That day became so memorable to the Rabbis that the Talmud says, "Whenever the expression 'On that day' appears, it means *that* day"—the one on which Gamaliel was deposed.

And on that day, the Sanhedrin voted after hot debate to include the Song of Songs in what we now call the Bible.

In the dispute over the Song, it was Rabbi Akiba who carried the day. He had the reputation of having been a poor, illiterate shepherd who had become a great scholar and had safely experienced a mystical entry into the Garden or Paradise—perhaps the grown-up Garden of the Song itself. Perhaps that is why his words in the Sanhedrin were so filled with passion and with deep and direct experience that he could sway his colleagues.

What did Akiba say? First of all, he attacked what was evidently a customary use of the Song as an erotic ballad, what we might call a "torch song": "Whoever trills and sings the Song of Songs in taverns and banquet halls has no share in the World to Come" (*Tosefta, Sanhedrin* 12:10; Babylonian Talmud, *Sanhedrin* 101a). He asserted, "The whole world is not worth the day on which the Song of Songs was given to Israel. All the Writings are holy, but the Song of Songs is the Holy of Holies [using the phrase for the innermost and most sacred room of the Holy Temple, which had been destroyed a generation earlier]" (*Mishnah Yadaim* 3:5).

Judging from later explication, Akiba probably eased the way for the Sanhedrin to approve the Song by defining it as an allegory, in which the woman who sings to her evanescent lover is Israel seeking God. Later rabbis added details that explained the Song as an allegory of the Exodus and Wilderness adventures, in which God and Israel reach out to each other, separate, rejoin, and vanish once again—a dance of love thwarted and never quite fulfilled. (For example, the two breasts of the Song's playful shepherdess were interpreted as Moses and Aaron, reaching out to God before the rest of Israel.) From this standpoint, it is not at all surprising that the Rabbis decided that the Song should be chanted during Passover.

In this way, just as the Rabbis through the Haggadah turned to airy words instead of bodily weapons as instruments of freedom, so by allegorizing the Song the Rabbis lifted erotic joy from the body to a purely spiritual experience, mirroring their own experience of the erotic joys of Torah study. Just as the sense of playful, joyful intertwining with the earth retreated for Jews who no longer had connection with the Land of Israel, so the play and joy of sex retreated into heaven.

In our own generation, many Jews have reconnected with the earth—both in the State of Israel and in far-flung Jewish communities around the world. And the Song's celebration of joyful equality between women and men and of loving sexuality that is sacred, not necessarily because it births more children but for its own joyful sake, have come into their own in many Jewish communities.

So perhaps in our own era, might the Song's subversive and liberating qualities come into Passover in a different way? Not, as in the biblical era, the Song as earth and eros alone. Not, as in the Rabbinic era, sex as only an allegory for spiritual love. But today, could a new springtime for earth and humankind beckon us into feeling earth and eros infused with the Spirit, the Breath of Life, "spirituality"—and feeling spirituality infused with earth and eros?

In the biblical story of the Freedom Journey, God's Name is constantly before our eyes and in our ears. In the Song of Songs, God's Name seems astonishingly absent. Could we hear the Song calling us to hear the absence of God's Name from any explicit mention as an invitation to sense God as fully present in every breath of the Song's music? Not in one of its particular characters and moments, but in all its form and all its content? And therefore could we hear the Song calling us to sense God as utterly present throughout our Freedom Journey? In every step, in every breath?

44

Exodus in the Life
and Death of Jesus

By Ched Myers and Russell Powell

*Be aware, sisters and brothers, that our ancestors were
all under the Cloud, and all passed through the Sea,
and all were baptized into Moses in the Cloud and in
the Sea.*

1 Corinthians 10:1–2

The Exodus story resonates just below the surface of the entire Second Testament. The apostle Paul (cited above) understood the journey "through the Cloud and the Sea" to be archetypal for all believers. We can hear Exodus echoes particularly in the synoptic Gospel narratives of the life and death of Jesus of Nazareth, from beginning to end. For example, Matthew's story of Jesus's birth (Matt. 2:13–18) is closely patterned after the Moses tale in Exodus 1:15–2:10. And as Jesus hung on an imperial cross, the sky darkened—just as it did over Pharaoh's Egypt (Exod. 10:21–29).

Here we look at Exodus allusions in the Gospel of Mark, which, as the earliest of the Second Testament narratives of Jesus's life, represents a "core sample" of early Christian faith. We focus on Mark's "Passion" narrative of Jesus's execution at the hands of the Romans as a nationalist dissident and then briefly on a theological understanding of the cross as "Passover midrash."

Nonviolence: Suffering Becomes Freedom

The Passion begins at the midpoint of Mark's story, where Jesus's disciples were unable (or unwilling) to embrace him as a leader who would face death on a Roman cross rather than bring military victory over the empire (Mark 8:27–31). This crisis occurred at the commencement of a long journey from northern Galilee to Jerusalem, during which Jesus instructed his followers in a "catechism" of nonviolence (Mark 8:34–11:1).

This was no ordinary pilgrimage to the Holy City, however. It represented a sort of archetypal *reversal* of the great Exodus. Rather than lead his followers *out* of imperial bondage, Jesus deliberately headed *into* a confrontation with the political authorities—a journey into the "heart of darkness" of empire in Roman-occupied Judea. _Both_ movements—to distance oneself from and to engage the powers—are necessary in the long history of struggles for justice.

And it is instructive that here, as in the Moses story where the Israelite slaves complained that Moses was bringing more oppression upon them, Jesus's followers were skeptical of this liberation march, full of dismissiveness (Mark 8:32) and fear (Mark 9:32, 10:32).

This long march culminated in the "Palm Sunday" demonstration at the gates of the city. Jesus, flanked by peasant supporters, entered the Holy City as a prophet intent on challenging the foundations of state power. Mark's so-called "Triumphal Entry" narrative (Mark 11:1–10) portrays carefully choreographed political street theater designed to repudiate the delusion of messianic triumphalism.

On one hand, the symbolism of the parade invoked several biblical precedents that seem to affirm messianic triumph. The colt recalls Jacob's prophetic blessing that a victorious Judah would celebrate with a donkey's colt and also recalls the return of the Ark to Israel (1 Sam. 6:7–12). The laying of cloaks alludes to Jehu's acclamation (2 Kings 9:13), and the chant echoes the royal processional hymn of Psalm 118:25–26. The parade's starting point "near the Mount of Olives" (Mark 11:1) brings to mind the apocalyptic battle between Israel and her enemies, prophetically imagined by Zechariah (14:1–5).

On the other hand, Jesus's symbolism also meant to *parody* messianic movements in more recent history. The parade mimics the military procession of Simon Maccabee, the guerilla general who liberated the Land of Israel from Hellenistic rule two centuries before (1 Macc. 13:51), and more immediately the pomp and circumstance of Roman procuratorial liturgies. But Mark's odd account of "commandeering" the colt, which takes up half the episode (Mark 11:2–6), reorganizes the symbolism around a different, expressly *anti-military* Zecharian image:

> Shout aloud, daughter of Jerusalem! Lo, your king comes to you; triumphant and victorious is he, humble and riding upon ... a colt, the foal of a donkey. He will cut off the chariot from Ephraim and the war horse from Jerusalem ... and shall command peace to the nations."
>
> ZECHARIAH 9:9–10

In this sense Jesus's parade reiterates the spirit of Moses's Exodus march: both liberation movements were unarmed, yet utterly subversive to empire!

Mark next narrates a sequence of conflict stories in the capital city (Mark 11–12). Jesus's "nonviolent siege" began at the Temple, which Jesus intended (unlike his nationalist Zealot contemporaries) not to *defend*, but to *disrupt* in the spirit of Jeremiah (11:15–19; see Jer. 7:3–15). He then locked horns in serial fashion with each stratum of Judean social and political power: chief priests (Mark 11:27–33), landowners (12:1–12, invoking Isaiah 5), Pharisees (Mark 12:13–17), Sadducees (12:18–27), scribes (12:28–40), wealthy patrons of the Temple (12:41–44), and eventually the Sanhedrin (14:53–65).

This sequence can be seen as an (obviously polemical) re-narration of Moses's repeated confrontations with Pharaoh—but now it is the *Judean* authorities who were exposed as oppressors of the poor. This critique is summarized in Jesus's famous lament concerning the destitute widow in Mark 12:43–44.

It must always be acknowledged that the fierce intra-Jewish debates portrayed in the Gospels were twisted by later Christian interpreters (especially after the church made its fateful alliance with Constantine in the fourth century) into a deadly rationale for anti-Semitism. This murderous hermeneutic legacy continues to require renunciation and resistance.

Pilate: Provincial Pharaoh/Caesar

The Second Testament evangelists, however, understood the true architecture of first-century Roman oppression, which is why in Mark's account, Jesus's final showdown happened facing Caesar's representative, the highest rung on the ladder of power (short of Rome itself) (Mark 15:1–15).

Like Pharaoh, Pilate is portrayed as duplicitous and politically calculating. Mark gives us a caricature of procuratorial pragmatism at work: Pilate managed to send a prominent dissident to the gallows, while dividing the nationalist crowd against itself. After Jesus refused to cooperate with his interrogation, Pilate defused the possibility of a popular uprising by granting a special "holiday" amnesty (Mark 15:6), a shrewd public relations ploy aimed at playing the unruly mob's patriotism off against itself. But as in the Exodus story (1–14) of plagues followed by Pharaoh's frightened kowtowing to God followed by his hardening of his heart, followed by more plagues and more reversals, this narrative is heavy with satire.

There are two elements of Mark's narrative that are, historically speaking, utterly implausible: the absurd scenario of a Roman procurator "consulting" a Jewish crowd (Mark 15:9, 15:12, 15:14), and the inconceivable spectacle of Jews calling for the crucifixion of one of their own (Mark 15:13–14).

Both, however, would be consistent with a literary *parody* of the notorious Roman gladiator tradition. These bloodthirsty games began with an elaborate procession into the amphitheater, then pitted criminals, prisoners of war, or dissidents against gladiators or animals. If the victim survived, the sponsor of the games would "consult" the crowd, which would indicate (thumbs up or thumbs down) whether the combatant should be finished off.

Exodus in the Key of Satire

In this light, Pilate's behavior becomes intelligible, as does Jesus's subsequent "death march" to Golgotha—in Aramaic, the "place of the skull" (Mark 15:21–22). This is bitter Markan political satire: populist Judean sentiment, caught between the conflicting revolutionary claims of the urban guerilla Barabbas and the nonviolent rural prophet Jesus, was co-opted by the imperial overlord and manipulated into the pagan ritual of a gladiatorial trade-off.

Rome prevailed, Judea remained under the boot, and the Nazarene became an imperial statistic.

The fact that all these events took place during the Passover festival provides the most dramatic analogue between Mark's Passion narrative and the Exodus account. These holy days always occasioned political turmoil in colonial Palestine, since it was a time when an oppressed populace reflected on their foundational story of liberation. In Mark's story, the "Last Supper" depicts a Pesach Seder truly "on the run," just as the Hebrew Bible describes the original hasty Exodus (Exod. 12:11): Jesus and his community were hunted fugitives (Mark 14:1), meeting clandestinely in the attic of a "safe house," at which they arrived through an underground network replete with "passwords" (Mark 14:12–16).

From the outset this memorial meal was fraught with anxiety, as Jesus announced he was aware that his community had been infiltrated; he underlined the breach of trust by alluding to the lament of Psalm 41:9 (Mark 14:18). The disciples reacted with self-doubt and recrimination—echoing the internal conflicts that plagued the Exodus community.

Nevertheless, Jesus affirmed his extraordinary solidarity with his betrayal-bound companions: his Pesach homily boldly related the elements of the meal not only to the Exodus story, but also to *himself* (Mark 14:2–24). *He* was the "paschal lamb" (Exod. 12) who renewed the "blood of the covenant" in his death (Exod. 24:8). In place of a Temple offering, he offered his "body as sacrifice," understood as the inevitable cost of his nonviolent practice of resistance to all oppression, Judean and Roman.

Jesus concluded his Pesach reflection by announcing that the feast had become a fast—until justice should prevail (Mark 14:25).

Sharing Bread and Justice

Significantly in the narratology and theology of Mark, the ritual described here—"taking, blessing, breaking, and giving bread"—is identical to Jesus's earlier wilderness feedings of the poor (Mark 14:22 = 6:41). That famous "loaves and fishes" episode was, in turn, a midrashic reenactment of both Elisha's provisioning during a time of famine (2 Kings 4:42–44) and the Exodus tale of manna in the wilderness (Exodus 16). The Eucharistic liturgy celebrated by Christians, therefore, *should* be about remembering the *life* of Jesus, not only his death, as a practice of "Jubilee justice"—something our churches practice poorly.

That death is the ultimate Exodus moment in the Gospel story. As Jesus languished on the executioner's cross, the last two plagues are re-narrated. "Darkness came over the whole land," Mark tells us, invoking *YHWH*'s judgment against empire and its solar gods (Mark 15:33; see Exod. 10:21–23). But here the old story receives its final twist in Mark: it was the firstborn of the Hebrew peasant girl Miriam, rather than those of the Egyptians (Exod. 11:4–6), who died for the cause of liberation.

From the Gospels' perspective, Jesus's death signaled a seismic shift (in Matthew's version we even get an earthquake [Matt. 27:51–52]) from Passover's symbolism of divine retribution against an intransigent enemy to the suggestion of divine solidarity with the sacrificial offering of the nonviolent warrior's life (see, e.g., 2 Cor. 5:16ff.).

Redemption, Reimagined

Taking Mark's lead, later Second Testament traditions identified Jesus as the Passover "lamb without blemish" (1 Pet. 1:19) who was slaughtered by empire but vindicated by God (Rev. 5:12) and whose blood now provided forgiveness of sins to all (Heb. 9:11–10:18). This brings us in conclusion to a controversial issue: the ways in which Jesus's death was (and is) interpreted by churches as *cosmically* consequential.

The Second Testament offers multiple metaphors for how Jesus's death might be understood as "redemptive." Those drawn from the Hebrew Bible include Levitical purity language, the semantics of Jubilee debt release, covenant symbols, and Jesus as the embodiment of Second Isaiah's "lamb led to the slaughter" (Isa. 53:7).

For the last millennium, however, Christian "atonement" theology has been dominated by problematic medieval metaphors (e.g., Jesus died "in our stead," resulting in a divine exoneration of otherwise sinful human beings). These views are currently undergoing much-needed critique and revision in Christian theology, and this conversation can be helped by recovering the centrality of the Gospel's portrayal of Jesus's death as a "new Passover" drama.

There are at least four advantages in this approach for Christians:

First, to see the Cross as a kind of Passover midrash preserves the Hebrew tradition of *remembrance* as fundamental to faith identity.

Second, it places what Marvin Wilson (in *Our Father Abraham: Jewish Roots of the Christian Faith*) calls God's "liberating involvement in the human predicament" at the center of both liturgy and practice, thus authorizing our ongoing participation in struggles for justice.

Third, it affirms the Exodus conviction that the God of the Bible is *always* identified with the poor, a solidarity Christians see embodied in the Jesus who lived and died on their behalf.

Fourth, part of the Exodus tradition is the prophetic anticipation of future redemption (e.g., Isa. 65:17–18; Mic. 4:1–5), when all remaining pharaohs will be brought low and *shalom* will again flourish here on earth. This resonates with Christian convictions about the resurrection of Jesus and eschatological hope of the world redeemed.

To read the Jesus story, around which the entire Second Testament revolves, is to "re-member" the Exodus, recontextualized in a different imperial epoch. To read these traditions *faithfully* is to recontextualize them in our *own* world, which again groans under the shadow of empire.[1] It is our hope that churches and synagogues might support one another in embracing this task; after all, "our ancestors *all* passed through the Sea."

45

Exodus in the Qur'an

Mercy, Compassion, and Forgiveness

By S. Ayse Kadayifci-Orellana

For the Qur'an, Moses and the Exodus are major themes. Among the twenty-five prophets whom the Qur'an names and whose stories it tells, the life of Moses and stories of the Hebrews in pharaonic Egypt, of the Exodus of the Children of Israel, and of their liberation under the leadership of Moses are particularly important. Indeed, Moses is the most often mentioned prophet in the Qur'an.

According to Islamic tradition, Moses—like Prophet Muhammad—also talked to God face-to-face. He is mentioned in at least forty suras, where his life is described in unusually long detail. For example, sura 28 narrates the story of Moses from his birth to the Exodus of the Children of Israel out of Egypt.

Quite similar to the biblical account, the Qur'anic account also includes his killing of the Egyptian, his sojourn in Midian, his revelation at the Burning Bush, his return as liberator, and the story of the Golden Calf as well as that of Korach.

Why is this story so central to Qur'anic narrative? How can this story guide Muslims today?

The Oppressive Pharaoh

There are many different ways to approach and understand the Qur'anic account of Moses's life and liberation of the Children of Israel. On the one hand, it is about Pharaoh's oppression, tyranny, and injustice. Unmistakably the Qur'an condemns arrogance, oppressors, and tyrants and warns them about the punishment they will face hereafter. In that respect, the Qur'anic account puts a special emphasis on the confrontation between Moses and the Pharaoh, with at least ten verses mentioning these dealings.

Indeed, Pharaoh, or Fira'vun, is often associated with the archenemy of God, the epitome of evil, the pinnacle of arrogance, tyranny, and oppression. Pharaoh, resembling modern despotic rulers, is criticized in the Qur'an for being corrupt, dividing Egypt's people based on their faith and ethnicity, tormenting them with extreme cruelty, and even killing some of them: "We recite to you with truth some news of Moses and Pharaoh for people who believe. Pharaoh exalted himself arrogantly in the land and divided its people into camps, oppressing one group of them by slaughtering their sons and letting their women live. He was one of the corrupters" (Qur'an 28:3–4; also 2:49).

He was not only an arrogant and hard-hearted tyrant who enslaved and oppressed the Children of Israel, but he also rebelled against God by building a tower to heaven, shooting arrows at God, and claiming divinity: "I am your Lord most high" (Qur'an 79:24).

Indeed, the Qur'an constantly warns believers not to oppress others and to be patient when faced with oppression. Oppression, persecution, and killing others for any reason are clearly condemned by God. God warns believers against oppression and injustice and explicitly urges Muslims to be just and treat *everyone* fairly, as is shown in the Qur'anic verses "O ye who believe! Stand out firmly for justice as witnesses to Allah even as against yourselves, your parents or your kin, and whether it be (against) the rich and poor" (4:135) and "To fair dealing, and let not the hatred of others to you make you swerve to wrong and depart from justice. Be just for it is next to piety" (5:8).

God promises that those who are unjust will be duly punished— "So those are their houses fallen down because they were unjust"— and adds that believers must learn from this example: "most surely there is a sign in this for a people who know" (Qur'an 27:52).

Furthermore, God asks believers to be steadfast and promises deliverance to those who endure these difficulties with patience: "And We made a people, considered weak (and of no account), inheritors of lands in both east and west—lands whereon We sent down Our blessings. The fair promise of thy Lord was fulfilled for the Children of Israel, because they had patience and constancy, and We leveled to the ground the great works and fine buildings that Pharaoh and his people erected [with such pride]" (Qur'an 7:137). Indeed, patience (*sabr*) is the direct focus of two hundred Qur'anic verses, and many others allude to it indirectly.

Merciful God, Merciful People

On the other hand, the account of Exodus in the Qur'an is not only about oppression but also about forgiveness, repentance, hope, redemption, God's infinite mercy, and compassion. Qur'anic verses about the Exodus stress time and again God's mercy and forgiveness for the Children of Israel, as God tells them, "Then, you turned back after that; and had it not been for the grace of Allah upon you and His mercy, you would surely have been among the losers" (2:64; see also 2:50–54).

Indeed, mercy, compassion, and forgiveness are central to the Qur'anic message, as it is stated in the Qur'an (6:54): "When those come to thee who believe in Our signs, say: 'Peace be on you: Your Lord hath inscribed for Himself (the rule of) Mercy: verily, if any of you did evil in ignorance, and thereafter repented, and amended (his conduct), lo! He is Oft-Forgiving, Most Merciful" (6:54). Also, in a famous Hadith, *al-Qudsi*, God states, "My mercy precedes my wrath."

Most unexpected and therefore most powerful is the Qur'an's oft-repeated understanding of God's response to the worship of the Golden Calf (2:50–56, 2:90–92, 7:148–158, 20:83–98). Even though this would seem to have been the worst sin by the entire People of Israel against God in the whole Wilderness journey—the one in which it would have seemed God would be least merciful—God forgave the community and there was no rain of violent attack on the calf creators, as is described by the Torah.

Mercifulness is also a key quality of prophets. For instance, God in the Qur'an tells Prophet Muhammad: "We sent you as a mercy to all worlds" (21:107). Indeed, there is a traditional story that Moses was declared a prophet after he had shown compassion to a ewe lamb that ran off to the desert and fell down exhausted. He compassionately said, "O hapless one, whither are you fleeing? Whom do you fear?" Afterward, he picked her up and carried her back to the flock.

Then God said to the angels: "Saw ye with tenderness [how] my servant treated that dumb ewe? Because he took trouble and harmed not the ewe, but rather had mercy on her, (I declare) by My glory that I will raise him up and make him My interlocutor; I will grant him prophet-hood and send him a book, and as long as the world exists, his name will be spoken."[1]

Besides reminding us that God is most forgiving, compassionate, and merciful, the Qur'an asks Muslims to be forgiving and compassionate to all creatures: animals, plants, and humans. This is also evident in the verse "Those who believe and urge each other to steadfastness and urge each other to compassion … those are the Companions of the Right Hand" (Qur'an 90:17–18).

Thus, Muslims cannot be insensitive to the suffering of other beings (physical, economic, psychological, or emotional), nor can they be cruel to any creature. They cannot torture, inflict suffering, or willfully hurt another human being irrespective of gender, ethnicity, or religious origins. The story of the Exodus in the Qur'an also reinforces this message by condemning oppression and emphasizing forgiveness, mercy, and compassion.

The Penitent Pharaoh

Perhaps the most momentous difference between the biblical and Qur'anic accounts of the Exodus is that according to the Quran, Pharaoh himself exclaimed in the last moment, as the Red Sea closed upon him, "I believe that there is no God but Him in whom the Children of Israel believe, and I am of those who submit to God" (Qur'an 10:90).

God responds to him by saying, "Now! When before you rebelled and were of the evildoers? But today we will save you in your body, so you may be a sign for those who come after" (Qur'an 10:91–92). Was Pharaoh's repentance accepted and was he forgiven—even though he was the symbol and archetype of evil, oppression, and rebellion against God—or was he condemned to hell?

Islamic scholars, philosophers, and mystics pondered the faith and fate of Pharaoh, realizing that there is a Pharaoh within all of us. Some scholars argued that Pharaoh did not believe sincerely and therefore was not forgiven, while others argued that God had granted Pharaoh belief and he died as a believer, pure and cleansed of his sins because God's mercy is infinite. For instance, in his book *Fusus al-Hiqam*, Ibn al-Arabi argued that God "made him a sign of His loving-kindness to whomever He wishes, so that no one may despair of the mercy of God. For indeed, no one but despairing folk despair of the spirit of God" (12:87).[2] Had Pharaoh been despairing, he would not have hastened to believe.

Jalal al-Din al-Dawwani and others also considered that the real issue was the breadth of divine mercy, which excludes no one who sincerely repents. In fact, the Qur'an undoubtedly states that God's mercy extends even to those who have done evil: "As for those who do evil, and later repent and have faith, such shall find their Lord All-Forgiving, All-Compassionate after [they repent and believe]" (7:153).

Pharaoh represents our carnal soul, our ego (*nafs*), which is arrogant, stubborn, and too proud to admit mistakes and submit to the will of God. Through the image of Pharaoh, the Qur'an warns us against our own *nafs* and calls us to become *muslim* (which means "one who submits to the will of God").

Therefore the Qur'anic story of Moses and Exodus clearly warns Muslims today against oppression, violence, corruption, and arrogance, reminding them that we all have a Pharaoh within us. Even when faced with injustice and persecution Muslims need to be just, compassionate, and patient.

But neither does the Qur'an ask Muslims to stay idle and accept injustice. On the contrary, the Qur'an asks Muslims to work hard and strive to ensure justice for all through active, creative, nonviolent ways that would restore harmony among God's creation. In this process, justice, compassion, mercy, and forgiveness should be central to the way Muslims deal with our current problems and conflicts, as the Qur'an explicitly states that God prefers forgiveness: "The recompense of an injury is the like thereof: but whosoever forgives and thereby brings about a reestablishment of harmony, his reward is with God; and God loves not the wrongdoers" (42:40) and "Repel evil [not with evil] but something that is better" (41:34). Adds the commentator Amin Ahsan Islahi, "That is, with forgiveness and amnesty."

Prophesying to the Prophet

There is another important difference in the Qur'anic account of the Exodus from that of the Bible: the Qur'an reports (*Sura al-Kahf*, Qur'an 18:65) on a companion of Moses named al-Khidr ("the Green One"). Al-Khidr constantly challenged Moses, first asking Moses to swear not to question him if he acted in ways that Moses found strange. Moses agreed, yet on three occasions did violate his vow. Finally al-Khidr explained his actions—which at first seemed unethical—as meeting a higher ethical need that was not at first apparent. For example, he destroyed a ship—and later explained to Moses that it was to protect those who were to sail in it from the hands of a piratical ruler.

Al-Khidr's function in the story seems to be that he instructed Moses in patience and forbearance even when Moses saw al-Khidr's acts as impulsive and himself acted impulsively, challenging al-Khidr despite his oath not to do so. Al-Khidr seems to have been teaching Moses to take the long view. Perhaps his very presence—even more than the explicit content of his teaching, the fact that he taught a great prophet—reminds us that even the great prophets needed to learn from their companions on the journey, and that just as there is an aspect of Pharaoh in everyone, so is there an aspect of the prophet in everyone.

Today, the story of ancient pharaonic Egypt seems to repeat itself in our experience. Wars, natural and man-made disasters like the ancient plagues—such as hurricanes, earthquakes, wildfires, tsunamis, oil spills, floods, extinction of species, changing weather patterns, and epidemics—plague our globe.

All around the world, oppressive and tyrannical systems and regimes inflict injustice and undermine human dignity. Higher levels of stress associated with the demands of contemporary lifestyles take a toll on the social and cultural fabric, leading to increased local and international violence. Pervasive hate, intolerance, and zealotry result in unimaginable cruelty. Vicious cycles of revenge and violence conflate victims and victimizers. In this chaotic world, Muslims are both victims and victimizers.

From Somalia to Afghanistan, from Iraq to Pakistan, many of the wars and violence today take place in the Muslim world. Bombs explode in the middle of cities, killing many innocent people, inflicting more pain and suffering. Poverty, corruption, and oppression cause more frustration. Violence and conflict in these societies lead to many environmental calamities, which in turn add to the conflict and violence.

Scarred by colonialist policies and exploitation, various Muslim groups have grown increasingly impatient and intolerant, responding to internal and external threats and criticism with violence. These reactions, however, are increasing anti-Muslim sentiment around the world. Mutual anger, mistrust, and resentment only serve to escalate the rift between the Muslim and non-Muslim communities. Then how should Muslims respond to violence, oppression, injustice, and under-development? Where do Muslims need to look for guidance in order to navigate through these difficult times?

Prophetic Patience and Persistence

The Qur'an, as the Divine Word, containing signs (*ayah*) and guidance from God, has always been the primary source for Muslims to find the "right path" (*al-sirat al-mustaqim*). The Qur'an includes theological statements, prophecies, and legal and ethical injunctions. But many of its messages are also transmitted by stories, especially stories of the prophets, like Moses, who came before Prophet Muhammad. These stories of the prophets—often told in the form of dialogue between God Almighty and Prophet Muhammad—play a central role in the Qur'anic narrative to provide Muslims with moral and spiritual guidance.

The Qur'an clearly states that both the Prophet and Muslims must learn from the examples presented in these stories as indicated in the verses "Bear patiently what they say, and remember Our servant David, the man of might; he was penitent" (38:17) and "And all what we relate to thee of the tidings of the messengers is that whereby We strengthen thy hearth: in these there has come to thee the truth and an admonition and a reminder to believers" (11:120).

The Qur'anic narrative—especially the narrative of the Exodus from pharaonic Egypt and the prophetic career of Moses—makes it clear that these stories aim to warn against wrongdoing, to strengthen the faith of Muslims, and to inspire patience but not passivity when faced with oppression, violence, and danger.

46

Exodus in African America

A Great Camp Meeting

By Vincent Harding

The magnificent biblical account of deliverance has entered into the African American religious and political experience, including my own. It is our joint ownership of that story that has helped to develop the strength and beauty of our own relationship in retelling the story in this book—and in the wider world as well, opening us all to shared dreams and common work over the years, offering the promise of much more to come.

For me, there is no way to approach the archetypal Exodus story without hearing in my heart and mind the powerful, evocative voice of Paul Robeson, singing these words:

> When Israel was in Egypt's land
> Let my people go
> Oppressed so hard they could not stand
> Let my people go
> Go down, Moses
> Way down in Egypt's land
> Tell old Pharaoh
> Let my people go.

Much of the African American appropriation of the story is fully gathered here. Beginning somewhere early in our own centuries-long experience with slavery in this strangely chosen land, the children of Africa clearly recognized that we were living the biblical story, that the cruelly forced labor experience of the Israelites in a strange land was unmistakably our story. And, as we did with so much of our lives, we expressed what we felt, what we knew, what we experienced, in the profound and creative beauty of our songs, songs pouring out of the people, songs that told the ancient story from our perspective, songs that stretched out our hands and our lives to the God of the Exodus and declared with great certainty that we, too, were authentic children of the Divine Deliverer.

Of course, Robeson was a perfect carrier of the tradition. Son of a once enslaved father who knew that deliverance most often required his own active participation ("Oh let us all from bondage flee," the first singers called) and who had run away from slavery in North Carolina, the great, politically committed artist combined masterful singing of the Exodus songs with persistent, costly work for social justice. As a result, even though he did not identify with the formal Black church appropriation of the story in the same ways that his ordained father and brother did, Robeson offered great, sacrificial encouragement to many of us in this country and elsewhere who knew that the struggle against bondage, for great freedom, continued into the twentieth (and twenty-first) century. For he reminded us that we are all ordained in the divine service of human freedom and compassionate justice.

In a very real sense then, my dear friend and sister Fannie Lou Hamer was a faithful child of Paul Robeson. When, in her early fifties, she entered the ranks of the southern freedom movement in her native Mississippi, her experience as a child of the Black churches meant that she was deeply grounded in the Exodus story and in the songs Black people had created to claim and retell it. She, too, had a magnificent singing voice and was one of the movement's most powerful song leaders and encouragers. At almost every mass meeting in the dangerous organizing days when women, men, and children (often led by teenagers and twentysomethings) were breaking out of the bondage of sharecropping, the terrorism of violent white supremacy, and the shackles of fear, Mrs. Hamer (as everyone called her) would lead the singing, usually including her own version of the old Christmas spiritual "Go Tell It on the Mountain." And instead of the traditional next phrase "... that Jesus Christ is born," she boldly transformed it to "Go tell it on the mountain ... to let my people go." By then, hundreds of years after the first songs of deliverance were raised among us, Mrs. Hamer reminded the people not only of their own claim to the Exodus story, but encouraged them to move bravely into their own vital roles in the liberation process. (Like Robeson and like her own younger sister–freedom singer Bernice Johnson Reagon, beloved Fannie Lou offered more than song leadership as encouragement. For she, too, lived her songs, continually sang them in jail, refusing to be silenced by the brutal violence of her jailers.)

Grounded as she was in the story, Mrs. Hamer, with her fourth-grade sharecropper's education, became a perfect companion for the college-educated, sophisticated master teacher of the movement, Ella Baker. For Hamer knew that Baker was right when she addressed the courageous Black folks and their white allies who met in Jackson in 1964 to give formal organizational reality to the Mississippi Freedom Democratic Party (MFDP). As the delegates met, anticipating the coming Democratic National Convention to be held in Atlantic City, New Jersey, one of their central purposes was to launch a legal challenge to the all-white, segregated "regular" Mississippi party. Indeed the MFDP organizers planned to seek to replace the delegates of the segregated Democrats at the national convention. In the course of the MFDP organizational gathering, Ms. Baker (as she was almost always called by younger movement leaders everywhere) urged the delegates to be willing "to open your membership to the children of your white landowners, as long as those children are prepared to subscribe to your principles."

At that point, only a few of the white children were ready, but their numbers would increase, and it was clear that Baker, following the African American traditions, had not only claimed the right to the Exodus story, but again was redefining it, re-creating it; indeed she was providing a radical, spirit-grounded revisioning of just who might share the Promised Land of a new Mississippi, a new America, a more perfect union.

Then, when Mrs. Hamer formally led the uninvited Black and white MFDP delegation onto the floor of the national Democratic Party convention, she brought with her the old song and Exodus story, now purified by the blood, sweat, and tears of the Mississippi movement and the heroic testimony of her own life. In that setting, standing against the opposition of President Johnson (and his determination to be the center of attention), this child of Paul Robeson and sister of Victoria Gray, this carrier of the memories not only of her enslaved forebearers, but of her recently murdered brothers, James Chaney, Andrew Goodman, and Mickey Schwerner, once again embodied and gave voice to the courage and historic determination of our people to move relentlessly toward freedom, revisioning the Promised Land as we march.

For not only did Mrs. Hamer seize the time at Atlantic City and lead members and friends of the MFDP delegation to sing and proclaim to the entire nation, "Go tell it on the mountain ... to let my people go," but she also taught the wisdom that had been painfully, joyfully acquired through all the terror and hope of Mississippi's long and costly wilderness struggle, representing the meaning of the southern movement's revival of the Exodus experience. Going beyond the music, for all those who could hear, the wisdom and reformulated hope of the new exodus were best expressed by Mrs. Hamer when a journalist at the convention asked her if she and her movement comrades had been carrying on their costly freedom struggle in order "to gain equality with the white man." Speaking for her ancestors, her co-workers, and her children's children (and her white landowner's children?), Mrs. Hamer straightened up her five-feet, four-inches-tall frame and replied, "No. What would I look like fighting for equality with the white man? I don't want to go down that low. I want the true democracy that will raise me and the white man up—raise America up."

She had made it clear for all who could hear. The former captives were not only determined to continue to move toward freedom, but they were committed to place their own definition on that word. At their best the pilgrim marchers were resolved to carry out a seemingly impossible mission: to transform the land of their captivity into a Promised Land of great hope and boundless human possibilities for us and for many unexpected others. In that transformative summer of 1964, such a vision was often hard to maintain, just as the first Exodus people found it difficult to keep their eyes on the prize of freedom, found it sometimes nearly impossible to believe in the promises of their Divine Deliverer. (Just as many members of your own part of the community must live amid a cloud of tormenting questions, denials, and fears after the Holocaust, my dear friends.)

But the spirited, sacrificial energies of the Mississippi freedom fighters and their allies in the Atlantic City convention hall, and across the nation, began to force open a new way before the final gavel came down. For the national Democratic Party officially committed itself to new rules that would make it impossible for the South's lily-white, segregated state delegations ever to be seated without challenge again. At the same time, courageous voter registration campaigns, especially in the South's Black Belt communities, played a crucial role in changing the character of the Democratic Party (both as a result of the influx of Black voters and the departure of many southern whites into the Republican ranks).

Even then, no one, not even Mrs. Hamer, Ms. Baker, or Bob Moses, nor any of their magnificent Mississippi versions of the Exodus people, could have dreamed then that the door they pushed open in Atlantic City would one day reemerge, even more amazingly ajar, in Denver, my own city—of all places—to become an unexpected passageway, creating dramatic space for the Democratic nomination of a son of Africa and America to become the party's presidential candidate in 2008. And of course, we know how *that* story is still being created, must be continuously created, by us all, with all the human complications, surprises, disappointments, dangers, and amazing possibilities that the Torah has taught us to expect.

Now I ask, what are the new songs? Will we still be able to create them and share them, as we once did (as we still do) with freedom seekers, democracy makers, all over the world? (Will I ever experience again anything like the amazing joy I felt in 1989 as the liberating people of Berlin tore down the wall, brick by brick, singing their freedom work song to the tune of "Go Tell It on the Mountain"?)

Of course, there is no way that we could explore the African American connections to the Torah's central story of deliverance without a deep encounter with my friend and brother, Martin King. For while he rarely referred to himself in the Moses role, Black people of all kinds—all over the country—especially those related to the churches, clearly chose to picture him that way in the post–Montgomery Bus Boycott years. In a sense, on that last night of his life, Martin connected his community's vision of its historic place in the iconic Exodus story with his own ever-deepening sense of foreboding. For he was clearly wrestling with thoughts concerning the ultimate cost he would need to pay for his insistence on speaking and living truth to all the war-making, empire-building, poor-people-neglecting American pharaohs. Martin was also unflinching in his recognition that anyone who insisted on following Rabbi Jesus, choosing to stand in solidarity with garbage workers, sharecroppers, maids and porters, Appalachian poor people, and Native American distressed communities—and every other kind and color of poor and exploited people—could not count on longevity.

So, together we can recollect so carefully the painful crying out of dear Martin when he closed his last lamentation/exhortation in Memphis, seizing the hope of Moses's experience, speaking in the language of a disciple of Jesus:

> Like anybody, I would like to live a long life. Longevity has its place. But I'm not concerned about that now. I just want to do God's will. And He's allowed me to go up to the mountain. And I've looked over. And I've seen the promised land. I may not get there with you. But I want you to know tonight that we, as a people, will get to the promised land.

In many ways, the words that followed, those last words before Martin slumped into the arms of his co-workers and sat down on his chair that final night of his life—these words might be understood as his own last valiant attempt to face the harshness of what he sensed might well be coming, the arrival of the relentless bullet that had been tracking him for such a long time.

And, like the perennial pastor that he was, he was surely hoping to encourage the people—as well as himself—when he said:

> I'm happy tonight. I'm not worried about anything. I'm not fearing any man. Mine eyes have seen the glory of the coming of the Lord.

As I consider those last words (a familiar crescendo that Martin often brought in from Julia Ward Howe's "Battle Hymn of the Republic"), a somewhat unorthodox thought comes to my mind. I want to take the risk of presuming on the deep brotherly love that Martin and I shared and thereby feel free to suggest that there was another Exodus-grounded African American spiritual that we must hear at the end, a song that Martin loved to quote, one that I often think of as I watch the films that captured that last night. (I was not in Memphis on April 3, 1968.) For only the memory of our friendship frees me more than forty years later to approach my dear brother and urge him to share with us again that other song of the marching, freedom-bound people:

> Walk together, children
> Don't you get weary
> There's a great camp meeting in the Promised Land.

Perhaps in the more than forty years of sojourn since that last night in Memphis (in the more than four hundred years since our earliest days of enslavement in this land), perhaps we have learned that the "Promised Land" is not so much a location, constrained by time and space, as it is a process, possibly an ongoing "great camp meeting," transforming us all as we seek to transform all around us into the best possible vision of our freedom-singing, freedom-loving, freedom-seeking, freedom-sharing ancestors.

If that is the living reality of our Exodus movement, then we may dare to respond to our beloved brother and remind him of how often he encouraged us not to get weary, how powerful was his invitation to the "great camp meeting." And then, loving him, enjoying him, displaying some of his own puckish sense of humor, we can surely ask, "What you mean, jelly bean? What you mean, 'I may not get there with you'? Who ever heard of a great camp meeting without you, without Fannie Lou, without Ella (even if she does give you a hard time sometime), without Bayard and his great tenor voice. You all *are* the camp meeting. And so are your beloved Yoki and Coretta. And yes, of course, sister Ann Braden (to make sure all the freedom-loving white folks are there) and dear Tom Merton and June Jordan (holding down the poet's corners) and, of course, your sister (and my dear wife) Rosemarie, and all the blessed children, starting with Addie May and the other Birmingham girls. Your magnificent marching (and praying) companion Rabbi Heschel is surely with the camp meeting, praying not only with his legs, as he once said after walking side by side with you, but with every part of his body. And did you ever meet Bawa Muhaiyadeen, the great Sufi mystic? Your spirits belong with each other in the campground.

"Yes, we're asking, what you mean, Martin? You know Gandhi and Dorothy Day will be asking for you, and Stokely/Kwame as well, with his big, loving grin, knowing how much you loved him. Do you hear Robeson and Nina, and feel Howard Thurman quieting us all? How, Martin, how are you going to tell Dr. Benjamin Mays, 'I may not get there with you'? And don't even think about trying it on Daddy King and your mama. Walk together, with us, Martin. Don't get weary. The camp meeting is going on, and we are the ones we've been waiting for. We have work to do in the great tasks of compassionate human fulfillment. We are the ones, including you, brother Martin, including you. There's a great camp meeting already begun. Let us continue."

The Beloved Community you called for, Martin, a marvelous community of hope! I'm very glad that we are the ones we've been waiting for. Let's continue the journey toward freedom.

Freedom Journey for the Planet?

The biblical story of the Freedom Journey out of Egypt taught us the two-step dance of God, the dance in which the steps of control and community must keep the world in balance. In the biblical story, Pharaoh as an organizing principle made it possible to nourish a stricken people even when a disastrous famine erupted. Power protected the people.

But when Pharaoh overran all boundaries of power and so toppled the balance of the world, the disaster of his control run amok led to the second step in the dance—formation of a new kind of community at Sinai and in the Wilderness.

The struggle for freedom from Caesar repeated the dance in a different way. Again, Rome brought order to an unruly world, economic "globalization" to disparate local societies, new science and cultural interchange to isolated provincial backwaters. But when successive Caesars and their legions made the Roman Empire into a juggernaut, they threw the world and the dance of God out of balance. This time two new kinds of community—Rabbinic Judaism and Christianity—emerged to set the balance right, along with the new community of Islam.

Today, What Are Pharaoh, Caesar, Sinai, Pentecost, the Night of Power?

Today we are in the midst of a third version of the two-step dance. Now it is Modernity, modern corporations, and the modern superstates that have brought unheard-of abundance, public health, successful science, and cultural interchange to large parts of the human race. They have encouraged transformations in the relationships of women and men; in family life and child rearing; in the transmission of information through mass media; in the sheer numbers of the human race—in every case, a boon to some; a curse to others.

And these same institutions have killed tens of millions of people in wars and genocides and have threatened the web of life upon the planet.

As a result, many who have benefited and suffered from their doings have come to believe these institutions have, like Pharaoh and Caesar before them, overstepped the bounds of power, thrown the whole world into earthquake. And now we see some of these people struggling to shape new forms of community adequate to repair what they see as newly radical imbalance.

When the Jewish people felt the disintegration of its customary forms under the pressure of the Roman Empire and faced the question of how to live free under Rome, the ancient biblical tales of winning freedom and reshaping community became not only a nostalgic memory but an urgent challenge.

Now that the classic forms of Jewish peoplehood and all the other ancient sacred communities of Earth are disintegrating under the pressure of Modernity, not only Jews but all the peoples face the question of how to secure the benefits provided by the benevolent aspects of modernity, at the same time achieving their freedom from modern forms of domination and shaping new forms of their communities.

For Jews and perhaps for all the nations, two prophetic teachings light up with urgent meaning—two lines about the Exodus that the ancient Rabbis never thought belonged in their Haggadah:

> "To Me," declares the Breath of Life, "are the Children of Israel not just like the Children of the Ethiopians? Have I not brought Israel up from the land of Egypt, and also the Philistines from Kaphtor and Aram from Kir?"
>
> AMOS 9:7

> In that day Israel shall be the third with Egypt and with Assyria, a blessing in the midst of the earth; for the Infinite Breath of Life has blessed them, saying: "Blessed be Egypt My people, and Assyria the work of My hands, and Israel My inheritance."
>
> ISAIAH 19:24–25

To the ancient Rabbis, these insights were irrelevant. The Jewish people stood alone, and if other peoples were ever to deserve deliverance and blessing, it would be far, far into the unfathomable future.

But now that future has come. As Amos (8:8) prophesies:

> Then shall not the whole earth shake, and all that dwell upon it mourn? Shall not all seas rise like the Nile—yes, surge and subside like the Nile?

Yes, in the generation when thousands of species die more swiftly than ever before during the life span of the human race, when the climate of the earth itself is changing, yes, that time has come.

And not only the time for new versions of crossing of the Sea, but the time to stand again at "Sinai." All the nations need new forms for their own communities and also new ways to share community with each other and with all the life-forms of the earth. Not only with crocodiles and krill, with redwoods and rare earths, but even with carbon dioxide and the snows of Kilimanjaro.

There are two aspects to this question: What does it mean to retell in new ways the stories as they were told on Passover and Shavuot? And what does it mean to redo in new ways the actual experience of Exodus and Sinai, liberation and community building? Are these the same question, as in some sense they became for Rabbinic Judaism and the Christian church? Or do study and action, memory and desire, the word and the body, stand across a chasm from each other now?

New Retellings of the Story

For the Rabbis, reframing the story was itself a way of reframing the community. Where once Passover had meant gathering millions of people, dragging a lamb-offering to God, it became a gathering of family and friends in homes, offering God words of midrash and prayer. Where Shavuot had once meant a gathering at the Temple to celebrate the spring wheat harvest, now it meant gathering in synagogues to celebrate the Torah. Words became both the medium and the message of a whole new path of peoplehood. Celebration of the Seder became a way of actually reasserting freedom in an unfree society where Jews felt buffeted on all sides. And the reframing of Shavuot strengthened the notion of an Oral Torah, of a moment when all Israel could stand again at Sinai and hear the squiggles on the letters of the Torah shape a new form of community.

But today, it is *all* the traditional communal forms that feel buffeted. Even beyond the human race, the whole weave of life-forms is torn and tearing—the weave within which the human race has lived for a million years. The reassertion of freedom will require new words and new ways of connecting words, but it will also require new challenges in body as well as words.

Joining Words to Body

Can the two forms be united, instead of having to be separate as body Judaism of the Bible was separated from word Judaism of the Talmud?

We are beginning to experiment.

In 1969, on the first anniversary of the death of Martin Luther King, which fell on the third night of Passover, about eight hundred Jews and Christians, white and Black, joined in the basement of a Black church in Washington, D.C., to celebrate a new kind of Seder—the Freedom Seder, it was called. The story of liberation from the ancient Pharaoh was told alongside stories of modern liberation, especially the struggle of Black Americans to resist slavery and racism and segregation in America.

The event was unprecedented because it interwove the ancient Jewish story with a modern non-Jewish story. It was also unprecedented in that it was itself a political event.

The next year, focusing on the U.S. war in Vietnam as well as the struggle against racism and on the Soviet Union's attack on freedom at home and in Eastern Europe, hundreds rose from the table at a Freedom Seder and marched to the White House, where they reenacted all but the last, most lethal of the ancient Ten Plagues—releasing blood, frogs, mice onto the White House grounds—and then marched toward the Soviet Embassy, which they regarded as a twin pharaoh.

Then an even bigger crowd—about four thousand—gathered in the field house at Cornell University for another Freedom Seder that was even more a political act in the deepest sense. This Seder celebrated two Catholic priests who had gone underground and were being hunted by the FBI because they had used direct nonviolent resistance to oppose the Vietnam War. One of them, Father Daniel Berrigan, actually rose from underground during the Seder itself and for a few hours established his freedom not only in words but also in body.

These events used the forms of Jewish festival celebration to challenge the powerful in public, not in private homes where freedom was limited to the dialogue of searching questions. These Freedom Seders sparked the writing of Haggadot seeking women's liberation, of animal-rights Haggadot, of Haggadot honoring the resistance of the mothers of Argentina to the military junta that "disappeared" their dissident husbands and children. They even sparked "Seders of the Children of Abraham," drawing on the Abrahamic saga rather than the Passover saga, to seek peace between Israelis and Palestinians.

They also presaged the use of Tu B'Shvat, the midwinter Jewish festival for the Rebirthday of the Trees, to challenge corporations that were logging ancient redwoods and despoiling the Everglades; the use of Sukkot prayers pleading with God to send rain and heal the rivers of the earth, to challenge General Electric for its poisoning of the Hudson River; the use of Tisha B'Av, the day of mourning for the destruction of the ancient Temples, to confront the U.S. Senate's failure to deal with the worldwide climate crisis that is endangering the universal Temple: earth itself.

And all these events—the Freedom Seders, the redwood plant-ins, the grieving fasts on the steps of the Capitol—involved not only Jews but also people from religious, spiritual, and ethical communities who were not Jewish.

Meanwhile, inside the Soviet Union, an old Jewish custom of dancing in the streets on the festival of Simchat Torah took on new life. Traditionally, dancers had carried Torah scrolls to celebrate the annual reading of the end and the beginning of the Torah. Traditionally, the dancing had been within the Jewish ghettos and neighborhoods. But suddenly the dancing spilled out into the public streets of Moscow and other Soviet cities, and the celebrations came "out of the closet" into public space. They became events not only of internal self-assertion but also of public affirmations of freedom and community, challenging oppressive behavior by the government.

Festivals in Multicultural Public Space

Why were all these festival celebrations coming out of the closet? For Jews, because the Rabbinic formulation of "nook-and-cranny" Judaism celebrated in ghettos no longer made sense. After the Holocaust, it became much clearer that there were no nooks and crannies.

The Jews of Europe did not threaten any empire; there was no Great Rebellion against the great powers, as there had been in 135 CE. Yet these "nook-and-cranny" Jews were annihilated. Indeed, during the next two generations it became clear that the great corporate powers of the world would not leave space even for the inoffensive Native Indigenous communities of the Amazon Valley or the Amish of central Pennsylvania (who were poised to be the first victims of a Three Mile Island nuclear meltdown, even though they did not use electric power).

At the same time, in the shadow of the Holocaust new and unexpected allies began to emerge who shared values of liberation and community that Jews also affirmed. Sometimes these alliances were explicitly on Jewish themes or on what had been Jewish cultural and religious turf. In America, for example, committed Christians and secular liberals joined demonstrations on behalf of freedom for Soviet Jews.

During the 1960s, after the Second Vatican Council of the Roman Catholic Church abandoned the charge of deicide against the Jewish people and opened up new relational possibilities, grassroots groups of Roman Catholics, especially in America, began to experiment with holding Passover Seders as a way of getting in touch with the Jewishness of Jesus. The more they did this, the more they also got in touch with the Jewishness of modern Jews.

Most Jews had almost always observed the Seder only with other Jews, as a kind of tribal family celebration. It was, after all, a retelling of the liberation of the Jewish people; why would anyone else be interested, or welcome?

But increasingly in the 1950s and 1960s, many American Jews were becoming friends with American Christians. They began to invite their friends who were not Jewish to join in the Seder.

And then in the 1960s, southern Black songs that had drawn on the biblical story of the Exodus in plaintive hope of freedom from slavery and segregation took on new urgency, new vigor, new militancy in a renewed struggle for liberation.

Some Jews—facing neighborhoods where no Jews could live, professions and businesses and clubs for "Gentiles only," and colleges where there was a "Jewish quota"—felt themselves only newly and hesitantly welcome in the American community. Some of them began to feel their own hopes and interests intertwined with those of the Black community that was even more uncertain of its welcome into "America."

And some Jews—including both rabbis who were deeply committed to Jewish learning, and some young folk who had found their synagogues boring enclaves of the past—were drawn by the passion for liberation they saw in the sit-in movement and in many Black southern ministers, typified by Dr. Martin Luther King.

Biblical passages, prayer, even religion as a whole took on new and electrifying meaning when prayer moved into the streets and was greeted with police dogs, when passages from Amos and Isaiah rolled off the tongues of people on their way to jail for freedom's sake.

In the summer of 1964, two young Jews and a young Black who had begun to work for voting rights in Mississippi were kidnapped and murdered—together—by the Ku Klux Klan. In the spring of 1965, in the voting-rights march near Selma, Alabama, Dr. King stood side by side with Rabbi Abraham Joshua Heschel, who astonished and exhilarated many young Jews by saying that he felt as if his legs had been praying on that march.

Confronting Power Anew

At the very same moment in 1965, teach-ins against the Vietnam War erupted on many American campuses. Many young people who had been involved somehow in the movement for civil rights began to see the U.S. government as an imperial conqueror because of its growing involvement in making war against Vietnam. By 1967, Dr. King was standing beside Rabbi Heschel at Riverside Church in New York City as leaders of "Clergy and Laity Concerned About Vietnam." In his speech there on April 4, Dr. King called the United States the greatest purveyor of violence in the world at that time.

So from these strands of transformation were emerging an amalgam of feelings and ideas that could easily fit into the vision of a people called by God to resist a modern pharaoh. Not the United States alone, but also a Soviet Union that sent tanks to smash the vision of "Prague Spring" and "socialism with a human face" in Czechoslovakia.

By May and June of 1968 and then 1970, uprisings of Black communities all across America in the wake of Dr. King's murder, the outbreak of massive student-worker unrest in France, the Czech uprising against Soviet rule, widespread strikes by American students after the U.S. government's invasion of Cambodia—all these gave the sense that new forms of action were spreading around the world in ways that could shake governments and powerful corporations. Pharaoh tottered.

And one version of pharaoh did fall—the Soviet Union vanished with but a minimum of bloodshed, as millions of people in a dozen countries went into the streets. The Berlin Wall dissolved as the Red Sea had divided.

But it soon became apparent that other forms of "pharaoh" had reasserted their top-down power and were doing even more damage to the fabric of human communities around the world and to the fabric of the planetary ecosystem. Scientists reported that dependence on burning fossil fuels to power modern civilization was endangering the global climate system. By 2010, catastrophic floods and droughts, rising sea levels and melting sheets of ice were fulfilling their warnings.

Religious Restoration

It might have been expected that the multireligious and transnational experiments toward new forms of community that emerged in the 1960s and 1970s would grow deeper and broader in the face of these developments. But instead, there was a wave of inward-looking, xenophobic energy in many religious communities and xenophobic violence by a number of national governments against various religious communities.

- In the United States, right-wing Christianity took on great political power—opposed to feminism, to governmental supports for the poor, to reductions of military spending even after the end of the Cold War and the collapse of the Soviet Union; ready to treat Muslims, Hispanics, and gay people as pariahs.
- In Israel, the union of religious fervor and state power produced militant Jewish settlers in Palestinian territories and the readiness to use military force not only for self-defense but for stringent measures of occupation, blockade, and invasion.
- In the Muslim world, especially in its Arabic- and Farsi-speaking segments, nationalist movements against Western, Israeli, and Russian power increasingly invoked Muslim rhetoric and adopted terrorist attacks on civilians as a favorite tactic, at first

directed chiefly against Israel and then against the United States, other Western countries, and Russia. In Iran, a revolutionary Islamic government became more and more repressive toward its own citizens and more hostile to what it saw as overweening Western and Israeli military might.

- Then, partly in response to the murderous attacks of September 11, 2001, carried out by self-proclaimed Muslims, and partly in the hope of getting major strategic and economic advantage in the oil-rich Middle East, the United States undertook wars against two Muslim-majority countries, increased its support for the Israeli occupation of Muslim-majority Palestinian territories, undertook deadly attacks on Pakistanis, threatened war against Iran, intervened against anti-Western Islamic movements in such other Muslim-majority countries as Yemen and Somalia, and experienced a wave of Islamophobia at home.

- In South Asia, Hindu religion and identity were mobilized by new political parties in India into a wave of religious nationalism in opposition to the more secular definition of India espoused by the Congress Party, and the rivalry between India and Pakistan over control of Kashmir took on increasingly religious rhetoric and fervor on both sides.

- In China, the government carried out brutal attacks on Buddhism in Tibet and on Muslim minorities in the northwest.

- In parts of Africa, life-threatening droughts and famines became the occasion for grasping for scarce food and farms by genocidal attacks by one ethno-religious community against another.

Religious Renewal

Yet there were also signs of new commitments to create new networks and communities transcending boundaries of religion, race, and nation:

- In 2009, to honor the fortieth anniversary of the Freedom Seder—forty years, perhaps a pregnant pause—again people gathered in a Black church in Washington, D.C., to celebrate the coming of Passover. But this time, Muslims, Buddhists, and a few Wiccans joined with Jews and Christians; and this time, the Haggadah was called a "Seder for the Earth." On its cover was the graphic of a globe made all of *matzah*, representing a new earth-wide consciousness of the need to turn the bread of affliction into a wider taste of freedom. And its focus was a call to end the repressive power of top-down corporations that were bringing new plagues upon the planet, as Pharaoh did long before.

- In the cathedral of Uppsala, Sweden, one hundred religious leaders from around the earth gathered for an Interfaith Summit on the Climate Crisis—leaders of communities that had warred for centuries explored how to work together for the planet's sake. The interfaith service honored in conventional ways the unique, specific prayers and practices of each tradition—strung together, one by one. Then in the midst of this single-file liturgy, a parade without a center, came a symbol that spoke for none of them—and all of them: a great green globe of moss, rolled down the center aisle in joyful reminder of why these former enemies had gathered.

- In the United States, multireligious and interfaith alliances, once almost wholly limited to Christian-Jewish connections, began to include Muslims and to actively oppose a wave of fear and rage aimed by some Americans toward Islam, American Muslims, and Muslims almost anywhere.

- In the Mediterranean, Jews, Christians, Muslims, and secular atheists joined to create "Freedom Flotillas," using mostly nonviolence to challenge the Israeli government's blockade of Gaza.

- In several thousand places in more than 150 countries, people gathered on a single day in 2009 and again in 2010 to demand deep cuts in the emissions of carbon dioxide that are bringing on a global climate crisis.

- The major science-fiction feature films *Avatar* and *WALL-E* and the documentary *An Inconvenient Truth*—challenging the destruction of earth's web of life—crossed all borders to win enormous audiences. (*Avatar* even hinted at a new amalgam of indigenous spirituality, hints of the Exodus story of the earth's rebellion against Pharaoh, and celebration of the Tree of Life evocative of Kabbalah.)

- Christian activists, with some Jewish allies, appealed to the biblical tradition of the Jubilee to press the World Bank to annul some debts owed by the poorest nations and by the same token to move away from lending to eco-destructive projects.

- The Internet began to offer hope of giving birth to a new sense of planetary community made up of many strands, each rooted in its own authenticity but ready to connect through overlapping electronic fringes.

All these are only hints of possibility. Their growth in the last generation may echo the Bible's story of the cluster of *Ivrim*, boundary crossers, Hebrews, who under the very nose of Pharaoh swiftly grew from seventy souls to a nascent newborn nation. These hints of possibility may—or may not—grow beyond the ability of the Tight and Narrow Place, *Mitzrayyim*, to contain their lively energy. We can expect attempts by those in power, like Pharaoh long ago, to drown these efforts in the cradle.

The need for a new form of planetary community seems clear. But the outcome is uncertain. We hear more questions than answers, and to hear deeply, heartfully, we may need to hush ourselves as the *Sh-sh-sh'ma* teaches us.

Questions—More Than the Seder's Four

Some questions that we hear from the stories we have reexamined:

- The midwives, Miriam, and Pharaoh's daughter are crucial to the beginning of the liberation story. Yet by the time of wandering in the Wilderness, the influence of women has been minimized. Can seeing the Exodus as birth help us make sure that women remain partners and leaders in our liberation struggles?
- Nonviolent civil disobedience plays an important part in the story, and even amid violence the stories remind us to honor and protect those who opt out of war and to purify those who take part in it. Can we learn from these stories to place far higher value on nonviolence as a means and goal of change?
- The story of the Ten Plagues emphasizes the close relationship between the freedom of human beings and the vitality of the web of life on earth. How can we integrate these stories in our own struggles toward freedom and community?
- The stories struggle to honor both the sacred individuality of people so focused on an inward "laser beam" of holiness that they cannot take part in communal celebration and the need of

the community for an all-embracing holiness. How can we define these boundaries and these connections today?

- The stories affirm edginess and fringes. How can we celebrate the inwardness and particular authenticity of each tradition while weaving threads of sacred connection between them?
- The stories seem to say that a new form of community can only emerge from an extraordinary shared experience—Sinai, Pentecost—that gives a new center to those who have been connecting only in a single-file procession. How could such a transformative center come to the myriad cultures and species of our planet?
- The stories teach that storytelling is crucial, if the stories are told with passion and with openness to midrash and revision. How can we speak and hear these stories with new depth and new excitement—new incitement?

As we comb through the ancient stories with ears more alert to hear their meaning, more than the Four Questions of the Haggadah will arise for us.

And these questions are central to our lives. For as the ancient Haggadah reminds us, in every generation some pyramidal power arises for destruction. And in every generation, every human being can join the Freedom Journey. Can—but will we choose to?

Acknowledgments

Among myriad beloved teachers in our lives, these names especially arise for us: Al Hajj Talib Abdur Rashid, Rebecca Alpert, Barbara Breitman, Saadi Shakur Chisti, Joan Chittister, David Cooper, Shoshana Cooper, Jeffrey Dekro, Marcia Falk, Laura Geller, Everett Gendler, Shefa Gold, Arlene Goldbard, Art Green, Jamie Hamilton, Vincent Harding, Iftekhar Hussain, Shaya Isenberg, Zia Inayat Khan, Liz Lerman, Michael Lerner, Mordechai Liebling, Anne McCarthy, Rachmiel O'Regan, Judith Plaskow, Marcia Prager, Jenny Rardin, Marc Raskin, Jeff Roth, Zalman Schachter-Shalomi, David Shneyer, Bob Smith, Bahira Sugarman, Esther Ticktin, Max Ticktin, Pat Tirone, Brian Walt, Howard Waskow, Grey Wolfe, and the dead who still live within us: Howard K. Beale, Dan Berman, William Sloane Coffin, Charles Curran, David Gracie, Paul Jacobs, Diane Levenberg, Shira Ruskay, Ira Silverman, David Wolfe-Blank, and our parents, Beatrice and Charles Berman, and Hannah and Henry Waskow.

We especially recommend two works that directly address the questions of this book: Martin Buber's *Moses*, a brilliant theological biography, and Michael Walzer's *Exodus and Revolution*, a powerful history of how the Exodus story has influenced many nationalist and social-class revolutionary movements.

More broadly, we have also learned from Martin Buber, *I and Thou*, *Paths in Utopia*, and *Pointing the Way*; Abraham Joshua Heschel, *The Sabbath*, *The Prophets*, and *Moral Grandeur and Spiritual Audacity* (edited by Susannah Heschel); Michael Lerner, *The Left Hand of God*; Marge Piercy, *He, She and It*; Judith Plaskow, *Standing Again at Sinai*; Zalman Schachter-Shalomi, *Paradigm Shift*; Ali Shariati, *Hajj*; Jim Wallis, *God's Politics*; and John Howard Yoder, *The Politics of Jesus*.

Wherever possible, we have drawn on Everett Fox's translations of the Hebrew Bible (sometimes with our own changes), because Fox tries hard to deliver the wordplays and breathing patterns of the Hebrew (see *The Five Books of Moses* [Schocken]).

We offer special thanks to Emily Wichland, Lauren Hill, and Stuart Matlins of Jewish Lights, whose wise editorial guidance has greatly enriched this book, and to Michael Bogdanow, whose art has enriched not only its cover but our hearts and souls.

The members of the board of The Shalom Center during the past six years and Nick Alpers, who was program coordinator of The Shalom Center, made it possible to turn many ideas, hopes, and wishes into living reality.

With each other we share the joy of having during the past two years of the writing of this book shared the depths of physical pain and the heights of spiritual, emotional, and intellectual connection.

May the Great Name—in which are these names and all the names of all the beings in the universe—bring joy and blessing to our teachers and their students and the students of their students, and to all who aim toward Wisdom, everywhere on earth. May they be blessed with peace and loving-kindness; with honorable and adequate livelihoods that arise from working not upon the backs of Earth or other human beings, but as part of earth and the human community; and with time to pause, to play, to sing, to love.

AOW and POB

Notes

8. Toward Freedom—or Toward Death?

1. See David Bakan, *The Duality of Human Existence* (Chicago: Rand McNally, 1966).

10. Who Hardened Pharaoh's Heart?

1. Andrew C. Revkin, "U.S. Sees Problems in Climate Change," *New York Times*, June 3, 2002.

2. Reuters, "Bush: Global Climate Report Is Bureaucratic Hot Air," June 5, 2002, www.bcas.net/EnvFeatures/ClimateChange/June2002/1%20to%2015.htm.

21. Sacred Time: The Seventh Year

1. See Everett Fox, trans., *The Five Books of Moses* (New York: Schocken, 1995).

33. From Genocide to Purification

1. See Penny Coleman, *Flashback: Posttraumatic Stress Disorder, Suicide, and the Lessons of War* (Boston: Beacon Press, 2006).

44. Exodus in the Life and Death of Jesus

1. For more detail on this understanding of the text, see these writings by Ched Myer: *Binding the Strong Man: A Political Reading of Mark's Story of Jesus* (Maryknoll, NY: Orbis Books, 2008); "The Gospel of the Cross Confronts the Powers: Mark's Passion Narrative," in *Consuming Passion: Why the Killing of Jesus Really Matters*, ed. Simon Barrow and Jonathan Bartley (London: Darton, Longman and Todd, 2005), pp. 61–73, which can also be found online at www.thewitness.org/agw/myers040704.html; *The Biblical Vision of Sabbath Economics* (Washington, DC: Tell the Word Press, 2001), chap. 2; and Ched Myers and Elaine Enns, *Ambassadors of Reconciliation*, vol. 1, *New Testament Reflections on Restorative Justice and Peacemaking* (Maryknoll, NY: Orbis Books, 2009), pp. 93–100. See also Marvin Wilson, *Our Father Abraham: Jewish Roots of the Christian Faith* (Grand Rapids, MI: Eerdmans, 1989), p. 251.

45. Exodus in the Qur'an

1. "The Story of Moses and the Lost Sheep," www.tebyan.net/Pearls_of_Wisdom/Anecdotates/2009/5/3/90917.html.

2. Ibn al-Arabi, *The Bezels of Wisdom* [Fusus al-Hiqam], trans. R. W. J. Austin (New York: Paulist Press, 1980).

Suggestions for Further Reading

Ali, Abdullah Yusuf, trans. *The Meaning of the Glorious Quran*. Cairo: Dar Al-Kitab Al-Masri, 1934.

Alpert, Rebecca. *Like Bread on the Seder Plate: Jewish Lesbians and the Transformation of Tradition*. New York: Columbia University Press, 1997.

Angel, Leonard. *The Book of Miriam*. Buffalo, NY: Mosaic Press, 1997.

Anisfeld, Sharon Cohen, Tara Mohr, and Catherine Spector, eds. *The Women's Passover Companion: Women's Reflections on the Festival of Freedom*. Woodstock, VT: Jewish Lights, 2003.

———. *The Women's Seder Sourcebook: Rituals & Readings for Use at the Passover Seder*. Woodstock, VT: Jewish Lights, 2003.

Arnow, David. *Creating Lively Passover Seders: A Sourcebook of Engaging Tales, Texts & Activities*. 2nd ed. Woodstock, VT: Jewish Lights, 2011.

Asad, Muhammad, ed. and trans. *The Message of the Qur'an*. Bitton, UK: Book Foundation, 2003.

Bakan, David. *The Duality of Human Existence*. Chicago: Rand McNally, 1966.

Berman, Phyllis, and Arthur Waskow. *Tales of Tikkun: New Jewish Stories to Heal the Wounded World*. Northvale, NJ: Jason Aronson, 1996.

Bloch, Ariel, and Chana Bloch, trans. *The Song of Songs*. New York: Random House, 1995.

Boulding, Kenneth. *The Meaning of the Twentieth Century: The Great Transition*. New York: Harper and Row, 1964.

Broner, Esther. *The Telling*. New York: Random House, 1993.

———. *The Women's Haggadah*. New York: HarperOne, 1994.

Buber, Martin. *I and Thou*. Translated by Walter Kaufmann. New York: Charles Scribner's Sons, 1970.

———. *Moses: The Revelation and the Covenant*. 1946. New York: Harper Torchbooks, 1958.

———. *Paths in Utopia*. Translated by R. F. C. Hull. London: Routledge & Kegan Paul, 1949.

———. *Pointing the Way*. Edited and translated by Maurice Friedman. New York: Harper, 1957.

Cameron, James, dir. *Avatar.* Twentieth Century Fox, 2010.

Cohen, Tamara. *The Journey Continues: The Ma'yan Passover Haggadah.* New York: Ma'yan: The Jewish Women's Project of the Jewish Community Center in Manhattan, 2002.

Coleman, Penny. *Flashback: Posttraumatic Stress Disorder, Suicide, and the Lessons of War.* Boston: Beacon Press, 2006.

Dykstra, Laurel A. *Set Them Free: The Other Side of Exodus.* Maryknoll, NY: Orbis Books, 2002.

Easwaran, Eknath. *Nonviolent Soldier of Islam: Badshah Khan, A Man to Match His Mountains.* 2nd ed. Tomales, CA: Nilgiri Press, 1999.

Eisenberg, Evan. *The Ecology of Eden.* New York: Knopf, 1998.

Elwell, Sue Levi, ed. *Kol-di-khefin/The Open Door: A Passover Haggadah.* New York: Central Conference of American Rabbis Press, 2002.

Falk, Marcia, trans. *The Song of Songs.* San Francisco: HarperSanFrancisco, 1990.

Feiler, Bruce. *America's Prophet: Moses and the American Story.* New York: William Morrow, 2009.

Finkelstein, Louis. *Akiba: Scholar, Saint, and Martyr.* New York: Atheneum, 1970.

Fox, Everett, trans. *The Five Books of Moses.* New York: Schocken, 1995.

———. *Give Us a King! Samuel, Saul, and David.* New York: Schocken, 1999.

Frankel, Ellen. *The Five Books of Miriam: A Woman's Commentary on the Torah.* San Francisco: HarperSanFrancisco, 1996.

Gold, Shefa. *Torah Journeys: An Inner Path to the Promised Land.* Teaneck, NJ: Ben Yehuda Press, 2006.

Green, Arthur. *Ehyeh: A Kabbalah for Tomorrow.* Woodstock, VT: Jewish Lights, 2003.

———. *Tormented Master: A Life of Rabbi Nahman of Bratslav.* Tuscaloosa, AL: University of Alabama Press, 1979. Reprint, Woodstock, VT: Jewish Lights, 1992.

Harding, Vincent. *There Is a River: The Black Struggle for Freedom in America.* New York: Harcourt Brace Jovanovich, 1981.

Heinlein, Robert. *Stranger in a Strange Land.* New York: Putnam, 1961.

Heschel, Abraham Joshua. *The Insecurity of Freedom.* New York: Schocken, 1972.

———. *Moral Grandeur and Spiritual Audacity.* Edited by Susannah Heschel. New York: Farrar, Straus, and Giroux, 1996.

———. *The Prophets.* Philadelphia: Jewish Publication Society of America, 1962.

———. *The Sabbath.* New York: Farrar, Straus, and Young, 1951.

Heschel, Susannah, ed. *On Being a Jewish Feminist.* New York: Schocken Books, 1983.

Hoffman, Lawrence A., and David Arnow, eds. *My People's Passover Haggadah: Traditional Texts, Modern Commentaries.* 2 vols. Woodstock, VT: Jewish Lights, 2008.

Huda, Qamar-ul, ed. *Crescent and Dove: Peace and Conflict Resolution in Islam.* Washington, DC: United States Institute of Peace Press, 2010.

Ibn al-Arabi. *The Bezels of Wisdom* [Fusus al-Hiqam]. Translated by R. W. J. Austin. New York: Paulist Press, 1980.

Koltun, Elizabeth, ed. *The Jewish Woman: New Perspectives*. New York: Schocken Books, 1976.

Laufer, Nathan. *Leading the Passover Journey: The Seder's Meaning Revealed, the Haggadah's Story Retold*. Woodstock, VT: Jewish Lights, 2005.

Lerner, Michael. *The Left Hand of God: Taking Back Our Country from the Religious Right*. San Francisco: HarperSanFrancisco, 2006.

Metzger, Deena. *What Dinah Thought*. New York: Viking, 1989.

Myers, Ched. *The Biblical Vision of Sabbath Economics*. Washington, DC: Tell the Word Press, 2001.

———. *Binding the Strong Man: A Political Reading of Mark's Story of Jesus*. 20th anniv. ed. Maryknoll, NY: Orbis Books, 2008.

———. "The Gospel of the Cross Confronts the Powers." In *Consuming Passion: Why the Killing of Jesus Really Matters*. Edited by Simon Barrow and Jonathan Bartley. London: Darton, Longman, and Todd, 2005.

———. "*The Passion*: The Gospel as Political Parody." *Witness Magazine*. www.thewitness.org/agw/myers040704.html.

Myers, Ched, and E. Enns. *Ambassadors of Reconciliation*. Vol. 1, *New Testament Reflections on Restorative Justice and Peacemaking*. Maryknoll, NY: Orbis Books, 2009.

New Jewish Agenda, comp. *The Shalom Seders*. New York: Adama Books, 1984.

Piercy, Marge. *He, She and It*. New York: Knopf, 1991.

Plaskow, Judith. *Standing Again at Sinai: Judaism from a Feminist Perspective*. New York: HarperCollins, 1990.

Rukeyser, Muriel. *The Collected Poems of Muriel Rukeyser*. Pittsburgh, PA: University of Pittsburgh Press, 2005.

Safi, Omid. *Memories of Muhammad: Why the Prophet Matters*. San Francisco: HarperCollins, 2009.

———, ed. *Progressive Muslims: On Justice, Gender and Pluralism*. Oxford: OneWorld, 2003.

Schachter-Shalomi, Zalman. *Paradigm Shift: From the Jewish Renewal Teachings of Reb Zalman Schachter-Shalomi*. Northvale, NJ: Jason Aronson, 1993.

Sells, Michael, trans. *Approaching the Qur'an: The Early Revelations*. Ashland, OR: White Cloud Press, 1999.

Shariati, Ali. *Hajj*. Translated by Ali A. Behzadnia and Najla Denny. Costa Mesa, CA: Evecina Cultural and Educational Foundation, 1993.

Soelle, Dorothee. *Death by Bread Alone: Texts and Reflections on Religious Experience*. Philadelphia: Fortress Press, 1978.

Wallis, Jim. *God's Politics: Why the Right Gets It Wrong and the Left Doesn't Get It*. San Francisco: HarperSanFrancisco, 2005.

Walzer, Michael. *Exodus and Revolution*. New York: Basic Books, 1985.

Waskow, Arthur. *Down-to-Earth Judaism*. New York: William Morrow, 1995.

———. *The Freedom Seder*. 2nd ed. New York: Holt, Rinehart, Winston, 1970.

———. *Godwrestling—Round 2: Ancient Wisdom, Future Paths*. Woodstock, VT: Jewish Lights, 1996.

———. *Interfaith Freedom Seder of the Earth*. Philadelphia: The Shalom Center, 2009. www.theshalomcenter.org.

———. "The Seder of the Children of Abraham, Hagar, and Sarah." *Tikkun*, March 1999, pp. 41–48.

———. "Tales and Songs of the New Hassidim." *Sing Shalom* [CD]. Philadelphia: The Shalom Center, 2006. www.theshalomcenter.org.

———, ed. *Torah of the Earth: Exploring 4,000 Years of Ecology in Jewish Thought*. 2 vols. Woodstock, VT: Jewish Lights, 2000.

Wildavsky, Aaron. *The Nursing Father: Moses as a Political Leader*. Tuscaloosa, AL: University of Alabama Press, 1984.

Wilson, Marvin. *Our Father Abraham: Jewish Roots of the Christian Faith*. Grand Rapids, MI: Eerdmans, 1989.

Wolfson, Ron. *Passover: The Family Guide to Spiritual Celebration*. With Joel Lurie Grishaver. 2nd ed. Woodstock, VT: Jewish Lights, 2003.

Yoder, John Howard. *The Politics of Jesus*. Grand Rapids, MI: Eerdmans, 1972.

Zornberg, Avivah Gottlieb. *The Particulars of Rapture: Reflections on Exodus*. New York: Doubleday, 2001.

About the Authors

Rabbi Arthur O. Waskow and **Rabbi Phyllis O. Berman** have been married since 1986. They have written two books together before this one—*Tales of Tikkun: New Jewish Stories to Heal the Wounded World* and *A Time for Every Purpose Under Heaven: The Jewish Life-Spiral as a Spiritual Path*. Together they have taught, spoken, and led study and prayer services for synagogues, retreat centers, campuses, and interfaith conferences throughout the United States and the world—Israel, Beijing, Edinburgh, Geneva, Vienna, Paris, Barcelona, Madrid, Sweden, New Delhi, and England.

Together they helped bring into being an interfaith spiritual retreat community, the Tent of Abraham, Hagar, and Sarah. With Sister Joan Chittister and Murshid Saadi Shakur Chisti, they co-authored *The Tent of Abraham: Stories of Hope and Peace for Jews, Christians, and Muslims*.

Between them they have four children, three children-in-law, and five grandchildren.

Since 1969, when he published the original *Freedom Seder*, Rabbi Waskow has been one of the creators and leaders of Jewish renewal and of several important interfaith projects addressing issues of peace, justice, and healing of the earth. In 1983 he founded and has since been director of The Shalom Center (www.theshalomcenter.org), a prophetic voice in Jewish, multireligious, and American life in seeking peace, social justice, and healing of the wounded earth.

He has written, co-authored, or edited more than a dozen books on Jewish thought and practice, including *Seasons of Our Joy; God-wrestling—Round 2: Ancient Wisdom, Future Paths; Torah of the Earth: Exploring 4,000 Years of Ecology in Jewish Thought;* and several others on eco-Judaism.

Since first visiting Israel and the Palestinian territories in 1969, Rabbi Waskow has worked steadfastly for a two-state peace settlement between Israel and Palestine in the context of a larger Middle East peace.

In 1995, Waskow was ordained a rabbi by a transdenominational rabbinical court under the auspices of ALEPH: Alliance for Jewish Renewal. He was named by the United Nations one of forty Wisdom-Keepers from around the world in connection with the Habitat II conference in 1995, and in 2005 was named by the *Forward*, the leading Jewish weekly in North America, as one of its "Forward Fifty." In 2007 *Newsweek* named him one of the fifty most influential American rabbis. He has taught at the Reconstructionist Rabbinical College, Hebrew Union College in New York, Swarthmore College, Vassar College, Temple University, and Drew University.

From 1959 to 1982, he worked on policy issues in Washington, D.C., as legislative assistant to Congressman Robert W. Kastenmeier, and at the Peace Research Institute, the Institute for Policy Studies, and the Public Resource Center. In 1963, he was granted a PhD in U.S. history by the University of Wisconsin in Madison. He was elected a delegate from the District of Columbia to the Democratic National Convention of 1968; co-authored "A Call to Resist Illegitimate Authority"; and wrote a number of books on race relations, military strategy, disarmament, and community-based renewable energy.

Rabbi Berman founded (1979) and has since been director of the Riverside Language Program (www.riversidelanguage.org), a unique and renowned intensive school (located in New York City) for teaching English language and American culture to newly arrived adult immigrants and refugees from all around the world.

Out of her work with immigrants, she co-authored a book of stories of their lives, *Getting Into It*, and several articles on the impact of American public policy on immigrants and refugees.

Berman has also, since the early 1980s, been a leading Jewish-renewal liturgist, prayer leader, story writer, and storyteller. Her articles on new ceremonies for women and new midrash have appeared in *Moment*, *Worlds of Jewish Prayer*, *Tikkun*, and *Good Housekeeping*.

From 1994 to 2005, Berman was director of the Summer Program of the Elat Chayyim Center for Healing and Renewal.

She was chair of the board of the P'nai Or Religious Fellowship from 1985 to 1993, and a member of the board of ALEPH: Alliance for Jewish Renewal from 1993 to 2002. She was ordained an *Eshet Chazon* (Woman of Vision) by the Jewish-renewal community in 1991 and rabbi by the ALEPH ordination program in 2004.

From its founding in 2002 through 2009, she has been the key facilitator for The Tent of Abraham, Hagar, and Sarah.

About the Contributors

Dr. Vincent Harding is chairperson of the Veterans of Hope Project: A Center for the Study of Religion and Democratic Renewal, located at the Iliff School of Theology in Denver. Harding taught at Spelman College and Swarthmore College and for two decades as professor of religion and social transformation at Iliff, where he is now emeritus professor. Harding and his late wife, Rosemarie Freeney Harding, traveled throughout the South in the early 1960s working with the Student Nonviolent Coordinating Committee, the Southern Christian Leadership Conference, and the Congress on Racial Equality to end racial segregation and bring closer "the Beloved Community." Harding occasionally drafted speeches for Martin Luther King, including King's famous anti–Vietnam War speech, "A Time to Break Silence," which King delivered on April 4, 1967, at Riverside Church in New York City, exactly a year before he was assassinated.

Dr. S. Ayse Kadayifci-Orellana is assistant professor of peace and conflict resolution at the School of International Service at American University, Washington, D.C. She is also one of the founding members and the associate director of Salam Institute for Peace and Justice, a not-for-profit organization for research, education, and practice on issues related to conflict resolution, nonviolence, and development with a focus on bridging differences between Muslim and non-Muslim communities.

She authored *Standing on an Isthmus: Islamic Narratives of War and Peace in the Palestinian Territories*, co-authored and edited the volume *Anthology on Islam and Peace and Conflict Resolution in Islam: Precept and Practice*, and has written on mediation and peace building, religion and conflict resolution, Islamic approaches to war and peace, and Islam and nonviolence. Dr. Kadayifci-Orellana has facilitated dialogues and conflict resolution workshops between Israelis and Palestinians and has conducted Islamic conflict resolution training workshops for imams and Muslim youth leaders in the United States.

Ched Myers is an activist and theological educator with Bartimaeus Cooperative Ministries (www.bcm-net.org) in southern California, where he focuses on building capacity for biblical literacy, church renewal, and faith-based witness for justice. His publications are listed at www.chedmyers.org. Over the past three decades he has worked with many religiously rooted peace and justice organizations and movements, including the American Friends Service Committee, the Pacific Concerns Resource Center, the Pacific Life Community, Christian Peacemaker Teams, the Catholic Worker movement, and Witness for Peace. He has taught at many seminaries, including the Fuller Theological Seminary and Claremont School of Theology.

Russell Powell is a student at Yale Divinity School and has been an intern for Bartimaeus Cooperative Ministries.

Notes

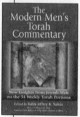

Congregation Resources

Empowered Judaism: What Independent Minyanim Can Teach Us about
Building Vibrant Jewish Communities
By Rabbi Elie Kaunfer; Foreword by Prof. Jonathan D. Sarna
Examines the independent minyan movement and the lessons these grassroots
communities can provide. 6 x 9, 224 pp, Quality PB, 978-1-58023-412-2 **$18.99**

Spiritual Boredom: Rediscovering the Wonder of Judaism *By Dr. Erica Brown*
Breaks through the surface of spiritual boredom to find the reservoir of meaning
within. 6 x 9, 208 pp, HC, 978-1-58023-405-4 **$21.99**

Building a Successful Volunteer Culture
Finding Meaning in Service in the Jewish Community
By Rabbi Charles Simon; Foreword by Shelley Lindauer; Preface by Dr. Ron Wolfson
Shows you how to develop and maintain the volunteers who are essential to the vitality
of your organization and community. 6 x 9, 192 pp, Quality PB, 978-1-58023-408-5 **$16.99**

The Case for Jewish Peoplehood: Can We Be One?
By Dr. Erica Brown and Dr. Misha Galperin; Foreword by Rabbi Joseph Telushkin
6 x 9, 224 pp, HC, 978-1-58023-401-6 **$21.99**

Inspired Jewish Leadership: Practical Approaches to Building Strong Communities
By Dr. Erica Brown 6 x 9, 256 pp, HC, 978-1-58023-361-3 **$24.99**

Jewish Pastoral Care, 2nd Edition: A Practical Handbook from Traditional &
Contemporary Sources *Edited by Rabbi Dayle A. Friedman, MSW, MAJCS, BCC*
6 x 9, 528 pp, Quality PB, 978-1-58023-427-6 **$30.00**

Rethinking Synagogues: A New Vocabulary for Congregational Life
By Rabbi Lawrence A. Hoffman, PhD 6 x 9, 240 pp, Quality PB, 978-1-58023-248-7 **$19.99**

The Spirituality of Welcoming: How to Transform Your Congregation into a
Sacred Community *By Dr. Ron Wolfson* 6 x 9, 224 pp, Quality PB, 978-1-58023-244-9 **$19.99**

Children's Books

Around the World in One Shabbat
Jewish People Celebrate the Sabbath Together
By Durga Yael Bernhard
Takes your child on a colorful adventure to share the many ways Jewish
people celebrate Shabbat around the world.
11 x 8½, 32 pp, HC, 978-1-58023-433-7 **$18.99** *For ages 3–6*

What You Will See Inside a Synagogue
By Rabbi Lawrence A. Hoffman, PhD, and Dr. Ron Wolfson; Full-color photos by Bill Aron
A colorful, fun-to-read introduction that explains the ways and whys of Jewish
worship and religious life.
8½ x 10½, 32 pp, Full-color photos, Quality PB, 978-1-59473-256-0 **$8.99** *For ages 6 & up*
(A book from SkyLight Paths, Jewish Lights' sister imprint)

Because Nothing Looks Like God
By Lawrence Kushner and Karen Kushner Introduces children to the possibilities of
spiritual life. 11 x 8½, 32 pp, Full-color illus., HC, 978-1-58023-092-6 **$17.99** *For ages 4 & up*

The Book of Miracles: A Young Person's Guide to Jewish Spiritual Awareness
Written and illus. by Lawrence Kushner
6 x 9, 96 pp, 2-color illus., HC, 978-1-879045-78-1 **$16.95** *For ages 9–13*

In God's Hands *By Lawrence Kushner and Gary Schmidt* 9 x 12, 32 pp, Full-color illus.,
HC, 978-1-58023-224-1 **$16.99** *For ages 5 & up*

In Our Image: God's First Creatures *By Nancy Sohn Swartz*
9 x 12, 32 pp, Full-color illus., HC, 978-1-879045-99-6 **$16.95** *For ages 4 & up*

The Kids' Fun Book of Jewish Time
By Emily Sper 9 x 7½, 24 pp, Full-color illus., HC, 978-1-58023-311-8 **$16.99** *For ages 3–6*

What Makes Someone a Jew? *By Lauren Seidman*
Reflects the changing face of American Judaism.
10 x 8½, 32 pp, Full-color photos, Quality PB, 978-1-58023-321-7 **$8.99** *For ages 3–6*

Children's Books by Sandy Eisenberg Sasso

Adam & Eve's First Sunset: God's New Day
Explores fear and hope, faith and gratitude in ways that will delight kids and adults—inspiring us to bless each of God's days and nights.
9 x 12, 32 pp, Full-color illus., HC, 978-1-58023-177-0 **$17.95** *For ages 4 & up*

Also Available as a Board Book: **Adam and Eve's New Day**
5 x 5, 24 pp, Full-color illus., Board Book, 978-1-59473-205-8 **$7.99** *For ages 0–4*
(A book from SkyLight Paths, Jewish Lights' sister imprint)

But God Remembered: Stories of Women from Creation to the
Promised Land   Four different stories of women—Lilith, Serach, Bityah and the Daughters of Z—teach us important values through their faith and actions.
9 x 12, 32 pp, Full-color illus., Quality PB, 978-1-58023-372-9 **$8.99** *For ages 8 & up*

Cain & Abel: Finding the Fruits of Peace
Shows children that we have the power to deal with anger in positive ways. Provides questions for kids and adults to explore together.
9 x 12, 32 pp, Full-color illus., HC, 978-1-58023-123-7 **$16.95** *For ages 5 & up*

For Heaven's Sake
Heaven is often found where you least expect it.
9 x 12, 32 pp, Full-color illus., HC, 978-1-58023-054-4 **$16.95** *For ages 4 & up*

God in Between
If you wanted to find God, where would you look? This magical, mythical tale teaches that God can be found where we are: within all of us and the relationships between us. 9 x 12, 32 pp, Full-color illus., HC, 978-1-879045-86-6 **$16.95** *For ages 4 & up*

God Said Amen
An inspiring story about hearing the answers to our prayers.
9 x 12, 32 pp, Full-color illus., HC, 978-1-58023-080-3 **$16.95** *For ages 4 & up*

God's Paintbrush: Special 10th Anniversary Edition
Wonderfully interactive, invites children of all faiths and backgrounds to encounter God through moments in their own lives. Provides questions adult and child can explore together. 11 x 8½, 32 pp, Full-color illus., HC, 978-1-58023-195-4 **$17.95** *For ages 4 & up*

Also Available as a Board Book: **I Am God's Paintbrush**
5 x 5, 24 pp, Full-color illus., Board Book, 978-1-59473-265-2 **$7.99** *For ages 0–4*
(A book from SkyLight Paths, Jewish Lights' sister imprint)

Also Available: **God's Paintbrush Teacher's Guide**
8½ x 11, 32 pp, PB, 978-1-879045-57-6 **$8.95**

God's Paintbrush Celebration Kit
A Spiritual Activity Kit for Teachers and Students of All Faiths, All Backgrounds
9½ x 12, 40 Full-color Activity Sheets & Teacher Folder w/ complete instructions
HC, 978-1-58023-050-6 **$21.95**
8-Student Activity Sheet Pack (40 sheets/5 sessions), 978-1-58023-058-2 **$19.95**

In God's Name
Like an ancient myth in its poetic text and vibrant illustrations, this award-winning modern fable about the search for God's name celebrates the diversity and, at the same time, the unity of all people.
9 x 12, 32 pp, Full-color illus., HC, 978-1-879045-26-2 **$16.99** *For ages 4 & up*

Also Available as a Board Book: **What Is God's Name?**
5 x 5, 24 pp, Full-color illus., Board Book, 978-1-893361-10-2 **$7.99** *For ages 0–4*
(A book from SkyLight Paths, Jewish Lights' sister imprint)

Also Available in Spanish: **El nombre de Dios**
9 x 12, 32 pp, Full-color illus., HC, 978-1-893361-63-8 **$16.95** *For ages 4 & up*

Noah's Wife: The Story of Naamah
When God tells Noah to bring the animals of the world onto the ark, God also calls on Naamah, Noah's wife, to save each plant on Earth. Based on an ancient text.
9 x 12, 32 pp, Full-color illus., HC, 978-1-58023-134-3 **$16.95** *For ages 4 & up*

Also Available as a Board Book: **Naamah, Noah's Wife**
5 x 5, 24 pp, Full-color illus., Board Book, 978-1-893361-56-0 **$7.95** *For ages 0–4*
(A book from SkyLight Paths, Jewish Lights' sister imprint)

Meditation

Jewish Meditation Practices for Everyday Life
Awakening Your Heart, Connecting with God
By Rabbi Jeff Roth
Offers a fresh take on meditation that draws on life experience and living life with greater clarity as opposed to the traditional method of rigorous study.
6 x 9, 224 pp, Quality PB, 978-1-58023-397-2 **$18.99**

The Handbook of Jewish Meditation Practices
A Guide for Enriching the Sabbath and Other Days of Your Life
By Rabbi David A. Cooper Easy-to-learn meditation techniques.
6 x 9, 208 pp, Quality PB, 978-1-58023-102-2 **$16.95**

Discovering Jewish Meditation: Instruction & Guidance for Learning an Ancient
Spiritual Practice *By Nan Fink Gefen, PhD* 6 x 9, 208 pp, Quality PB, 978-1-58023-067-4 **$16.95**

Meditation from the Heart of Judaism: Today's Teachers Share Their Practices,
Techniques, and Faith *Edited by Avram Davis*
6 x 9, 256 pp, Quality PB, 978-1-58023-049-0 **$16.95**

Ritual/Sacred Practices

The Jewish Dream Book: The Key to Opening the Inner Meaning of
Your Dreams *By Vanessa L. Ochs, PhD, with Elizabeth Ochs; Illus. by Kristina Swarner*
Instructions for how modern people can perform ancient Jewish dream practices and dream interpretations drawn from the Jewish wisdom tradition.
8 x 8, 128 pp, Full-color illus., Deluxe PB w/ flaps, 978-1-58023-132-9 **$16.95**

God in Your Body: Kabbalah, Mindfulness and Embodied Spiritual Practice
By Jay Michaelson
The first comprehensive treatment of the body in Jewish spiritual practice and an essential guide to the sacred.
6 x 9, 272 pp, Quality PB, 978-1-58023-304-0 **$18.99**

The Book of Jewish Sacred Practices: CLAL's Guide to Everyday &
Holiday Rituals & Blessings *Edited by Rabbi Irwin Kula and Vanessa L. Ochs, PhD*
6 x 9, 368 pp, Quality PB, 978-1-58023-152-7 **$18.95**

Jewish Ritual: A Brief Introduction for Christians
By Rabbi Kerry M. Olitzky and Rabbi Daniel Judson
5½ x 8½, 144 pp, Quality PB, 978-1-58023-210-4 **$14.99**

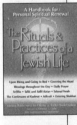

The Rituals & Practices of a Jewish Life: A Handbook for Personal Spiritual
Renewal *Edited by Rabbi Kerry M. Olitzky and Rabbi Daniel Judson*
6 x 9, 272 pp, Illus., Quality PB, 978-1-58023-169-5 **$18.95**

The Sacred Art of Lovingkindness: Preparing to Practice
By Rabbi Rami Shapiro 5½ x 8½, 176 pp, Quality PB, 978-1-59473-151-8 **$16.99**
(A book from SkyLight Paths, Jewish Lights' sister imprint)

Science Fiction/Mystery & Detective Fiction

Criminal Kabbalah: An Intriguing Anthology of Jewish Mystery &
Detective Fiction *Edited by Lawrence W. Raphael; Foreword by Laurie R. King*
All-new stories from twelve of today's masters of mystery and detective fiction—sure to delight mystery buffs of all faith traditions.
6 x 9, 256 pp, Quality PB, 978-1-58023-109-1 **$16.95**

Mystery Midrash: An Anthology of Jewish Mystery & Detective Fiction
Edited by Lawrence W. Raphael; Preface by Joel Siegel
6 x 9, 304 pp, Quality PB, 978-1-58023-055-1 **$16.95**

Wandering Stars: An Anthology of Jewish Fantasy & Science Fiction
Edited by Jack Dann; Introduction by Isaac Asimov
6 x 9, 272 pp, Quality PB, 978-1-58023-005-6 **$18.99**

More Wandering Stars: An Anthology of Outstanding Stories of Jewish Fantasy and
Science Fiction *Edited by Jack Dann; Introduction by Isaac Asimov*
6 x 9, 192 pp, Quality PB, 978-1-58023-063-6 **$16.95**

Holidays/Holy Days

Who by Fire, Who by Water—Un'taneh Tokef
Edited by Rabbi Lawrence A. Hoffman, PhD
Examines the prayer's theology, authorship and poetry through a set of lively essays, all written in accessible language.
6 x 9, 272 pp, HC, 978-1-58023-424-5 **$24.99**

All These Vows—Kol Nidre
Edited by Rabbi Lawrence A. Hoffman, PhD
The most memorable prayer of the Jewish New Year—what it means, why we sing it, and the secret of its magical appeal.
6 x 9, 300 pp (est), HC, 978-1-58023-430-6 **$24.99**

Rosh Hashanah Readings: Inspiration, Information and Contemplation
Yom Kippur Readings: Inspiration, Information and Contemplation
Edited by Rabbi Dov Peretz Elkins; Section Introductions from Arthur Green's These Are the Words
Rosh Hashanah: 6 x 9, 400 pp, Quality PB, 978-1-58023-437-5 **$19.99**; HC, 978-1-58023-239-5 **$24.99**
Yom Kippur: 6 x 9, 368 pp, Quality PB, 978-1-58023-438-2 **$19.99**; HC, 978-1-58023-271-5 **$24.99**

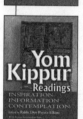

Jewish Holidays: A Brief Introduction for Christians
By Rabbi Kerry M. Olitzky and Rabbi Daniel Judson
5½ x 8½, 176 pp, Quality PB, 978-1-58023-302-6 **$16.99**

Reclaiming Judaism as a Spiritual Practice: Holy Days and Shabbat
By Rabbi Goldie Milgram 7 x 9, 272 pp, Quality PB, 978-1-58023-205-0 **$19.99**

Shabbat, 2nd Edition: The Family Guide to Preparing for and Celebrating the Sabbath
By Dr. Ron Wolfson 7 x 9, 320 pp, Illus., Quality PB, 978-1-58023-164-0 **$19.99**

Hanukkah, 2nd Edition: The Family Guide to Spiritual Celebration
By Dr. Ron Wolfson 7 x 9, 240 pp, Illus., Quality PB, 978-1-58023-122-0 **$18.95**

The Jewish Family Fun Book, 2nd Edition
Holiday Projects, Everyday Activities, and Travel Ideas with Jewish Themes
By Danielle Dardashti and Roni Sarig; Illus. by Avi Katz
6 x 9, 304 pp, 70+ b/w illus. & diagrams, Quality PB, 978-1-58023-333-0 **$18.99**

Passover

My People's Passover Haggadah
Traditional Texts, Modern Commentaries
Edited by Rabbi Lawrence A. Hoffman, PhD, and David Arnow, PhD
A diverse and exciting collection of commentaries on the traditional Passover Haggadah—in two volumes!
Vol. 1: 7 x 10, 304 pp, HC, 978-1-58023-354-5 **$24.99**
Vol. 2: 7 x 10, 320 pp, HC, 978-1-58023-346-0 **$24.99**

Freedom Journeys: The Tale of Exodus and Wilderness across Millennia
By Rabbi Arthur O. Waskow and Rabbi Phyllis O. Berman
Explores how the story of Exodus echoes in our own time, calling us to relearn and rethink the Passover story through social-justice, ecological, feminist and interfaith perspectives. 6 x 9, 288 pp, HC, 978-1-58023-445-0 **$24.99**

Leading the Passover Journey: The Seder's Meaning Revealed, the Haggadah's Story Retold *By Rabbi Nathan Laufer*
Uncovers the hidden meaning of the Seder's rituals and customs.
6 x 9, 224 pp, Quality PB, 978-1-58023-399-6 **$18.99**; HC, 978-1-58023-211-1 **$24.99**

Creating Lively Passover Seders, 2nd Edition: A Sourcebook of Engaging Tales, Texts & Activities *By David Arnow, PhD* 7 x 9, 464 pp, Quality PB, 978-1-58023-444-3 **$24.99**

Passover, 2nd Edition: The Family Guide to Spiritual Celebration
By Dr. Ron Wolfson with Joel Lurie Grishaver 7 x 9, 416 pp, Quality PB, 978-1-58023-174-9 **$19.95**

The Women's Passover Companion: Women's Reflections on the Festival of Freedom
Edited by Rabbi Sharon Cohen Anisfeld, Tara Mohr and Catherine Spector; Foreword by Paula E. Hyman
6 x 9, 352 pp, Quality PB, 978-1-58023-231-9 **$19.99**; HC, 978-1-58023-128-2 **$24.95**

The Women's Seder Sourcebook: Rituals & Readings for Use at the Passover Seder
Edited by Rabbi Sharon Cohen Anisfeld, Tara Mohr and Catherine Spector
6 x 9, 384 pp, Quality PB, 978-1-58023-232-6 **$19.99**

Life Cycle
Marriage/Parenting/Family/Aging

The New Jewish Baby Album: Creating and Celebrating the Beginning of a Spiritual Life—A Jewish Lights Companion
By the Editors at Jewish Lights; Foreword by Anita Diamant; Preface by Rabbi Sandy Eisenberg Sasso
A spiritual keepsake that will be treasured for generations. More than just a memory book, *shows you how—and why it's important*—to create a Jewish home and a Jewish life. 8 x 10, 64 pp, Deluxe Padded HC, Full-color illus., 978-1-58023-138-1 **$19.95**

The Jewish Pregnancy Book: A Resource for the Soul, Body & Mind during Pregnancy, Birth & the First Three Months *By Sandy Falk, MD, and Rabbi Daniel Judson, with Steven A. Rapp* Medical information, prayers and rituals for each stage of pregnancy. 7 x 10, 208 pp, b/w photos, Quality PB, 978-1-58023-178-7 **$16.95**

Celebrating Your New Jewish Daughter: Creating Jewish Ways to Welcome Baby Girls into the Covenant—New and Traditional Ceremonies *By Debra Nussbaum Cohen; Foreword by Rabbi Sandy Eisenberg Sasso* 6 x 9, 272 pp, Quality PB, 978-1-58023-090-2 **$18.95**

The New Jewish Baby Book, 2nd Edition: Names, Ceremonies & Customs—A Guide for Today's Families *By Anita Diamant* 6 x 9, 320 pp, Quality PB, 978-1-58023-251-7 **$19.99**

Parenting as a Spiritual Journey: Deepening Ordinary and Extraordinary Events into Sacred Occasions *By Rabbi Nancy Fuchs-Kreimer, PhD*
6 x 9, 224 pp, Quality PB, 978-1-58023-016-2 **$17.99**

Parenting Jewish Teens: A Guide for the Perplexed
By Joanne Doades Explores the questions and issues that shape the world in which today's Jewish teenagers live and offers constructive advice to parents.
6 x 9, 176 pp, Quality PB, 978-1-58023-305-7 **$16.99**

Judaism for Two: A Spiritual Guide for Strengthening and Celebrating Your Loving Relationship   *By Rabbi Nancy Fuchs-Kreimer, PhD, and Rabbi Nancy H. Wiener, DMin; Foreword by Rabbi Elliot N. Dorff, PhD*
Addresses the ways Jewish teachings can enhance and strengthen committed relationships. 6 x 9, 224 pp, Quality PB, 978-1-58023-254-8 **$16.99**

The Creative Jewish Wedding Book, 2nd Edition: A Hands-On Guide to New & Old Traditions, Ceremonies & Celebrations *By Gabrielle Kaplan-Mayer*
9 x 9, 288 pp, b/w photos, Quality PB, 978-1-58023-398-9 **$19.99**

Divorce Is a Mitzvah: A Practical Guide to Finding Wholeness and Holiness When Your Marriage Dies *By Rabbi Perry Netter; Afterword by Rabbi Laura Geller*
6 x 9, 224 pp, Quality PB, 978-1-58023-172-5 **$16.95**

Embracing the Covenant: Converts to Judaism Talk About Why & How
By Rabbi Allan Berkowitz and Patti Moskovitz 6 x 9, 192 pp, Quality PB, 978-1-879045-50-7 **$16.95**

The Guide to Jewish Interfaith Family Life: An InterfaithFamily.com Handbook
Edited by Ronnie Friedland and Edmund Case
6 x 9, 384 pp, Quality PB, 978-1-58023-153-4 **$18.95**

A Heart of Wisdom: Making the Jewish Journey from Midlife through the Elder Years
Edited by Susan Berrin; Foreword by Rabbi Harold Kushner
6 x 9, 384 pp, Quality PB, 978-1-58023-051-3 **$18.95**

Introducing My Faith and My Community: The Jewish Outreach Institute Guide for the Christian in a Jewish Interfaith Relationship
By Rabbi Kerry M. Olitzky 6 x 9, 176 pp, Quality PB, 978-1-58023-192-3 **$16.99**

Making a Successful Jewish Interfaith Marriage: The Jewish Outreach Institute Guide to Opportunities, Challenges and Resources *By Rabbi Kerry M. Olitzky with Joan Peterson Littman*
6 x 9, 176 pp, Quality PB, 978-1-58023-170-1 **$16.95**

A Man's Responsibility: A Jewish Guide to Being a Son, a Partner in Marriage, a Father and a Community Leader *By Rabbi Joseph B. Meszler*
6 x 9, 192 pp, Quality PB, 978-1-58023-435-1 **$16.99**; HC, 978-1-58023-362-0 **$21.99**

So That Your Values Live On: Ethical Wills and How to Prepare Them
Edited by Rabbi Jack Riemer and Rabbi Nathaniel Stampfer
6 x 9, 272 pp, Quality PB, 978-1-879045-34-7 **$18.99**

Judaism / Christianity / Interfaith

Christians & Jews—Faith to Faith: Tragic History, Promising Present, Fragile Future *By Rabbi James Rudin*
A probing examination of Christian-Jewish relations that looks at the major issues facing both faith communities. 6 x 9, 288 pp, HC, 978-1-58023-432-0 **$24.99**

How to Do Good & Avoid Evil: A Global Ethic from the Sources of Judaism *By Hans Küng and Rabbi Walter Homolka* Explores how the principles of Judaism provide the ethical norms for all religions to work together toward a more peaceful humankind. 6 x 9, 224 pp, HC, 978-1-59473-255-3 **$19.99***

Getting to the Heart of Interfaith: The Eye-Opening, Hope-Filled Friendship of a Pastor, a Rabbi and a Sheikh
By Rabbi Ted Falcon, Pastor Don Mackenzie and Sheikh Jamal Rahman
Presents ways we can work together to transcend the differences that have divided us historically. 6 x 9, 192 pp, Quality PB, 978-1-59473-263-8 **$16.99***

Claiming Earth as Common Ground: The Ecological Crisis through the Lens of Faith *By Rabbi Andrea Cohen-Kiener* 6 x 9, 192 pp, Quality PB, 978-1-59473-261-4 **$16.99***

Modern Jews Engage the New Testament: Enhancing Jewish Well-Being in a Christian Environment *By Rabbi Michael J. Cook, PhD* 6 x 9, 416 pp, HC, 978-1-58023-313-2 **$29.99**

The Changing Christian World: A Brief Introduction for Jews
By Rabbi Leonard A. Schoolman 5½ x 8½, 176 pp, Quality PB, 978-1-58023-344-6 **$16.99**

Christians & Jews in Dialogue: Learning in the Presence of the Other
By Mary C. Boys and Sara S. Lee
6 x 9, 240 pp, Quality PB, 978-1-59473-254-6 **$18.99**; HC, 978-1-59473-144-0 **21.99***

Disaster Spiritual Care: Practical Clergy Responses to Community, Regional and National Tragedy *Edited by Rabbi Stephen B. Roberts, BCJC, and Rev. Willard W. C. Ashley Sr., DMin, DH*
6 x 9, 384 pp, HC, 978-1-59473-240-9 **$40.00**

Healing the Jewish-Christian Rift: Growing Beyond Our Wounded History
By Ron Miller and Laura Bernstein 6 x 9, 288 pp, Quality PB, 978-1-59473-139-6 **$18.99***

How to Be a Perfect Stranger, 5th Edition: The Essential Religious Etiquette Handbook *Edited by Stuart M. Matlins and Arthur J. Magida*
6 x 9, 432 pp, Quality PB, 978-1-59473-294-2 **$19.99***

InterActive Faith: The Essential Interreligious Community-Building Handbook
Edited by Rev. Bud Heckman with Rori Picker Neiss
6 x 9, 304 pp, Quality PB, 978-1-59473-273-7 **$16.99**; HC, 978-1-59473-237-9 **$29.99***

Introducing My Faith and My Community
The Jewish Outreach Institute Guide for the Christian in a Jewish Interfaith Relationship *By Rabbi Kerry M. Olitzky* 6 x 9, 176 pp, Quality PB, 978-1-58023-192-3 **$16.99**

The Jewish Approach to Repairing the World (*Tikkun Olam*)
A Brief Introduction for Christians *By Rabbi Elliot N. Dorff, PhD, with Rev. Cory Willson*
5½ x 8½, 256 pp, Quality PB, 978-1-58023-349-1 **$16.99**

The Jewish Connection to Israel, the Promised Land: A Brief Introduction for Christians *By Rabbi Eugene Korn, PhD* 5½ x 8½, 192 pp, Quality PB, 978-1-58023-318-7 **$14.99**

Jewish Holidays: A Brief Introduction for Christians *By Rabbi Kerry M. Olitzky and Rabbi Daniel Judson* 5½ x 8½, 176 pp, Quality PB, 978-1-58023-302-6 **$16.99**

Jewish Ritual: A Brief Introduction for Christians *By Rabbi Kerry M. Olitzky and Rabbi Daniel Judson* 5½ x 8½, 144 pp, Quality PB, 978-1-58023-210-4 **$14.99**

A Jewish Understanding of the New Testament *By Rabbi Samuel Sandmel; Preface by Rabbi David Sandmel* 5½ x 8½, 368 pp, Quality PB, 978-1-59473-048-1 **$19.99***

Righteous Gentiles in the Hebrew Bible: Ancient Role Models for Sacred Relationships *By Rabbi Jeffrey K. Salkin; Foreword by Rabbi Harold M. Schulweis; Preface by Phyllis Tickle* 6 x 9, 192 pp, Quality PB, 978-1-58023-364-4 **$18.99**

Talking about God: Exploring the Meaning of Religious Life with Kierkegaard, Buber, Tillich and Heschel *By Rabbi Daniel F. Polish, PhD* 6 x 9, 160 pp, Quality PB, 978-1-59473-272-0 **$16.99***

We Jews and Jesus: Exploring Theological Differences for Mutual Understanding
By Rabbi Samuel Sandmel; Preface by Rabbi David Sandmel
6 x 9, 192 pp, Quality PB, 978-1-59473-208-9 **$16.99**

*A book from SkyLight Paths, Jewish Lights' sister imprint

Inspiration

God of Me: Imagining God throughout Your Lifetime
By Rabbi David Lyon Helps you cut through preconceived ideas of God and dogmas that stifle your creativity when thinking about your personal relationship with God. 6 x 9, 192 pp, Quality PB, 978-1-58023-452-8 **$16.99**

The God Upgrade: Finding Your 21st-Century Spirituality in Judaism's 5,000-Year-Old Tradition *By Rabbi Jamie Korngold; Foreword by Rabbi Harold M. Schulweis* A provocative look at how our changing God concepts have shaped every aspect of Judaism. 6 x 9, 240 pp (est), Quality PB, 978-1-58023-443-6 **$16.99**

The Seven Questions You're Asked in Heaven: Reviewing and Renewing Your Life on Earth *By Dr. Ron Wolfson* An intriguing and entertaining resource for living a life that matters. 6 x 9, 176 pp, Quality PB, 978-1-58023-407-8 **$16.99**

Happiness and the Human Spirit: The Spirituality of Becoming the Best You Can Be *By Rabbi Abraham J. Twerski, MD* Shows you that true happiness is attainable once you stop looking outside yourself for the source. 6 x 9, 176 pp, Quality PB, 978-1-58023-404-7 **$16.99**; HC, 978-1-58023-343-9 **$19.99**

A Formula for Proper Living: Practical Lessons from Life and Torah *By Rabbi Abraham J. Twerski, MD* 6 x 9, 144 pp, HC, 978-1-58023-402-3 **$19.99**

The Bridge to Forgiveness: Stories and Prayers for Finding God and Restoring Wholeness *By Rabbi Karyn D. Kedar* 6 x 9, 176 pp, Quality PB, 978-1-58023-451-1 **$16.99**

The Empty Chair: Finding Hope and Joy—Timeless Wisdom from a Hasidic Master, Rebbe Nachman of Breslov *Adapted by Moshe Mykoff and the Breslov Research Institute* 4 x 6, 128 pp, Deluxe PB w/ flaps, 978-1-879045-67-5 **$9.99**

The Gentle Weapon: Prayers for Everyday and Not-So-Everyday Moments— Timeless Wisdom from the Teachings of the Hasidic Master, Rebbe Nachman of Breslov *Adapted by Moshe Mykoff and S. C. Mizrahi, together with the Breslov Research Institute* 4 x 6, 144 pp, Deluxe PB w/ flaps, 978-1-58023-022-3 **$9.99**

God Whispers: Stories of the Soul, Lessons of the Heart *By Rabbi Karyn D. Kedar* 6 x 9, 176 pp, Quality PB, 978-1-58023-088-9 **$15.95**

God's To-Do List: 103 Ways to Be an Angel and Do God's Work on Earth *By Dr. Ron Wolfson* 6 x 9, 144 pp, Quality PB, 978-1-58023-301-9 **$16.99**

Jewish Stories from Heaven and Earth: Inspiring Tales to Nourish the Heart and Soul *Edited by Rabbi Dov Peretz Elkins* 6 x 9, 304 pp, Quality PB, 978-1-58023-363-7 **$16.99**

Life's Daily Blessings: Inspiring Reflections on Gratitude and Joy for Every Day, Based on Jewish Wisdom *By Rabbi Kerry M. Olitzky* 4½ x 6½, 368 pp, Quality PB, 978-1-58023-396-5 **$16.99**

Restful Reflections: Nighttime Inspiration to Calm the Soul, Based on Jewish Wisdom *By Rabbi Kerry M. Olitzky and Rabbi Lori Forman* 4½ x 6½, 448 pp, Quality PB, 978-1-58023-091-9 **$15.95**

Sacred Intentions: Daily Inspiration to Strengthen the Spirit, Based on Jewish Wisdom *By Rabbi Kerry M. Olitzky and Rabbi Lori Forman* 4½ x 6½, 448 pp, Quality PB, 978-1-58023-061-2 **$15.95**

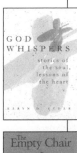

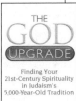
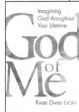

Kabbalah/Mysticism

Jewish Mysticism and the Spiritual Life: Classical Texts, Contemporary Reflections *Edited by Dr. Lawrence Fine, Dr. Eitan Fishbane and Rabbi Or N. Rose* Inspirational and thought-provoking materials for contemplation, discussion and action. 6 x 9, 256 pp, HC, 978-1-58023-434-4 **$24.99**

Ehyeh: A Kabbalah for Tomorrow *By Rabbi Arthur Green, PhD* 6 x 9, 224 pp, Quality PB, 978-1-58023-213-5 **$18.99**

The Gift of Kabbalah: Discovering the Secrets of Heaven, Renewing Your Life on Earth *By Tamar Frankiel, PhD* 6 x 9, 256 pp, Quality PB, 978-1-58023-141-1 **$16.95**

Seek My Face: A Jewish Mystical Theology *By Rabbi Arthur Green, PhD* 6 x 9, 304 pp, Quality PB, 978-1-58023-130-5 **$19.95**

Zohar: Annotated & Explained *Translation & Annotation by Dr. Daniel C. Matt; Foreword by Andrew Harvey* 5½ x 8½, 176 pp, Quality PB, 978-1-893361-51-5 **$15.99** *(A book from SkyLight Paths, Jewish Lights' sister imprint)*

See also *The Way Into Jewish Mystical Tradition* in The Way Into... Series.

Spirituality

Repentance: The Meaning and Practice of *Teshuvah*
By Dr. Louis E. Newman; Foreword by Rabbi Harold M. Schulweis; Preface by Rabbi Karyn D. Kedar
Examines both the practical and philosophical dimensions of *teshuvah*, Judaism's core religious-moral teaching on repentance, and its value for us—Jews and non-Jews alike—today. 6 x 9, 256 pp, HC, 978-1-58023-426-9 **$24.99**

Tanya, the Masterpiece of Hasidic Wisdom
Selections Annotated & Explained
Translation & Annotation by Rabbi Rami Shapiro; Foreword by Rabbi Zalman M. Schachter-Shalomi
Brings the genius of *Tanya*, one of the most powerful books of Jewish wisdom, to anyone seeking to deepen their understanding of the soul.
5½ x 8½, 240 pp, Quality PB, 978-1-59473-275-1 **$16.99**
(A book from SkyLight Paths, Jewish Lights' sister imprint)

Aleph-Bet Yoga: Embodying the Hebrew Letters for Physical and Spiritual Well-Being
By Steven A. Rapp; Foreword by Tamar Frankiel, PhD, and Judy Greenfeld; Preface by Hart Lazer
7 x 10, 128 pp, b/w photos, Quality PB, Lay-flat binding, 978-1-58023-162-6 **$16.95**

A Book of Life: Embracing Judaism as a Spiritual Practice
By Rabbi Michael Strassfeld 6 x 9, 544 pp, Quality PB, 978-1-58023-247-0 **$19.99**

Bringing the Psalms to Life: How to Understand and Use the Book of Psalms
By Rabbi Daniel F. Polish, PhD 6 x 9, 208 pp, Quality PB, 978-1-58023-157-2 **$16.95**

Does the Soul Survive? A Jewish Journey to Belief in Afterlife, Past Lives & Living with Purpose *By Rabbi Elie Kaplan Spitz; Foreword by Brian L. Weiss, MD*
6 x 9, 288 pp, Quality PB, 978-1-58023-165-7 **$16.99**

First Steps to a New Jewish Spirit: Reb Zalman's Guide to Recapturing the Intimacy & Ecstasy in Your Relationship with God *By Rabbi Zalman M. Schachter-Shalomi with Donald Gropman* 6 x 9, 144 pp, Quality PB, 978-1-58023-182-4 **$16.95**

Foundations of Sephardic Spirituality: The Inner Life of Jews of the Ottoman Empire
By Rabbi Marc D. Angel, PhD 6 x 9, 224 pp, Quality PB, 978-1-58023-341-5 **$18.99**

God & the Big Bang: Discovering Harmony between Science & Spirituality
By Dr. Daniel C. Matt 6 x 9, 216 pp, Quality PB, 978-1-879045-89-7 **$16.99**

God in Our Relationships: Spirituality between People from the Teachings of Martin Buber *By Rabbi Dennis S. Ross* 5½ x 8½, 160 pp, Quality PB, 978-1-58023-147-3 **$16.95**

The Jewish Lights Spirituality Handbook: A Guide to Understanding, Exploring & Living a Spiritual Life *Edited by Stuart M. Matlins*
What exactly is "Jewish" about spirituality? How do I make it a part of my life? Fifty of today's foremost spiritual leaders share their ideas and experience with us.
6 x 9, 456 pp, Quality PB, 978-1-58023-093-3 **$19.99**

Judaism, Physics and God: Searching for Sacred Metaphors in a Post-Einstein World
By Rabbi David W. Nelson 6 x 9, 352 pp, Quality PB, inc. reader's discussion guide, 978-1-58023-306-4 **$18.99**; HC, 352 pp, 978-1-58023-252-4 **$24.99**

Meaning & Mitzvah: Daily Practices for Reclaiming Judaism through Prayer, God, Torah, Hebrew, Mitzvot and Peoplehood *By Rabbi Goldie Milgram*
7 x 9, 336 pp, Quality PB, 978-1-58023-256-2 **$19.99**

Minding the Temple of the Soul: Balancing Body, Mind, and Spirit through Traditional Jewish Prayer, Movement, and Meditation *By Tamar Frankiel, PhD, and Judy Greenfeld*
7 x 10, 184 pp, Illus., Quality PB, 978-1-879045-64-4 **$18.99**

One God Clapping: The Spiritual Path of a Zen Rabbi *By Rabbi Alan Lew with Sherril Jaffe*
5½ x 8½, 336 pp, Quality PB, 978-1-58023-115-2 **$16.95**

The Soul of the Story: Meetings with Remarkable People
By Rabbi David Zeller 6 x 9, 288 pp, HC, 978-1-58023-272-2 **$21.99**

There Is No Messiah ... and You're It: The Stunning Transformation of Judaism's Most Provocative Idea *By Rabbi Robert N. Levine, DD*
6 x 9, 192 pp, Quality PB, 978-1-58023-255-5 **$16.99**

These Are the Words: A Vocabulary of Jewish Spiritual Life
By Rabbi Arthur Green, PhD 6 x 9, 304 pp, Quality PB, 978-1-58023-107-7 **$18.95**

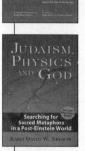

Spirituality/Prayer

Making Prayer Real: Leading Jewish Spiritual Voices on Why Prayer Is Difficult and What to Do about It *By Rabbi Mike Comins*
A new and different response to the challenges of Jewish prayer, with "best prayer practices" from Jewish spiritual leaders of all denominations.
6 x 9, 320 pp, Quality PB, 978-1-58023-417-7 **$18.99**

Witnesses to the One: The Spiritual History of the *Sh'ma*
By Rabbi Joseph B. Meszler; Foreword by Rabbi Elyse Goldstein
6 x 9, 176 pp, Quality PB, 978-1-58023-400-9 **$16.99**; HC, 978-1-58023-309-5 **$19.99**

My People's Prayer Book Series: Traditional Prayers, Modern Commentaries *Edited by Rabbi Lawrence A. Hoffman, PhD*
Provides diverse and exciting commentary to the traditional liturgy. Will help you find new wisdom in Jewish prayer, and bring liturgy into your life. Each book includes Hebrew text, modern translations and commentaries from all perspectives of the Jewish world.

Vol. 1—The *Sh'ma* and Its Blessings
　7 x 10, 168 pp, HC, 978-1-879045-79-8 **$24.99**
Vol. 2—The *Amidah* 7 x 10, 240 pp, HC, 978-1-879045-80-4 **$24.95**
Vol. 3—*P'sukei D'zimrah* (Morning Psalms)
　7 x 10, 240 pp, HC, 978-1-879045-81-1 **$29.99**
Vol. 4—*Seder K'riat Hatorah* (The Torah Service)
　7 x 10, 264 pp, HC, 978-1-879045-82-8 **$23.95**
Vol. 5—*Birkhot Hashachar* (Morning Blessings)
　7 x 10, 240 pp, HC, 978-1-879045-83-5 **$24.95**
Vol. 6—*Tachanun* and Concluding Prayers
　7 x 10, 240 pp, HC, 978-1-879045-84-2 **$24.95**
Vol. 7—Shabbat at Home 7 x 10, 240 pp, HC, 978-1-879045-85-9 **$24.95**
Vol. 8—*Kabbalat Shabbat* (Welcoming Shabbat in the Synagogue)
　7 x 10, 240 pp, HC, 978-1-58023-121-3 **$24.99**
Vol. 9—Welcoming the Night: *Minchah* and *Ma'ariv* (Afternoon and
　Evening Prayer) 7 x 10, 272 pp, HC, 978-1-58023-262-3 **$24.99**
Vol. 10—Shabbat Morning: *Shacharit* and *Musaf* (Morning and
　Additional Services) 7 x 10, 240 pp, HC, 978-1-58023-240-1 **$24.99**

Spirituality/Lawrence Kushner

I'm God; You're Not: Observations on Organized Religion & Other Disguises of the Ego
6 x 9, 256 pp, HC, 978-1-58023-441-2 **$21.99**

The Book of Letters: A Mystical Hebrew Alphabet
Popular HC Edition, 6 x 9, 80 pp, 2-color text, 978-1-879045-00-2 **$24.95**
Collector's Limited Edition, 9 x 12, 80 pp, gold-foil-embossed pages, w/ limited-edition silkscreened print, 978-1-879045-04-0 **$349.00**

The Book of Miracles: A Young Person's Guide to Jewish Spiritual Awareness
6 x 9, 96 pp, 2-color illus., HC, 978-1-879045-78-1 **$16.95** *For ages 9–13*

The Book of Words: Talking Spiritual Life, Living Spiritual Talk
6 x 9, 160 pp, Quality PB, 978-1-58023-020-9 **$18.99**

Eyes Remade for Wonder: A Lawrence Kushner Reader *Introduction by Thomas Moore*
6 x 9, 240 pp, Quality PB, 978-1-58023-042-1 **$18.95**

God Was in This Place & I, i Did Not Know: Finding Self, Spirituality and
Ultimate Meaning 6 x 9, 192 pp, Quality PB, 978-1-879045-33-0 **$16.95**

Honey from the Rock: An Introduction to Jewish Mysticism
6 x 9, 176 pp, Quality PB, 978-1-58023-073-5 **$16.95**

Invisible Lines of Connection: Sacred Stories of the Ordinary
5½ x 8½, 160 pp, Quality PB, 978-1-879045-98-9 **$15.95**

Jewish Spirituality: A Brief Introduction for Christians
5½ x 8½, 112 pp, Quality PB, 978-1-58023-150-3 **$12.95**

The River of Light: Jewish Mystical Awareness
6 x 9, 192 pp, Quality PB, 978-1-58023-096-4 **$16.95**

The Way Into Jewish Mystical Tradition
6 x 9, 224 pp, Quality PB, 978-1-58023-200-5 **$18.99**; HC, 978-1-58023-029-2 **$21.95**

Theology/Philosophy/The Way Into... Series

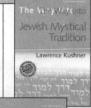

The Way Into... series offers an accessible and highly usable "guided tour" of the Jewish faith, people, history and beliefs—in total, an introduction to Judaism that will enable you to understand and interact with the sacred texts of the Jewish tradition. Each volume is written by a leading contemporary scholar and teacher, and explores one key aspect of Judaism. The Way Into... series enables all readers to achieve a real sense of Jewish cultural literacy through guided study.

The Way Into Encountering God in Judaism
By Rabbi Neil Gillman, PhD
For everyone who wants to understand how Jews have encountered God throughout history and today.
6 x 9, 240 pp, Quality PB, 978-1-58023-199-2 **$18.99**; HC, 978-1-58023-025-4 **$21.95**
Also Available: **The Jewish Approach to God:** A Brief Introduction for Christians
By Rabbi Neil Gillman, PhD
5½ x 8½, 192 pp, Quality PB, 978-1-58023-190-9 **$16.95**

The Way Into Jewish Mystical Tradition
By Rabbi Lawrence Kushner
Allows readers to interact directly with the sacred mystical texts of the Jewish tradition. An accessible introduction to the concepts of Jewish mysticism, their religious and spiritual significance, and how they relate to life today.
6 x 9, 224 pp, Quality PB, 978-1-58023-200-5 **$18.99**; HC, 978-1-58023-029-2 **$21.95**

The Way Into Jewish Prayer
By Rabbi Lawrence A. Hoffman, PhD
Opens the door to 3,000 years of Jewish prayer, making anyone feel at home in the Jewish way of communicating with God.
6 x 9, 208 pp, Quality PB, 978-1-58023-201-2 **$18.99**

The Way Into Jewish Prayer Teacher's Guide
By Rabbi Jennifer Ossakow Goldsmith
8½ x 11, 42 pp, PB, 978-1-58023-345-3 **$8.99**
Download a free copy at www.jewishlights.com.

The Way Into Judaism and the Environment
By Jeremy Benstein, PhD
Explores the ways in which Judaism contributes to contemporary social-environmental issues, the extent to which Judaism is part of the problem and how it can be part of the solution.
6 x 9, 288 pp, Quality PB, 978-1-58023-368-2 **$18.99**

The Way Into Tikkun Olam (Repairing the World)
By Rabbi Elliot N. Dorff, PhD
An accessible introduction to the Jewish concept of the individual's responsibility to care for others and repair the world.
6 x 9, 304 pp, Quality PB, 978-1-58023-328-6 **$18.99**

The Way Into Torah
By Rabbi Norman J. Cohen, PhD
Helps guide you in the exploration of the origins and development of Torah, explains why it should be studied and how to do it.
6 x 9, 176 pp, Quality PB, 978-1-58023-198-5 **$16.99**

The Way Into the Varieties of Jewishness
By Sylvia Barack Fishman, PhD
Explores the religious and historical understanding of what it has meant to be Jewish from ancient times to the present controversy over "Who is a Jew?"
6 x 9, 288 pp, Quality PB, 978-1-58023-367-5 **$18.99**; HC, 978-1-58023-030-8 **$24.99**

Theology/Philosophy

The God Who Hates Lies: Confronting and Rethinking Jewish Tradition
By Dr. David Hartman with Charlie Buckholtz
The world's leading Modern Orthodox Jewish theologian probes the deepest questions at the heart of what it means to be a human being and a Jew.
6 x 9, 275 pp (est), HC, 978-1-58023-455-9 **$24.99**

Jewish Theology in Our Time: A New Generation Explores the Foundations and Future of Jewish Belief *Edited by Rabbi Elliot J. Cosgrove, PhD; Foreword by Rabbi David J. Wolpe; Preface by Rabbi Carole B. Balin, PhD*
A powerful and challenging examination of what Jews can believe—by a new generation's most dynamic and innovative thinkers.
6 x 9, 240 pp, HC, 978-1-58023-413-9 **$24.99**

Maimonides, Spinoza and Us: Toward an Intellectually Vibrant Judaism
By Rabbi Marc D. Angel, PhD A challenging look at two great Jewish philosophers and what their thinking means to our understanding of God, truth, revelation and reason. 6 x 9, 224 pp, HC, 978-1-58023-411-5 **$24.99**

The Death of Death: Resurrection and Immortality in Jewish Thought
By Rabbi Neil Gillman, PhD 6 x 9, 336 pp, Quality PB, 978-1-58023-081-0 **$18.95**

Doing Jewish Theology: God, Torah & Israel in Modern Judaism *By Rabbi Neil Gillman, PhD*
6 x 9, 304 pp, Quality PB, 978-1-58023-439-9 **$18.99**

Hasidic Tales: Annotated & Explained *Translation & Annotation by Rabbi Rami Shapiro*
5½ x 8½, 240 pp, Quality PB, 978-1-893361-86-7 **$16.95***

A Heart of Many Rooms: Celebrating the Many Voices within Judaism
By Dr. David Hartman 6 x 9, 352 pp, Quality PB, 978-1-58023-156-5 **$19.95**

The Hebrew Prophets: Selections Annotated & Explained
Translation & Annotation by Rabbi Rami Shapiro; Foreword by Rabbi Zalman M. Schachter-Shalomi
5½ x 8½, 224 pp, Quality PB, 978-1-59473-037-5 **$16.99***

A Jewish Understanding of the New Testament *By Rabbi Samuel Sandmel; Preface by Rabbi David Sandmel* 5½ x 8½, 368 pp, Quality PB, 978-1-59473-048-1 **$19.99***

Jews and Judaism in the 21st Century: Human Responsibility, the Presence of God and the Future of the Covenant *Edited by Rabbi Edward Feinstein; Foreword by Paula E. Hyman*
6 x 9, 192 pp, Quality PB, 978-1-58023-374-3 **$19.99**

A Living Covenant: The Innovative Spirit in Traditional Judaism
By Dr. David Hartman 6 x 9, 368 pp, Quality PB, 978-1-58023-011-7 **$25.00**

Love and Terror in the God Encounter: The Theological Legacy of Rabbi Joseph B. Soloveitchik *By Dr. David Hartman* 6 x 9, 240 pp, Quality PB, 978-1-58023-176-3 **$19.95**

A Touch of the Sacred: A Theologian's Informal Guide to Jewish Belief
By Dr. Eugene B. Borowitz and Frances W. Schwartz
6 x 9, 256 pp, Quality PB, 978-1-58023-416-0 **$16.99**; HC, 978-1-58023-337-8 **$21.99**

Traces of God: Seeing God in Torah, History and Everyday Life *By Rabbi Neil Gillman, PhD*
6 x 9, 240 pp, Quality PB, 978-1-58023-369-9 **$16.99**

Your Word Is Fire: The Hasidic Masters on Contemplative Prayer
Edited and translated by Rabbi Arthur Green, PhD, and Barry W. Holtz
6 x 9, 160 pp, Quality PB, 978-1-879045-25-5 **$15.95**

I Am Jewish
Personal Reflections Inspired by the Last Words of Daniel Pearl
Almost 150 Jews—both famous and not—from all walks of life, from all around the world, write about many aspects of their Judaism.
Edited by Judea and Ruth Pearl 6 x 9, 304 pp, Deluxe PB w/ flaps, 978-1-58023-259-3 **$18.99**
Download a free copy of the *I Am Jewish Teacher's Guide* at www.jewishlights.com.

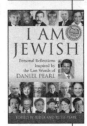

Hannah Senesh: Her Life and Diary, The First Complete Edition
By Hannah Senesh; Foreword by Marge Piercy; Preface by Eitan Senesh; Afterword by Roberta Grossman
6 x 9, 368 pp, b/w photos, Quality PB, 978-1-58023-342-2 **$19.99**

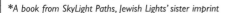

*A book from SkyLight Paths, Jewish Lights' sister imprint

Ecology/Environment

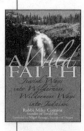

A Wild Faith: Jewish Ways into Wilderness, Wilderness Ways into Judaism
By Rabbi Mike Comins; Foreword by Nigel Savage 6 x 9, 240 pp, Quality PB, 978-1-58023-316-3 **$16.99**

Ecology & the Jewish Spirit: Where Nature & the Sacred Meet
Edited by Ellen Bernstein 6 x 9, 288 pp, Quality PB, 978-1-58023-082-7 **$18.99**

Torah of the Earth: Exploring 4,000 Years of Ecology in Jewish Thought
Vol. 1: Biblical Israel & Rabbinic Judaism; Vol. 2: Zionism & Eco-Judaism
Edited by Rabbi Arthur Waskow Vol. 1: 6 x 9, 272 pp, Quality PB, 978-1-58023-086-5 **$19.95**
Vol. 2: 6 x 9, 336 pp, Quality PB, 978-1-58023-087-2 **$19.95**

The Way Into Judaism and the Environment *By Jeremy Benstein, PhD*
6 x 9, 288 pp, Quality PB, 978-1-58023-368-2 **$18.99**; HC, 978-1-58023-268-5 **$24.99**

Graphic Novels/History

The Adventures of Rabbi Harvey: A Graphic Novel of Jewish Wisdom and Wit in the Wild West *By Steve Sheinkin* 6 x 9, 144 pp, Full-color illus., Quality PB, 978-1-58023-310-1 **$16.99**

Rabbi Harvey Rides Again: A Graphic Novel of Jewish Folktales Let Loose in the Wild West *By Steve Sheinkin* 6 x 9, 144 pp, Full-color illus., Quality PB, 978-1-58023-347-7 **$16.99**

Rabbi Harvey vs. the Wisdom Kid: A Graphic Novel of Dueling Jewish Folktales in the Wild West *By Steve Sheinkin*
Rabbi Harvey's first book-length adventure—and toughest challenge.
6 x 9, 144 pp, Full-color illus., Quality PB, 978-1-58023-422-1 **$16.99**

The Story of the Jews: A 4,000-Year Adventure—A Graphic History Book
By Stan Mack 6 x 9, 288 pp, Illus., Quality PB, 978-1-58023-155-8 **$16.99**

Grief/Healing

Facing Illness, Finding God: How Judaism Can Help You and Caregivers Cope When Body or Spirit Fails *By Rabbi Joseph B. Meszler*
Will help you find spiritual strength for healing amid the fear, pain and chaos of illness. 6 x 9, 208 pp, Quality PB, 978-1-58023-423-8 **$16.99**

Midrash & Medicine: Healing Body and Soul in the Jewish Interpretive Tradition *Edited by Rabbi William Cutter, PhD; Foreword by Michele F. Prince, LCSW, MAJCS*
Explores how midrash can help you see beyond the physical aspects of healing to tune in to your spiritual source. 6 x 9, 352 pp, HC, 978-1-58023-428-3 **$29.99**

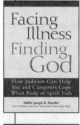

Healing from Despair: Choosing Wholeness in a Broken World
By Rabbi Elie Kaplan Spitz with Erica Shapiro Taylor; Foreword by Abraham J. Twerski, MD
5½ x 8½, 208 pp, Quality PB, 978-1-58023-436-8 **$16.99**

Healing and the Jewish Imagination: Spiritual and Practical Perspectives on Judaism and Health *Edited by Rabbi William Cutter, PhD*
6 x 9, 240 pp, Quality PB, 978-1-58023-373-6 **$19.99**

Grief in Our Seasons: A Mourner's Kaddish Companion *By Rabbi Kerry M. Olitzky*
4½ x 6½, 448 pp, Quality PB, 978-1-879045-55-2 **$15.95**

Healing of Soul, Healing of Body: Spiritual Leaders Unfold the Strength & Solace in Psalms *Edited by Rabbi Simkha Y. Weintraub, LCSW*
6 x 9, 128 pp, 2-color illus. text, Quality PB, 978-1-879045-31-6 **$16.99**

Mourning & Mitzvah, 2nd Edition: A Guided Journal for Walking the Mourner's Path through Grief to Healing *By Rabbi Anne Brener, LCSW*
7½ x 9, 304 pp, Quality PB, 978-1-58023-113-8 **$19.99**

Tears of Sorrow, Seeds of Hope, 2nd Edition: A Jewish Spiritual Companion for Infertility and Pregnancy Loss *By Rabbi Nina Beth Cardin*
6 x 9, 208 pp, Quality PB, 978-1-58023-233-3 **$18.99**

A Time to Mourn, a Time to Comfort, 2nd Edition: A Guide to Jewish Bereavement *By Dr. Ron Wolfson; Foreword by Rabbi David J. Wolpe*
7 x 9, 384 pp, Quality PB, 978-1-58023-253-1 **$19.99**

When a Grandparent Dies: A Kid's Own Remembering Workbook for Dealing with Shiva and the Year Beyond *By Nechama Liss-Levinson, PhD*
8 x 10, 48 pp, 2-color text, HC, 978-1-879045-44-6 **$15.95** *For ages 7–13*

Social Justice

Confronting Scandal
How Jews Can Respond When Jews Do Bad Things
By Dr. Erica Brown
A framework to transform our sense of shame over reports of Jews committing crime into actions that inspire and sustain a moral culture.
6 x 9, 192 pp, HC, 978-1-58023-440-5 **$24.99**

There Shall Be No Needy
Pursuing Social Justice through Jewish Law and Tradition
By Rabbi Jill Jacobs; Foreword by Rabbi Elliot N. Dorff, PhD; Preface by Simon Greer
Confronts the most pressing issues of twenty-first-century America from a deeply Jewish perspective. 6 x 9, 288 pp, Quality PB, 978-1-58023-425-2 **$16.99**
There Shall Be No Needy Teacher's Guide 8½ x 11, 56 pp, PB, 978-1-58023-429-0 **$8.99**

Conscience
The Duty to Obey and the Duty to Disobey
By Rabbi Harold M. Schulweis
Examines the idea of conscience and the role conscience plays in our relationships to government, law, ethics, religion, human nature, God—and to each other.
6 x 9, 160 pp, Quality PB, 978-1-58023-419-1 **$16.99**; HC, 978-1-58023-375-0 **$19.99**

Judaism and Justice
The Jewish Passion to Repair the World
By Rabbi Sidney Schwarz; Foreword by Ruth Messinger
Explores the relationship between Judaism, social justice and the Jewish identity of American Jews. 6 x 9, 352 pp, Quality PB, 978-1-58023-353-8 **$19.99**

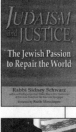

Spirituality/Women's Interest

New Jewish Feminism
Probing the Past, Forging the Future
Edited by Rabbi Elyse Goldstein; Foreword by Anita Diamant
Looks at the growth and accomplishments of Jewish feminism and what they mean for Jewish women today and tomorrow.
6 x 9, 480 pp, Quality PB, 978-1-58023-448-1 **$19.99**; HC, 978-1-58023-359-0 **$24.99**

The Divine Feminine in Biblical Wisdom Literature
Selections Annotated & Explained
Translation & Annotation by Rabbi Rami Shapiro
5½ x 8½, 240 pp, Quality PB, 978-1-59473-109-9 **$16.99**
(A book from SkyLight Paths, Jewish Lights' sister imprint)

The Quotable Jewish Woman
Wisdom, Inspiration & Humor from the Mind & Heart
Edited by Elaine Bernstein Partnow
6 x 9, 496 pp, Quality PB, 978-1-58023-236-4 **$19.99**

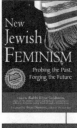

The Women's Haftarah Commentary
New Insights from Women Rabbis on the 54 Weekly Haftarah Portions, the 5 Megillot & Special Shabbatot
Edited by Rabbi Elyse Goldstein
Illuminates the historical significance of female portrayals in the Haftarah and the Five Megillot. 6 x 9, 560 pp, Quality PB, 978-1-58023-371-2 **$19.99**

The Women's Torah Commentary
New Insights from Women Rabbis on the 54 Weekly Torah Portions
Edited by Rabbi Elyse Goldstein
Over fifty women rabbis offer inspiring insights on the Torah, in a week-by-week format.
6 x 9, 496 pp, Quality PB, 978-1-58023-370-5 **$19.99**; HC, 978-1-58023-076-6 **$34.95**

See Passover for *The Women's Passover Companion: Women's Reflections on the Festival of Freedom* and *The Women's Seder Sourcebook: Rituals & Readings for Use at the Passover Seder.*

About Jewish Lights

People of all faiths and backgrounds yearn for books that attract, engage, educate, and spiritually inspire.

Our principal goal is to stimulate thought and help all people learn about who the Jewish People are, where they come from, and what the future can be made to hold. While people of our diverse Jewish heritage are the primary audience, our books speak to people in the Christian world as well and will broaden their understanding of Judaism and the roots of their own faith.

We bring to you authors who are at the forefront of spiritual thought and experience. While each has something different to say, they all say it in a voice that you can hear.

Our books are designed to welcome you and then to engage, stimulate, and inspire. We judge our success not only by whether or not our books are beautiful and commercially successful, but by whether or not they make a difference in your life.

For your information and convenience, at the back of this book we have provided a list of other Jewish Lights books you might find interesting and useful. They cover all the categories of your life:

Bar/Bat Mitzvah
Bible Study / Midrash
Children's Books
Congregation Resources
Current Events / History
Ecology / Environment
Fiction: Mystery, Science Fiction
Grief / Healing
Holidays / Holy Days
Inspiration
Kabbalah / Mysticism / Enneagram

Life Cycle
Meditation
Men's Interest
Parenting
Prayer / Ritual / Sacred Practice
Social Justice
Spirituality
Theology / Philosophy
Travel
Twelve Steps
Women's Interest

Stuart M. Matlins

Stuart M. Matlins, Publisher